THE CRESCENT AND THE CROSS

Other books published at the instigation of the Council on Christian Approaches to Defence and Disarmament

Geoffrey Goodwin (*editor*)
ETHICS AND NUCLEAR DETERRENCE

A. E. Harvey
RETALIATION: A Political and Strategic Option under Moral and Religious Scrutiny

Arthur Hockaday
THE STRATEGIC DEFENCE INITIATIVE: New Hope or New Peril?

Barrie Paskins (*editor*)
ETHICS AND EUROPEAN SECURITY

Brian Wicker (*editor*)
CHEMICAL WEAPONS: Are Britain's Reservations Still Justified?

Roger Williamson
PROFIT WITHOUT HONOUR? Ethics and the Arms Trade

SOME CORNER OF A FOREIGN FIELD: Intervention and World Order (*editor*)

The Crescent and the Cross

Muslim and Christian Approaches to War and Peace

Edited by

Harfiyah Abdel Haleem

Oliver Ramsbotham

Saba Risaluddin

and

Brian Wicker

for the Council on Christian Approaches to Defence and Disarmament

Foreword by HRH Crown Prince Hassan of Jordan

Published by
PALGRAVE
Houndmills, Basingstoke, Hampshire RG21 6XS and
175 Fifth Avenue, New York, N.Y. 10010
Companies and representatives throughout the world

PALGRAVE is the new global academic imprint of
St. Martin's Press LLC Scholarly and Reference Division and
Palgrave Publishers Ltd (formerly Macmillan Press Ltd).

Outside North America
ISBN 0–333–63811–5

Inside North America
ISBN 0–312–21304–2

This book is printed on paper suitable for recycling and
made from fully managed and sustained forest sources.

A catalogue record for this book is available
from the British Library.

Library of Congress Cataloging-in-Publication Data
The Crescent and the cross : Mulsim and Christian approaches to war
and peace / edited by Harfiyah Abdel Haleem ... [et al.].
p. cm
Includes bibliographical references and index.
ISBN 0–312–21304–2 (cloth)
1. War—Religious aspects—Islam. 2. War—Religious aspects–
–Christianity. 3. Islam—Relations—Christianity. 4. Christianity
and other religions—Islam. I. Haleem, Harfiyah Abdel.
BP190.5.W35C74 1998
261.8'73—dc21   97–38806
                                                      CIP

10   9   8   7   6   5   4   3
07   06   05   04   03   02   01

Printed and bound in Great Britain by
Antony Rowe Ltd, Chippenham, Wiltshire

Contents

Foreword

This project comes at a time when most Western defence establishments are reorienting their policies. The advent of the post-Cold War era and the concomitant changes in the security environment have had a profound impact upon the thinking of the peace community. In this period, Islam appears to be perceived in some quarters as a threat. The presumption appears to be that a future conflict between 'Islam' and 'the West' is inevitable.

Academic studies cannot in themselves prevent conflicts, but they can provide the insight and analysis necessary for reasoned discussion and action. They can show us how to find commonalities, and how to handle differences without resorting to violence.

This project achieves these vital objectives. It expands our understanding of the Christian and Muslim heritage in relation to the questions of war and peace. Furthermore, it examines the present applications and relevance of religious tenets, providing evidence that future conflict is by no means inevitable. This sensitive material is treated in an admirably neutral and analytical manner.

It is extremely encouraging to see Muslim and Christian scholars working together to better human civilization. The Council for Christian Approaches to Defence and Disarmament are to be highly commended. Informative, high calibre and original studies of this sort represent a welcome contribution to the pursuit of a deeper understanding between the two faiths, and to the search for global peace and security in the post-Cold War era.

His Royal Highness Crown Prince Hassan bin
Talal of the Hashemite Kingdom of Jordan,
The Royal Palace, Amman, Jordan

Introduction

This book is the product of a dialogue between scholars in Britain drawn from two traditions: Christianity and Islam. It is the latest in a series of studies initiated by the Council on Christian Approaches to Defence and Disarmament (CCADD). The Council was formed to discuss the ethics of defence and disarmament during the Cold War. The ending of the confrontation between two 'blocs' has led it to study new problem-areas. One of these is humanitarian intervention, resulting in the recently published study *Some Corner of a Foreign Field* (edited by Roger Williamson, 1997).

The present book has emerged out of another post-Cold War pattern of conflict: namely that between the 'Christian' West and Islamic 'fundamentalism'. For some in the West, Islamic 'fundamentalism' has replaced communism as the principal threat to global security. Conversely, many Muslims living as minorities within 'Christian' countries have felt increasingly insecure as a result of fears stoked up by the spectre of religious conflict on their own doorstep as well as in the wider international world.

CCADD therefore decided to begin a dialogue between Christian and Muslim scholars in Britain, to study how far these fears were justified in terms of fundamental religious beliefs and attitudes. Both traditions have accumulated, over the centuries, many false or irrelevant accretions, misunderstandings, superstitions; both have left profound scars on human history of which they are, or ought to be, frankly ashamed; both are in need of perpetual renewal and reformation if they are to remain true to their own spiritual heritage.

One result of our joint study has been to uncover several strands of thought and feeling within 'fundamentalism'. There is first of all the need, in every religious community, to go back to spiritual roots. Islam and Christianity are both religions of 'scripture', and each is obliged for the sake of its own integrity to return constantly, with scholarly integrity, to the true meaning of 'the book'. This is the first and deepest meaning of 'fundamentalism'.

But a second meaning is implicit in the first. For both traditions, a spiritual return to basics entails a commitment to 'justice, peace and the integrity of creation'. This becomes ever more necessary in our increasingly globalized, fractured and polluted planet. And what is more, in a world where weapons of mass destruction and the means to propagate ideologies are always in danger of falling into irresponsible hands, there is less and less space or time left for unnecessary rivalries. Humanity has to live together if it is not to die together.

Unfortunately 'fundamentalism' can easily be tempted to go astray through false, over-simplified and, in the end, violent solutions to the real problems of the world. This is the third, political and ideological, strand in 'fundamentalism', whether of the Islamic or the Christian variety. It is the aspect which has attracted most of the publicity in recent years, and the source of the insecurity that many have felt, whether out of fear of Islamist extremist movements in the Middle East and the Maghrib, or from the Christian right in America and church-sponsored xenophobia in the former Soviet-controlled territories of Europe. This false 'fundamentalism' is usually rooted more in popular myth and bigotry than in serious scholarly analysis. Hence in this book the authors have tried to show that a true return to the roots of faith can be used, not merely to expose false versions, but to ensure that the commitment to justice which follows from fidelity to the foundations of faith is employed for the common good of all.

After a brief survey of the history of Christian/Muslim conflicts and confrontations, two chapters follow, devoted respectively to the Christian and Muslim teachings on war and peace, treated historically. These have been contributed by the scholars from the respective traditions in the group. A chapter then follows in which an attempt is made to draw together the themes which emerge as common to both traditions, and to indicate those points at which the two traditions clearly diverge. Following from these studies, the results are then applied to two cases of conflict: the 'Gulf War' over Kuwait in 1990–1 CE (henceforth all dates refer to the Common Era) and the current problem of humanitarian intervention, including military intervention, in Bosnia. Finally, some conclusions are drawn for the future in the last chapter of the book.

The translation of the Qur'an preferred by the contributors to this book is *The Holy Qur'an, Text, Translation and Commentary*, by A. Yusuf Ali, Almana Publications, USA. Some adaptations have been made to bring the meaning closer to the Arabic.

The members of the study group responsible for this book are the following:

Zaki Badawi, Principal, the Muslim College, London; Chairman of the Imams and Mosques Council UK, Chairman of the Muslim Law (Shari'ah) Council UK, Vice-Chairman of the World Congress of Faiths.

Sir Hugh Beach, retired General in the British Army, formerly Warden, St George's House, Windsor; Director of the Council for Arms Control; formerly Chair of the Board of the Church Army; chairman of the Board of the Society for Promoting Christian Knowledge; a member of the Third Order of the Society of St Francis for 50 years.

David Fisher, Deputy Head of the Defence and Overseas Affairs Secretariat in the Cabinet Office. He has been responsible for Defence equipment in the Ministry of Defence and helped NATO revise its policies after the Cold War. He is author of *Morality and the Bomb* (London, 1985).

Muhammad A. S. Abdel Haleem, Professor of Arabic and Islamic Studies, and Director of the Centre of Islamic Studies, School of Oriental and African Studies, University of London.

Harfiyah Abdel Haleem, formerly Chair of the Oxford Development Education Trust, now works for the IQRA Trust dedicated to providing accurate information about Islam. She writes for *Muslim World Book Review* and for Radio Asia on a regular basis.

Abdul Ali Hamid, of the Muslim College.

Reverend Anthony Harvey, Canon, Sub-Dean and Librarian of Westminster Abbey; formerly Lecturer in Theology, University of Oxford. Author of several books on the New Testament and Christian ethics, and of the study *Retaliation*.

Sir Arthur Hockaday, Chairman of the British group of CCADD. Second Permanent Under-Secretary at the Ministry of Defence 1976–82; Director-General of the Commonwealth War Graves Commission 1982–9.

Haifa Jawad, Senior Lecturer in Middle East and Islamic Studies, Westhill College, Birmingham; former lecturer in politics and international relations at Al-Mustansiriya University, Baghdad; specialist in Euro-Arab relations, Islam and the West, and women's issues in Islam.

George Joffé, Director of Studies at the Royal Institute for International Affairs, Chatham House.

Salim Kemal, Chair of Philosophy, University of Dundee.

Robert Markus, Professor Emeritus, University of Nottingham; author of *Saeculum: History and Society in the Theology of St Augustine* (Cambridge, 1970).

Oliver Ramsbotham, Senior Lecturer in Peace Studies, University of Bradford; Director of Research in the Centre for Conflict Resolution. His recent books include *Choices: Nuclear and Non-Nuclear Defence Options* (1987), *Modernizing Nato's Nuclear Weapons* (1989), *Beyond Deterrence: Britain, Germany and the New European Security Debate* (1991, with Hugh Miall), and *Humanitarian Intervention in Contemporary Conflict* (1996, with Tom Woodhouse).

Saba Risaluddin, President of the World Conference on Religions for Peace, Director of the Calamus Foundation, currently working in Sarajevo.

Reverend Edwin Robertson, a Baptist Minister, and former Assistant Head of Religious Broadcasting for the BBC; former member of Department of Study, World Council of Churches and Executive Director of World Association for Christian Communication.

Reverend Patrick Sookhdeo, Director, International Institute for the Study of Islam and Christianity, London.

Brian Wicker, Honorary Secretary of CCADD, Convenor of its Research Group; President of the Catholic Theological Association; Convenor of the Security and Disarmament Commission of Pax Christi International, Vice-President of Pax Christi in Great Britain.

Roger Williamson, Assistant Secretary for International Affairs, Board for Social Responsibility, Church of England General Synod. Author of *Profit Without Honour?* (on the arms trade) and editor of *Some Corner of a Foreign Field* (on humanitarian intervention)

Written contributions have also been incorporated from the following:

The late **Sydney Bailey,** a former Chairman and latterly Vice-President of CCADD, a well-known Quaker authority on the United Nations and on international conflict resolution, author of *How Wars End.*

Ali Bin Ghanim Ali-Shahwani Al-Hajri, member of the Shari'ah Higher Court in Qatar, Qatar Delegation for Higher Studies, and an International Observer.

Stanley Harakas, of the Holy Cross Greek Orthodox School of Theology, Brookline, Massachusetts.

Some sections of this book have been contributed by individual authors, though always after discussion within the group. Other sections represent the work of diverse hands, fitted into a single text by the editors, who would like to acknowledge particularly the following contributions to the common task:

Hebrew and Christian scriptures (pp. 22–32) *Anthony Harvey*
Augustine and early Western Christianity (pp. 32–6) *Robert Markus*
Eastern Orthodoxy (pp. 36–7 and 54–6) *Stanley Harakas*
Islam and Christianity: Shared History (pp. 5–21), Aquinas (pp. 37–41) and Grotius (pp. 44–6) *Sir Arthur Hockaday*
Ibn Rushd (pp. 78–81) *Salim Kemal*
Some nineteenth-century humanitarians (pp. 46–8) and the humanitarian laws of war (pp. 133–8) *Sir Hugh Beach*
Varieties of pacifism (pp. 48–50) the late *Sydney Bailey*
Abu'l A'la Mawdudi (pp. 82–4) *George Joffe*
Sayyid Qutb (pp. 87–91) *Haifa Jawad*
The Gulf War: Desert Justice (pp. 144–57) *David Fisher*
The Gulf War: Another Christian View (pp. 157–62), together with material on pp. 50–4 *Roger Williamson*
The Invasion of Kuwait (pp. 162–3) *Judge Al-Hajri*

In addition, the editors themselves have contributed as follows:

Islam and Christianity: Shared Heritage (pp. 1–5) was written by *Saba Risaluddin*
Material on Vitoria (pp. 42–4), and some of 'Another Christian View' of the Gulf War (pp. 50–4) was provided by *Brian Wicker*, who also produced the final draft of Chapter 4.
Harfiyah Haleem, with Abdul Haleem, compiled Chapter 3 together with pp. 92–9 and pp. 164–71.
Oliver Ramsbotham wrote Chapters 7 and 8.

Finally the editors wish to thank *Teresa Wicker* for invaluable help with the index.

It should be pointed out that contributions to this book have been provided in a personal capacity, and do not necessarily reflect the thinking of any organisations to which their authors belong.

1 Islam and Christianity: a Shared Heritage and History

Islam and Christianity have much in common; yet our assumptions about each other are coloured, and indeed often distorted, by a shared but differently perceived theological, intellectual and social heritage, and by almost fourteen hundred years of shared history, at times painful, at times fruitful. Throughout that history we have disputed much of the same territory – not only in the Middle East, where both religions have their roots, but also in Asia, Africa and Mediterranean Europe.

The Prophet Muhammad (Peace Be Upon Him) was born six centuries after Jesus, during which time Christianity had developed from its tentative beginnings, as the faith of a persecuted minority, to worldly success. However, the Byzantine Empire was in increasing disarray, and the rapid expansion of Islam into its territories was experienced by Christendom as profoundly threatening. That sense of threat did not begin to dissipate – the Crusades and the Reconquista notwithstanding – until in the seventeenth century of the Common Era the might of the Ottoman Empire began to wane. In the post-colonial, post-Cold War period, when Islam is again being perceived, or presented, as a threat to Christendom's inheritors (the 'West'), there is a rich seam of historical encounters, fear and conflicts to be mined. Muslims, in turn, are able to draw on the memory of Islamic weakness during the colonial period and the sense of threat posed by Western cultural hegemony to foster resentments and mistrust.

Despite these political rivalries, there were, from the first, creative as well as polemical interchanges between the philosophers, theologians, poets and politicians of the two traditions. Yet it is the polemic that lingers in the mind, while the creativity is claimed by each civilization as its original contribution to succeeding generations. The debt which Christian thought and the Enlightenment alike owe to Muslims is too little acknowledged, hardly recognized outside the realms of academia; while present-day Muslim weakness and defensiveness have too often served to close minds to the possibility of a new

1

cross-fertilization of thought from which both Muslims and Christians – to say nothing of humanists and secularists – might be intellectually and spiritually renewed.

Although both Islam and Christianity arose in the Middle East in very specific local circumstances, neither is local, but both are universalist in self-perception, holding to the notion that there is a single truth for all mankind and that it is their duty to transmit it to others. Their shared spiritual and intellectual heritage is extensive and complex, encompassing Jewish monotheism, prophecy, scripture and revelation; Greek science and philosophy; Roman law and government; and ancient Semitic traditions.

Central to Islam's self-perception is the notion of a continuum of prophecy from Abraham, encompassing the great prophets of the Hebrew Bible and Jesus (as prophet, not as the Son of God), and culminating in the Prophet Muhammad. Just as Jesus came not 'to destroy the law or the prophets ... but to fulfil' (Matthew 5: 7), so the Qur'an affirms the oneness of revelation, calling on Muslims to say, 'We believe in God, and the revelation given to us, and to Abraham, Ismail, Isaac, Jacob and the Tribes, and that given to Moses and Jesus' (Qur'an 2: 136). As early Islamic thinkers began to reflect on their holy texts, they drew upon many strands of thought including those of Christian theologians, while both Muslims and Christians turned to the Neo-Platonists for philosophical insights.

Along with the Muslims' rapid worldly success came an extraordinary degree of intellectual curiosity, a hunger for knowledge, of which the *Bayt al-Hikmah* or House of Wisdom, founded by the Caliph al-Ma'mun in the early ninth century in Baghdad, is the outstanding expression. This state-funded enterprise was dedicated to gathering and translating into Arabic every available work of knowledge from the Hellenic world – though not its literature; Muslim interest was above all in philosophy and the natural sciences. The work of translation, especially that of philosophy, led to the development of an entirely new vocabulary to represent the new, Islamic, understanding of these alien modes of reasoning, and to a flowering of Muslim thought. Greek philosophy was not merely preserved and transmitted by Muslim philosophers such as Ibn Sina (Avicenna) (980–1037), who was renowned in Europe above all as a physician; it was elaborated on and developed, profoundly influencing European thinking.

The other great intellectual centre of Islam during this period was its westernmost outpost in the Iberian peninsula. The first half of the almost eight-hundred-year period of Muslim rule in Spain, or, as the Muslims call it, al-Andalus, was characterized by *convivencia*, Muslims living together in harmony with Christians and Jews, lasting broadly from soon after the conquest in the eighth century to around 1250. During this time, al-Andalus was a centre of learning for the Christians of the rest of Europe, as well as for the Muslims, Christians and Jews who lived there. Almost any European scholar worthy of the name would, sooner or later, find his way to al-Andalus to study with the theologians and philosophers of that extraordinarily rich culture.

This was a very different encounter from that of the crusades: for the Christians here found themselves relating to Muslims, not as the infidel to be banished from the holy sites by the sword, but as sophisticated and subtle thinkers to be admired and emulated, even if only in the sense of learning from them how to sustain and develop a different theology.

The culture of al-Andalus was remarkable in architecture, with distinctive arches, facades and decorations and imaginative use of water features, as in the Alhambra at Granada; in philosophy, as illustrated most impressively in the work of Ibn Rushd (Averroes, 1126–98), the 'Great Commentator' on Aristotle, who followed the path of Ibn Sina in seeking to reconcile prophetic revelation and dialectical reason; in scholarship, where the flame of knowledge of Greek was kept alive before breaking out in the Western Renaissance; and in poetry, where the subjects of the *muwashshah* ranged from romantic love (as in the poems of Ibn Zaydun (1003–71), a forerunner of the medieval troubadours of southern France) through descriptions of nature to the exaltation of God and the search for mystical knowledge of Him.

The establishment of institutions of learning that started with the *Bayt al-Hikmah* spread through North Africa to Spain and Italy where new Christian universities were established, on the model of Muslim establishments such as Al-Azhar in Cairo, Al-Zaytuna in Tunis, and Al-Qarawiyin in Fez. Thomas Aquinas (*c.* 1224–74), who studied at the universities of Naples and Paris, was deeply indebted to Muslim philosophers such as Ibn Sina and Ibn Rushd; indeed their work prompted him in his *Summa Contra Gentiles* to challenge some of their interpretation of Aristotle from a Christian perspective. The Qur'an itself, the holy scripture of Islam, was first translated into Latin in 1143 at the request of the Abbot of Cluny in France, and must have been of interest to scholars like Aquinas, in such close proximity with Muslims. Indeed the Renaissance, the very foundation of modern European thought, culture and political structures, could not have happened if Muslims had not preserved, developed and transmitted much more than just Greek philosophy. Furthermore, early European writers on international law – especially those such as Vitoria, Gentili and others, from the Spanish or Italian schools – can hardly have avoided a degree of familiarity with Islamic jurisprudence. There is also evidence that Grotius was familiar with Muslim international law, and Martin Luther was a scholar in Arabic.

The Christians of al-Andalus nurtured the understandable resentment of the conquered, and sought to regain what they saw as their lands from the Muslims, a long-drawn-out struggle known as *la reconquista*, marked by successes and defeats, by shifting alliances which sometimes brought together Christian and Muslim against their own co-religionists, and finally by the fall of the last Muslim stronghold, Granada, in 1492. In that year the Jews were expelled from Spain, and nearly half a million of them sought refuge in Islamic lands, encouraged by Sultan Bayazid II. Some of them established themselves in the Balkans, notably in Sarajevo, capital of Bosnia. Bosnia, in the heart of the Balkan peninsula, lies on a centuries-old double faultline between Western or Catholic, and Eastern or Orthodox, Christianity and between Christendom and Islam. Until the recent conflict, Bosnia was a bridge between these faiths, a country where people of different cultures and religions lived together in harmony, the inheritors of *la convivencia*. The destruction of this uniquely tolerant plural society is not only a tragedy for the people of Bosnia but a challenge to Christians and Muslims which has an impact far beyond its implications in Europe.

This challenge to members of both faiths becomes the more pressing when Christians and Muslims find themselves faced by their own shared history – a history replete with conflicts marring the spirit of reconciliation and co-operation to which the founders of both faiths subscribed. Throughout the nearly fourteen centuries since the death of Muhammad there have been many conflicts between essentially Christian and essentially Muslim entities – tribes, empires, nation-states, sects or warlords. Some of these could fairly be described as 'conflicts of civilizations' – the initial Muslim expansion into the Byzantine and former Roman Empires, the crusades to recover the Holy Places for Christendom, the 're-conquest' of Spain, the Ottoman capture of Constantinople and the success and final decline of the Western colonial enterprises in Asia and Africa. But in few of them is it easy to disentangle the threads of political, religious, economic and demographic factors; or to discern how far religion may have been a determinant element and how far a convenient label or an emotive rallying-cry, as to a very considerable extent it has been in Bosnia or Northern Ireland today.

THE MUSLIM 'BIG BANG'

As Muhammad came to preach the revelations which have formed the basis of Islam, he and his followers suffered persecution from the 'polytheists' who saw a threat to the pagan shrine which they maintained in Makkah (Mecca). At first he emigrated to Madinah (Medina), where he attracted a larger following and began to prescribe devotional practices and standards of conduct. But Mecca remained the prime objective and by the year 630 Muhammad and his supporters had secured the right of pilgrimage to Mecca and the submission and conversion of the local Bedouin.

In Muhammad's disputes with his immediate neighbours he sought to secure freedom of worship and to remove the grievance of persecution. But after his death in 632 the restlessness and vitality of the Arab tribes produced an explosive expansion – no longer directed against specific grievances but motivated principally by a conviction of a mission to spread the true faith of Islam as widely as possible, and perhaps also in part as one of the historic movements of peoples that from time to time have marked the record of mankind.

By 638, the Caliph Umar had entered Jerusalem. Although the Muslims hoped to convert as many as possible of the conquered peoples to Islam, and did not hesitate to take a hard line with pagans and 'polytheists', they did not interfere with the religions of the Book (Judaism and Christianity) so long as their adherents accepted a subordinate position and paid the taxes that were demanded from them. For example, after first paying respect to the site in Jerusalem whence Muhammad is believed to have ascended into heaven, Umar asked to see the Christian shrines. He was in the Church of the Holy Sepulchre when the Muslim hour of prayer approached. The Patriarch Sophronius invited him to spread his prayer-rug where he was; but Umar went out to the porch lest, he said, his followers should claim for Islam the place where he had prayed.

After breaking out from Arabia, the Muslim tide flowed in three main directions. North-eastwards their advance into Mesopotamia, Persia and Central Asia beyond the Oxus resulted eventually in the establishment of the Abbasid Caliphate in Baghdad in 750 and the flowering of a culture rich in mathematics, astronomy, medicine, jurisprudence and philosophy; Ibn Sina came from Bokhara. North-westwards, after the establishment of the Umayyad Caliphate in Damascus in 661, a steady process of attrition against the Byzantine Empire culminated in the great but still unsuccessful siege of Constantinople in 717–18. Westwards the Arabs invaded Egypt in 639. The Roman systems of administration and finance continued under Arab masters, but from the naval base now established at Alexandria, Cyprus was conquered and the subjection of North Africa proceeded to the final capture of Carthage in 698 and the subjugation of what are now Algeria and Morocco. From this springboard Tariq crossed to the rock that still bears his name (Jabal Tariq, Gibraltar) and, like the Romans in their invasion of Britain seven centuries earlier, took advantage of dissension among local rulers to complete the conquest of the Iberian peninsula by 720. In 732 the offensive was resumed, and the Muslims advanced as far as Tours where Charles Martel, the 'mayor of the palace' in the Merovingian kingdom of the Franks, inflicted a decisive defeat. This marked the limit of the Muslim advance into Western Europe, but did not preclude the development in al-Andalus of the remarkable culture described earlier in this chapter.

THE HOLY PLACES AND THE FIRST CRUSADE

As indicated in the anecdote of the Caliph Umar and the Patriarch Sophronius, Jerusalem is a Holy City for Christian, Jew and Muslim alike. Under the Umayyad Caliphs, a largely Hellenistic and Christian culture flourished under Arab rule: the Dome of the Rock has been described as a supreme example of Byzantine architecture, with its mosaics illustrating Byzantine art while respecting the Muslim prohibition of the depiction of living creatures. Within this culture the Christian Holy Places became increasingly a focus of pilgrimage and interest in Western Europe. Charlemagne, for example, showed a particular interest in their welfare, and the Abbasid Caliph Harun al-Rashid, perhaps seeing him as a possible ally against Byzantium, encouraged him to establish Latin foundations and send alms for their support. Charlemagne's interest gave rise over time to an increasing belief among the Franks that some right of rule in Jerusalem had somehow been established.

The decline of the Abbasid Caliphate in the ninth and tenth centuries enabled the Byzantines to retake much of what had been conquered in the seventh century, while Palestine and Syria became subject to the Fatimid dynasty in Cairo, from which the eccentric Caliph Hakim (reigned 996–1021) persecuted both Christians and Jews, and in 1009 ordered the destruction of the Church of the Holy Sepulchre itself. But he continued to employ Christian administrators and towards the end of his reign restored full liberty of conscience to Christians and Jews while forbidding his own co-religionists to observe the Ramadan fast or to make their pilgrimage to Mecca. Meanwhile, the demographic pressures of Central Asia were pushing the Turkic tribes, many of whose peoples had been converted to Islam in the tenth century, westwards. In particular the Seljuk clan penetrated in 1055 to Baghdad, where their leader Tughril was given supreme temporal power over the lands that owed spiritual allegiance to the Abbasid Caliph.

The massive defeat inflicted upon the Byzantines by Tughril's successor Alp Arslan at Manzikert in 1071 produced a lasting change in the balance of power in the Near East. Nevertheless, and despite the breakdown of confidence between the Churches of East and West in 1054, the Byzantine Emperor Alexius Comnenus (r. 1081–1118) sent a friendly embassy to the council convened at Piacenza in 1095 by the new and powerful Pope Urban II. He requested papal influence in recruiting fighting men from Western Europe to help relieve the hardships allegedly suffered by Christians under infidel rule. This appeal met a positive response. At the Council of Clermont later the same year Urban preached the Crusade, which he presented as a righteous war, designed not only to overcome the difficulties which the fighting and disorder in Asia Minor placed in the way of pilgrims, but to free Eastern Christians and even the shrines of Jerusalem itself from the Turks who had taken the city from the Fatimids soon after Manzikert. He promised absolution and remission of sins to those who died in battle against the infidel, and no doubt many who took the Cross saw it as a supreme penitential act rather than, or even as well as, a simple righting of wrong or an opportunity for plunder.

Despite the false start of the 'People's Crusade' led by Peter the Hermit, a large and impressive force made its way to Constantinople, where the Emperor secured from the Frankish leaders oaths of allegiance and promises to hand over any reconquered land that had previously been his. The crusaders won a succession of military victories, but the tensions between Eastern and Western Christendom re-emerged in 1098 with the establishment of Frankish principalities in Edessa and Antioch. In July 1099 Jerusalem fell to the crusaders after a siege of one month and, as was customary with cities that resisted, was sacked and put to the sword.

The First Crusade had been proclaimed in Augustinian fashion as a righteous war fought on the command of God and launched with the authority of the Pope in response to a request from the Byzantine Emperor for help, with what were seen as the 'just cause' of recovering territory wrongly taken from the Empire and the 'right intention' of bringing the Christian Holy Places back under Christian rule.[1] By August 1099 Pope Urban II was dead; the Emperor Alexius Comnenus had been alienated; territory had indeed been recovered from the Muslims, but little of it was restored to its previous sovereign; and the capture of Jerusalem had been accompanied initially by a brutal form of 'ethnic cleansing', though Muslims were still permitted to pray in part of the al-Aqsa mosque, and they and Jews could visit such sites of special religious significance as the tombs of the patriarchs at Hebron.

THE LATER CRUSADES

The establishment of a Kingdom of Jerusalem in 1101 stimulated other Western warriors to come out and help consolidate what had been achieved, while the Muslim rulers of Damascus, Mosul and other emirates kept the Christian settlements under constant pressure, and pilgrims were still at risk of death or slavery. The recapture of Edessa by the Muslims in 1144 caused consternation in the West and led to the proclamation of the Second Crusade by St Bernard of Clairvaux under the authority of Pope Eugenius III. Although this crusade attracted the participation of crowned heads – King Louis VII of France, the Hohenstaufen Emperor Conrad III, and King Roger II of Norman Sicily – it ended in total failure and the consolidation of the Muslim emirates in Syria and Palestine under Nur-al-Din, Emir of Aleppo.

Nur-al-Din's designs to obtain control of Egypt, still under the Fatimid Caliphs who were now allied with the Kingdom of Jerusalem, brought to prominence the famous Salah-al-Din (Saladin), a Kurd who was determined to drive the Christians into the sea and bring Palestine and Syria back within the fold of Islam. Following the collapse of the Fatimid Caliphate, his skilful diplomacy and generalship established an empire extending from Mosul to Egypt, from Libya to the Yemen, under the spiritual sway of the Abbasids in Baghdad.

A flagrant breach of truce in 1187, when a trading caravan from Egypt to Damascus was seized by Reynald of Chatillon, a bandit-knight whose earlier exploits had included a naval expedition in the Red Sea in 1182, during which he had sunk a ship carrying pilgrims bound for Mecca, galvanized Salah-al-Din into action, and he led a massive army into Palestine. The vacillations of Guy of Lusignan, King of Jerusalem, brought the Franks face to face with Salah-al-Din's army at the Horns of Hattin, near the Sea of Galilee, but in an ill-chosen tactical position lacking water. A crushing defeat led to the capture of King Guy and numerous other chieftains, and was followed within three months by the surrender of Jerusalem and Salah-al-Din's entry on the day celebrated as the anniversary of the Prophet's ascension to Heaven. By contrast with the Christian conquest in 1099, but consistently with the conventions for cities that surrendered, not a building was looted nor a person injured, though many who could not be ransomed were taken into slavery.

Salah-al-Din acquired a considerable reputation for chivalrous treatment of non-combatants, but he could be ruthless when he felt that justice so demanded. When the Frankish leaders were brought to his tent after the Horns of Hattin, defeated and parched with thirst, his first action was to hand to King Guy a goblet of rose-water iced with snow. After drinking, Guy passed the goblet to Reynald of Chatillon, the truce-breaker and desecrator of pilgrims. Salah-al-Din immediately made clear that he had not given Reynald drink or incurred any obligations of hospitality to him, and after a brief exchange of words he himself struck off Reynald's head.

The loss of Jerusalem led immediately to the launch of the Third Crusade. Among those who took the Cross were the Emperor Frederick Barbarossa and the Kings Philippe Auguste of France and Richard Coeur de Lion of England – with Salah-al-Din, a constellation unmatched until the early sixteenth century. But earlier weaknesses reappeared and earlier mistakes were repeated. Barbarossa proceeded from Germany by the overland route and, like others before him, found himself at loggerheads with the Byzantine Emperor before accidentally drowning in Cilicia in 1190. Philippe and Richard sailed by sea, but had been enemies before they started and now backed rival candidates for the Latin throne. Philippe fell ill and returned to France; Richard showed that Salah-al-Din was not invincible by defeating him at Arsuf in 1191 and Jaffa in 1192, but stained his reputation by ordering a massacre of Saracen prisoners after the capture of Acre. He did not succeed in retaking Jerusalem,

and his conquest of Cyprus during his outward voyage, at the expense
of Byzantium, merely exacerbated the intermittent hostility between
Eastern and Western Christians.

This hostility produced its most notorious manifestation in the
Fourth Crusade. For purposes of the present study, suffice it to say
that the atrocities at Jerusalem in 1099 pale almost into insignificance
alongside the sack of Constantinople in April 1204; while the French
and Flemings gave themselves over to destruction, rape and pillage,
the Venetians concentrated on the removal of the artistic treasures of
which so many still adorn their own city. Sir Steven Runciman cites
the contemporary Greek historian Nicetas Choniates as saying that
'even the Saracens' would have been more merciful.[2] And Christendom's strongest bulwark against Islam and the Turks, already in
decline, had been further and fatally weakened.

Yet papal enthusiasm for a crusade genuinely directed towards the
Holy Places survived the fiasco of the Fourth Crusade, and before his
death in 1216 Innocent III had spurred the Lateran Council of the
preceding year to declare the Fifth Crusade. Although no less bedev-
illed by internal dissensions than its predecessors, this crusade in some
respects came closer to success than any since the First. The crusaders
directed their main thrust towards Egypt and pressed the siege of
Damietta to the point that the Sultan offered to leave Jerusalem and
all of central Palestine and Galilee to the Franks if they would
evacuate Egypt. Many of the crusading leaders would gladly have
accepted this deal, but the papal legate and the Patriarch of Jerusalem
thought it wrong to come to terms with the infidel and the opportunity was lost. The legate hoped for total victory with the help of the
great Hohenstaufen Emperor Frederick II, who had taken the Cross
in 1215; but Frederick never came, the tide of battle turned in favour
of the Muslims, Damietta was relieved, and the Fifth Crusade ended
in failure.

By this time, with a state of relatively peaceful co-existence between
Muslims and Christians in the Near East, the crusading ardour of the
Catholic West was directed more against the Muslims in Spain, the
Albigensian heretics in southern France, and even the Emperor Frederick himself. Excommunicated in 1227 for further delay in joining the
crusade, Frederick nevertheless pulled a typically flamboyant stunt by
sailing to the Levant in 1228 and using the crusading army as a 'force
in being' to exert diplomatic pressure. Without striking a blow, he
secured a treaty whereby Jerusalem was returned to the Frankish
kingdom, the Dome of the Rock remained in Muslim hands, all

prisoners were released on both sides, and a peace for ten years was declared. But this did not avail to release him from his excommunication: some even regretted that no infidels had been slain. Indeed upon the expiry of the ten-year treaty in 1239, Pope Gregory IX preached a fresh crusade, and a large group of French noblemen led an expedition determined (as Runciman sardonically puts it) not to follow Frederick II's disgraceful example but to fight.[3] A decisive defeat by an Egyptian army at Gaza opened the way for the final loss of Jerusalem five years later, with further murder and pillage.

In December 1244, four months after the fall of Jerusalem, King Louis IX of France (St Louis) vowed that if he recovered from a malarial infection he would make a crusade; but two unsuccessful campaigns ended in his death from sickness. The future King Edward I of England had taken the Cross too late to join Louis's crusade. He found little crusading enthusiasm among the Franks of Syria and Palestine, and almost lost his life when stabbed with a poisoned dagger by an assassin, though the story of how his wife Eleanor sucked the poison from his wound did not appear until a century later.

Although St Louis's last words are said to have been 'Jerusalem, Jerusalem',[4] the Crusade to the Holy Land effectively petered out with the destruction of Acre by the Muslims in 1291. The conviction that the defeat of Muslim forces in battle must be in accordance with God's will and in furtherance of Christ's intentions nevertheless persisted for several more centuries in at least some of the theatres to which we now turn.

SPAIN AND THE MEDITERRANEAN

After their defeat at Tours in 732 at the hands of Charles Martel, the Arabs withdrew into Spain and generally preferred to settle south of the northern limit of the olive, leaving the mountainous areas of northern Spain to the Christians. The powerful Abd-al-Rahman established a military despotism strong enough to render abortive an expedition launched in 778 by Charles Martel's grandson Charlemagne and famous chiefly for the cutting-off of the Frankish rearguard (by Basques, not Muslims) and the death of the hero Roland.

For subsequent centuries the rich Andalusian culture described earlier in this chapter flourished, alike under the Muslim rulers in Cordoba or Granada and under Christian kings like Alfonso X of

Castile ('the Learned', r. 1252–84), and even within the context of continuing military conflict. But the military tide gradually came to flow with the Christians, and was reinforced by matrimonial diplomacy which reached its apogee with the marriage in 1469 of Ferdinand of Aragon and Isabella of Castile, and the subsequent unions which brought their grandson Charles V to the thrones of Spain in 1516 and the Holy Roman Empire in 1519. Ferdinand and Isabella, 'the Catholic Kings of the Spains', were determined to complete the unity of Spain, to which the Moorish kingdom of Granada represented the principal remaining obstacle. When Granada at last surrendered in 1492 Muslims and Jews were given the choice of conversion or expulsion, and mention has already been made of the exodus of Jews to Bosnia. Within Spain itself religious 'purity' was enforced by the newly founded Inquisition.

Also in 1492, the 'Catholic Kings' supported the voyage of Columbus across the Atlantic which, together with the Portuguese explorations that took Bartholomew Diaz round the Cape of Good Hope in 1488 and Vasco da Gama to India in 1498, was to diminish the commercial and geo-strategic importance of the Mediterranean. The Mediterranean nevertheless remained a theatre of maritime conflict in which Italian trading states like Venice and Genoa played a prominent part, though in mutual rivalry more often than in concert against the Muslims.

The maritime wars of the mid-sixteenth century reflected rivalries within Christendom itself and could only in the broadest sense be described as conflicts between Christianity and Islam. During the remarkable period in which Charles V, Henry VIII of England, Francis I of France and Sulayman the Magnificent reigned simultaneously over their respective empires and kingdoms, the principal actors formed and broke alliances with little scruple. Both France, with her endemic hostility to the Habsburg Empire, and Venice, for whom commercial interests always came first, were as liable to reach amicable accommodations with the Turks as to join coalitions against them. And in so far as there was an underlying conflict between Spain and Turkey, it was pursued in the intervals of Turkish embroilments with Persia and Spanish disputes with France or England. But the virtual destruction of the Turkish fleet by Spanish, Venetian and Genoese squadrons in the great naval battle of Lepanto in 1571 was a turning-point in psychological terms. Far more than their failure to capture Vienna in 1529, the scale of their naval losses at Lepanto showed that the Turks were not invincible; and both of these successes did something to keep the flickering spirit of the crusades alive.

CONSTANTINOPLE AND THE OTTOMAN EMPIRE

The migratory pressures westward from Central Asia, mentioned above in connection with the Seljuk Turks, continued throughout the Middle Ages. Among the most formidable were the incursions of the Mongols under Genghis Khan and his successors. The Mongols are only tangentially relevant to a study of the interaction between Christendom and Islam, but many of them, including daughters-in-law of Genghis Khan, were Christians of the Nestorian persuasion, and from time to time Christians and Mongols each saw the other as a possible ally against the Arabs or the Seljuk Turks. The illusions current on both sides are illustrated by the mission sent by Pope Innocent IV to the court of the Great Khan in 1245 with a papal letter requiring the Khan to accept Christianity. The Khan received the mission kindly but replied by ordering the Pope to acknowledge his suzerainty and come with all princes of the West to do him homage.

Of much more direct relevance to the present study is a Turkish clan that settled in Asia Minor in the thirteenth century, and in the early fourteenth extended its territory to the sea of Marmora under a chieftain, Osman (Uthman in Arabic transliteration) from whom the name of Ottoman derives. In 1354 Osman's son Orhan crossed the Dardanelles to take Gallipoli; and by the time of his death in 1359 Adrianople had been captured, and Constantinople cut off from its European hinterland. Orhan's son Murad I advanced further into Europe, annihilating the Serbian army in the battle of Kossovo in 1389, still a legendary date in Serb history, but was assassinated by a Serb on the day of the battle, the very same day on which 525 years later the Archduke Franz Ferdinand was to meet a similar fate at Sarajevo.

Constantinople fell at last to the formidable Sultan Muhammad II in 1453. Little help was available from the West; and after a siege of two months the walls of the imperial city yielded to artillery of unprecedented power. The last Emperor Constantine XI died in the fighting, the Byzantine Empire perished in another bout of massacre and pillage, and Istanbul ('The City') became the capital of a Turkish empire stretching far into both Europe and Asia. It did not take long for Muhammad II to complete the conquest of Serbia and Bosnia, where the seeds of conflicts far in the future were sown when the majority of Bosnians were converted to Islam while most Serbs retained the Orthodox faith. The modern Romania finally came under Turkish suzerainty in 1513. With the fall of Rhodes in 1523 and Cyprus in 1570, the whole of Eastern Christendom, which the crusades had been launched to save from the Muslims, was under Muslim rule.

A further expansion of the Ottoman Empire occurred under two remarkable Sultans more than fifty years after the fall of Constantinople. Selim I (r. 1512–20) conquered Egypt, Syria, Palestine and Arabia from the Mamelukes; brought the sacred city of Mecca under Ottoman control; and assumed the Caliphate. His son Sulayman the Magnificent (r. 1520–66), now undisputed ruler of most of the Muslim world, resumed the offensive in Europe and at Mohacs in 1526 gained a decisive victory which brought most of Hungary under Turkish rule for more than a century and carried Sulayman forward to the gates of Vienna. But Vienna held out against the siege of 1529, marking the westernmost limit of Turkish advance.

During the seventeenth century a succession of weak Ottoman Sultans and Habsburg Emperors saw the reins of power in Istanbul pass to a series of vigorous and efficient grand viziers, while John Sobieski, elected King of Poland in 1673, emerged as the strongest character in Catholic Europe after Louis XIV of France. In 1683 the ambitious Grand Vizier Kara Mustafa was invested with the standard of Muhammad, designating him in effect as the leader of Islam in a 'counter-crusade', and led a large Turkish army through Hungary to a second investment of Vienna, whence the Emperor Leopold I and a large proportion of the population fled before the siege began. Despite an appeal from the Pope, Louis felt no impulsion to come to the aid of his long-standing Habsburg rival: it was Sobieski who rose to the challenge. His arrival raised the two-month-old siege, and a ferocious battle ended in the precipitate retreat of the Turks. The relief of Vienna brought the end of any Muslim 'threat' to Central Europe, and the beginning of the Turkish withdrawal from the Balkans. The significance of Sobieski's victory for Catholic Europe is perhaps reflected in the prominent position assigned within the Vatican Museum to an indifferent painting of the battle.

The continuing decline of the Ottoman Empire gave rise to several crises between Christians and Muslims in the nineteenth and early twentieth centuries, but the welfare of its remaining Christian minorities was only one factor along with Russia's desire for free access to the Mediterranean and Britain's concern for the maintenance of her Indian empire and its lines of communication. Thus, when a crisis arose out of an apparently trivial dispute between Catholic and Orthodox monks over the custody of the Holy Places, France and Russia backed their respective co-religionists, and the Crimean War followed from British and French support for Turkey's rejection of a high-handed set of demands from Russia. Twenty years later, when rebellions against Turkish rule in Bulgaria were brutally suppressed and a Russian army advanced to the outskirts of Constantinople, political opinion in Britain was sharply divided: the High Anglican Gladstone gave first priority to the human rights of Turkey's Christian subjects and campaigned eloquently against 'Bulgarian atrocities', while Prime Minister Disraeli, Jewish by birth but Christian by conversion, dominated the Congress of Berlin in 1878 to secure a settlement which, while liberating some eleven million Christians from the 'Turkish yoke', advanced Austro-Hungarian rather than Russian interests in the Balkans. The Balkan wars of 1912–13 finally reduced 'Turkey-in-Europe' to a small enclave around Constantinople.

But by this time a new actor had come upon the stage. In his love–hate relationship with Britain the German Kaiser Wilhelm II, like Russian Tsars before him, saw India as both Britain's most precious possession and a point of vulnerability. In 1896 he ostentatiously dissociated himself from Western protests against Turkey's heavy-handed suppression of uprisings in Armenia, and two years later he accepted an invitation from Sultan Abdul Hamid II to visit Constantinople and tour the Ottoman Empire. He made what looked like a triumphal entry into Jerusalem mounted on a black charger, and in Damascus he laid a wreath at the tomb of Salah-al-Din and made a speech assuring the Muslim world of his perpetual friendship. Over the next decade German influence in Constantinople was consolidated with military missions and the scheme for the Berlin–Baghdad railway.

In August 1914 this political influence, which had been maintained with Enver Pasha and the 'Young Turks' after the abdication of Abdul Hamid in 1909, was reinforced by the arrival of the German battlecruiser *Goeben* off Constantinople; and at the end of October Turkey entered the war on the side of the Central Powers. The Turkish and Russian armies locked horns in the Caucasus in a campaign which acquired a specifically Christian/Muslim dimension early in 1915 when the Turkish government, alleging Armenian collaboration with the Russians as the cause of military defeat more plausibly attributable to Enver's strategic incompetence, launched on a much larger scale than heretofore what was interpreted and condemned throughout the West as a fresh wave of genocide ultimately involving more than one million deaths.

Meanwhile Sultan Muhammad V, in his capacity as Caliph, had in November 1914 proclaimed a Holy War against the Entente powers.

His proclamation was addressed to Muslims throughout the world, but above all, no doubt, to Muslim subjects of the British and Russian Empires. The British were sensitive to the loyalty of Muslim units of the Indian Army, and held some back from the front line at Gallipoli; the only serious mutiny, of a unit in Singapore in February 1915 whose soldiers believed wrongly that they were being sent to fight against Turkey, was attributed by the subsequent board of enquiry to the indifferent leadership of its British officers. The campaigns against the Turks in Gallipoli, Palestine and Mesopotamia were inspired not by crusading ambitions but by the strategic objectives of knocking Turkey out of the war, opening up a line of supply to Russia, and guarding the flanks of the route to India. Religious symbolism nevertheless played its part, as when in December 1917 General Allenby entered Jerusalem on foot in deliberate contrast to the style of the Kaiser's entry in 1898. The capture of Jerusalem in 1917, like that of 1099, created more problems than it solved: but this time they related not to the creation of a Christian kingdom (though the French and British were granted mandates for the time being over Syria, Lebanon, Jordan, Iraq and Palestine) but to the reconciliation of the claims of Arabs and Jews and the promises made to both parties by the Allies.

WESTERN EMPIRES

So far we have been concerned mainly with the Muslim expansion into territories under Christian rule, or to which Christians thought they had some sort of right; and with the attempts of Christian powers, with varying degrees of success, to regain the lost ground. The most recent five hundred years have also been marked by Western, if not explicitly Christian, expansion into territories under Muslim rule or peopled largely by Muslims, and in the twentieth century by a retreat from Western imperial hegemony.

In addition to their encounters with Christians around the Mediterranean and in south-eastern Europe the Muslims extended their sway into regions of which Christendom was then only dimly, if at all, aware. From the Arabian heartland and the Gulf, Arab and Persian traders voyaged to the shores of India and down the east coast of Africa in search of spices, gold or slaves. The west coast of Africa was reached by caravan across the Sahara. After the Muslim penetrations of central Asia mentioned earlier, the continuing migratory pressures in that continent impelled a succession of conquerors towards India, from Tamerlane in 1398 to the establishment of the Mughul Empire in 1526. And from India the merchants and adventurers pressed on towards the territories that we now know as Malaysia and Indonesia.

The pioneers of Western expansion into these regions were the Portuguese. With the blessing of a Bull issued by Pope Nicholas V, Prince Henry the Navigator sponsored a series of voyages further and further southward until at last Bartholomew Diaz rounded the Cape of Good Hope in 1488 and ten years later Vasco da Gama crossed the Indian ocean to Calicut. In 1509 the Portuguese admiral Almeida decisively defeated a mainly Egyptian fleet (constructed with Venetian assistance) at Diu, off the Gujarati coast, and established dominance over the sea routes of the Indies. But the Portuguese hegemony did not last: first the Dutch in the East Indies, then the British in India (who also saw off some competition from the French), established firmer foundations, first for trade and then for government, which matured into polities under imperial rule but much too substantial to be described merely as colonies. Colonies were established by the British, Germans and Portuguese in East and West Africa, while the French regarded their territories in North and West Africa almost as overseas departments of metropolitan France, and the Russian expansion into the Caucasus and Central Asia was treated simply as an extension of the land mass of the Russian Empire.

It is difficult to say how far this process should be treated as 'Christian' expansion. The pioneering voyages of the Portuguese set out from a strongly Catholic country (Prince Henry was head of the Order of Christ, a militant religious society) at a time when the spirit of the crusades was still alive. The Bull of Nicholas V commended Prince Henry for bringing within the Catholic fold 'the perfidious enemies of God and of Christ, such as the Saracens and the infidels', and authorized him to invade and conquer their territories.[5] Within the Russian Empire, although the frameworks of Muslim religion, law and education in the Caucasus and the Central Asian Khanates were left largely untouched, the close identification of the imperial structure with the Orthodox Church helped to make Islamic consciousness a focus of opposition to peasant settlements, economic modernization or (provoking a major insurrection in 1916) conscription for military service.

With Protestant imperial powers, like Britain or the Netherlands subsequent to the Reformation, the nuances are different again. The rejection of papal authority and the emphasis on individual salvation diminished the relevance of the historical concept of Christendom. Evangelical zeal was still manifest, but the spreading of the gospel was left primarily to the churches or to individual missionaries, with governments exercising not much more than a benevolent neutrality. In a rather different spirit from the Bull of Nicholas V, Warren Hastings in India was content 'to leave their religious creed to the Being who has so long endured it, and who will in his own time reform it'.[6] There were, of course, increasingly during the nineteenth century, individual servants of the Raj who were also enthusiastic evangelists. Captain Conolly, one of the two British emissaries executed as spies by the Emir of Bokhara in 1842, was well known as a strong believer in the civilizing mission of Christianity; but his rejection of Islam upon the scaffold availed him no more than his companion Colonel Stoddart's earlier acceptance of a forcible conversion. The suppression of slavery certainly had close links with the evangelical movement: for example, after Sayyid Said (Sultan of Muscat, Oman and Zanzibar 1806–56) had spent his long reign successfully evading the attempts of British Residents and the Royal Navy to put down the slave trade between Zanzibar and Arabia, the imposition upon his successor in 1873 of a treaty requiring the closure of the Zanzibav slave market (where the Anglican cathedral now stands) 'was largely a response to public outrage in Britain at the descriptions David Livingstone had sent back about the horrors of the slave trade in Africa's interior'.[7] Nevertheless evangelism was in general no part of the policy of Western governments

This was, of course, how it appeared through Western eyes. For Muslims, accustomed to the concept of the *ummah*, the worldwide Muslim community, and steeped in the historical tradition of the Caliphates of Damascus, Baghdad, Cairo, Cordoba or Istanbul, the perception was rather different. Observing the parallel thrusts of imperial expansion and Christian evangelism, and remembering the crusading spirit of medieval Catholic Christendom, it was difficult for Muslims to disentangle the threads. And one person's error can only too easily become someone else's conspiracy. For example, it is generally accepted that the thoughtless decision of the Ordnance authorities in England in January 1857, to extend to India the introduction of cartridges greased with the fat of animals sacred for Hindus or unclean for Muslims, was, even though rescinded within days in response to the representations of regimental officers, one of the proximate causes of the Mutiny later in the same year. As an historian of the Indian army has put it:

Conscious of their own good intentions, the British simply could not believe that anyone would credit them with anything so ridiculous as a plot to convert the Sepoys by fraud – yet every move they made confirmed the Sepoys in this belief. Officers and men alike simply did not understand each other's way of thinking. One British officer, addressing Indian troops, told them that he and his fellow countrymen were *Protestants*, and it was therefore unthinkable that they would try to convert anyone by fraud; they would accept only converts whose *reason* led them to accept the faith. The Sepoys are said to have nodded to show they understood.[8]

Similarly, the apportionment of colonies or spheres of influence among the colonial powers, while in their own eyes simply an attempt to balance their own interests on the basis of 'you win some, you lose some', could only too easily appear as an attempt to fragment the *ummah* and advance specifically Christian interests by dividing Islam. The sense of nationalism which has accompanied the progress to independence of so many peoples formerly subject to colonial or imperial rule may have been conditioned partly by the boundaries defined between colonies and mandates, partly by an increasingly secular political climate. Religion has, however, strongly coloured the political scene in the conflicts between Israel and her Arab neighbours: in the constitutional arrangements for power-sharing within the mixed population of Lebanon; and in the partition of the Indian empire with the emergence of Pakistan, and later Bangladesh.

Since 1945 there have been three major incidents of conflict involving Christians and Muslims – the Suez affair of 1956, the Kuwait war of 1990–1, and the more recent fighting in Bosnia. Kuwait and Bosnia are treated in depth in later chapters. Suffice it here to remark that the Kuwait war was not about Christianity and Islam as such: it was about oil, about international law and order, and about hegemony in the Middle East. Nor was it a war between Christians on one side and Muslims on the other. On one side was one Muslim state with political support from some others; on the other was a coalition of several Western and several Muslim states, with Saudi Arabia playing an indispensable role with her own armed forces and with provision of base facilities. The strongly Muslim character of the Saudi state was nevertheless recognized by the prudent decision of the Western forces to conduct in a low key their exercise of Christian ministry and their celebration of the Christmas festival. Nor was the misguided Suez adventure about Christianity and Islam. Its origins were entirely secular, springing from judgements, all subsequently shown to be mistaken, that Nasser was another Hitler, that free use of the Suez canal was a strategic necessity for the Western powers, and that the Egyptians could not operate the canal efficiently.

In addition, recent decades have seen continuing conflict in Sudan and East Timor between Muslim governments and Christian dissidents, involving in the former case serious allegations of interference with Christian worship, but in East Timor probably more closely linked with continuing local resentment at Indonesia's seizure of the territory from Portugal. There have also been periodic declarations of hostility to the West (sometimes specifically the United States) from so-called 'fundamentalist' governments or individuals and sporadic acts of terrorism in which the involvement of some Muslim governments has sometimes been suspected but not conclusively proved. The causes most frequently adduced for these words and deeds have sometimes derived from perceptions of Western (mainly American) support for Israel or (in the case of Iran) the late Shah, sometimes from fear of the corrosive effects of Western (again largely American) 'culture' upon traditional Islamic values.

CONCLUSIONS

This brief and necessarily superficial survey has catalogued many instances of conflict over the past fourteen centuries, with Muslims and Christians in opposition. What is much less clear, and what has varied greatly between the different occasions and different eras, is how far they could be described as conflicts between Christendom and Islam, or how far they have been generated by a host of other factors – political, geo-strategic, economic, migratory – and simply happen to have been fought out between two groups of opponents, one of which happened to consist essentially of Muslims, the other essentially of Christians. If the narrative appears to have placed disproportionate emphasis upon the crusades, this is precisely because, more than any of the other conflicts described, they had a specifically religious context. We have seen, however, that much of this history will have been interpreted differently from Christian and Muslim viewpoints within their respective traditions. What we have also seen, and on this both Muslims and Christians will sorrowfully agree, is that all too frequently the conduct of adherents of both traditions has fallen woefully short of their respective ideals and the teachings of their founders.

Those teachings and ideals are set out and discussed in the following chapters.

NOTES

1. For discussion of these terms, see Chapter 2 below, pp. 39–40.
2. Steven Runciman, *A History of the Crusades*, Vol. 3 (Cambridge: Cambridge University Press, 1954), p. 123.
3. Ibid., p. 213.
4. Ibid., p. 292.
5. Quoted in K. M. Panikkar, *Asia and Western Dominance: A Survey of the Vasco da Gama Epoch of Asian History, 1498–1945* (London: Allen and Unwin, 1953), pp. 30–1.
6. Quoted in Philip Mason, *The Men Who Ruled India* (London: Jonathan Cape, 1985), p. 143.
7. Richard Hall, *Empires of the Monsoon: A History of the Indian Ocean and its Invaders* (London: HarperCollins, 1996), p. 451.
8. Philip Mason, *A Matter of Honour: An Account of the Indian Army, its Officers and Men* (London and Basingstoke: Papermac, 1986), pp. 267–8 (first published by Jonathan Cape, 1974).

2 Christian Perspectives on War and Peace

Before introducing the scriptural basis of Christian thinking with regard to war, justice and peace it is necessary to say something about the place which scripture holds in Christian theology and the authority it exercises over believers.

Until at least the end of the Middle Ages the matter could be expressed quite simply. God was believed to have revealed his nature and his demands in scripture, which was regarded as both verbally inspired and literally true (though with other and often more important levels of meaning beneath the surface). But the Bible consists in large part of narrative, poetry and exhortation and contains little systematic teaching; nor does it cover by any means every matter on which guidance is needed. Therefore God has given to human beings the power of reason with which to supplement and confirm the scriptural revelation. Thus reason, according to this scheme, is strictly subservient to revelation, though a necessary adjunct to it.

This simple account gave place to considerable divergence of view after the Enlightenment, particularly among Protestants. Some tended to minimize the contribution of reason because of the overwhelming importance of the truth which they perceived to be revealed in the Bible; others came to think of the Christian religion as essentially a product of enlightened reason, requiring scripture only to give it particular and historical form.

In the nineteenth century the traditional view came under further attack as a result of critical study of the Bible. The complex literary interrelationships of the different writings, the selectivity and – at times – evident partiality if not factual error with which they record events known from other historical sources, the diverse genres of composition which need to be recognized before the intention of the author can be determined, the successive strata of editorial activity discernible in many of the books – these and other factors revealed by critical study made any simple account of divine inspiration and literal truth seem no longer sustainable. Christians now have reason to marvel at the sheer variety of literary and historical materials through which the revelation has been given but they can no longer expect any simple definition or simple criterion to tell them whether, and to what extent, any particular text is 'inspired' or 'true'.

It follows that in modern times reason has taken on considerable importance. Scripture continues to exercise its authority in the Church, not least because it affords the closest possible access to the events regarded by faith as crucial for religious history. But in the eyes of the majority of reflective Christians it is no longer regarded either as inerrant (for it contains inconsistencies, historical errors and instances of moral immaturity) or as the direct result of divine inspiration transmitted through an individual (for many of the writings can be shown to have been often worked over and to be the product of a community as much as of a single author). If it is to continue to play its part in the life of the Church it requires a constant effort of interpretation; its meaning must be correctly determined and faithfully expressed in a modern idiom; and its application to modern situations must be carefully assessed. In this matter, again, there is a divergence of opinion and practice in all the major churches. John Macquarrie, in his widely used *Principles of Christian Theology*, expresses it thus:

> If the demand for relevance and intelligibility is to be met, then there will always be a danger of infringing the autonomous – and even judgemental – character of the primordial revelation; but this must be weighed against the other danger of so insulating the revelation against all contact with the changing forms of secular culture, that it becomes encapsulated, and shut off from everything else in life.[1]

In what follows, an attempt is made to strike a balance between these extremes, and to give some account of the way in which different Christian traditions have sought to come to terms with those texts which bear most directly upon fundamental decisions about war and peace.

The basic texts

'Do not resist evil' (Matthew 5: 39). These words, reported to have been spoken by the founder of Christianity in the context of his most sustained discourse on moral issues (the Sermon on the Mount), might be expected to provide the fundamental text on which Christians would base their position on questions of peace and war. Placed alongside another equally radical and apparently unqualified command, to 'love your enemies' (Matthew 5: 44), it appears to settle for ever the question whether a Christian may engage in acts of violence and warfare. Taken on their own, these two commands seem to prove beyond all doubt that Christianity is a pacifist religion.

And so it has always been taken to be by a certain number of Christians. Of course, those who in the name of Christ have refused to take up arms or to countenance the use of force to resist attack have usually based their position on a wider range of texts than this. They have pointed, in addition, to Jesus's command to pray for (and implicitly not to resist) one's persecutors (Matthew 5: 44); his blessing of those who are peacemakers and 'meek' (Matthew 5: 5, 9); his saying (whatever its precise import) that those who take up the sword shall perish by the sword (Matthew 26: 52); above all his own refusal to offer active resistance to those who threatened him and in the end killed him (1 Peter 2: 23). And more than this: they have drawn practical consequences from the fundamental place occupied by love in the Christian ethic, a love which is a necessary response to the God who showed his love for us in Christ (1 John 5: 10) and which must extend to all our fellow human beings. Such a love seems necessarily to preclude acts of violence, even against an aggressor.

It is true that God is also a God of justice, who may visit on human beings the violent consequences of their own misdeeds. But 'Vengeance is mine; I will repay, says the Lord': this text from Deuteronomy was taken by St Paul (Romans 12: 19; Deuteronomy 32: 35) as reserving the exercise of forceful retribution to God alone. The followers of Christ must adopt only non-violent means of influencing others. They must altogether renounce the use of force.

But this simple and apparently well-founded response to the teaching and example of Jesus and to the gospel of love which was proclaimed by the cross has not been accepted or endorsed by the majority of Christians at any time in the history of the Church. There have been Christian soldiers, Christian armies and even Christian wars ('crusades'). For most of the centuries of church history, adherence to the letter of Christ's commands in this matter seems to have been practised only by a small minority of Christians.

Does this mean that the majority of Christian people have always been simply unfaithful to the clear teaching of their scriptures? The answer to this question will reveal something of the way in which scripture is handled by the Christian community and exerts its authority through different processes of interpretation.

Jesus's inheritance: The Hebrew scriptures

It is accepted by almost all Christian traditions that the New Testament needs to be read as a continuation of the Hebrew scriptures. Whatever modifications Jesus may have brought to the faith which he inherited from his Jewish background – and these are indeed substantial and significant – there is nevertheless no doubt whatever that the God whom he worshipped and called his Father is the same God as is witnessed to in the Hebrew scriptures. This God certainly issued the command, Thou shalt not kill (Exodus 20: 13), and we must attend to the implications of that in a moment. But he was also a God who violently overthrew the power of Pharaoh in order to liberate his people from slavery in Egypt (Exodus 14), who commanded them to occupy their land beyond the Jordan by force (if necessary, exterminating the inhabitants) (Joshua 8 and elsewhere), and who encouraged them to undertake a long series of military exploits. At no stage in Israel's history was any form of pacifism regarded as an appropriate response to God's commands. A prophet might advise them to rely on God rather than on their armies (Isaiah 31: 1), but this was certainly not held to imply that maintaining an army was wrong in itself. The nearest the Jews came to deliberately renouncing armed combat was in the Maccabean revolt, when for a time they refused to fight on the Sabbath and received heavy casualties as a result (1 Maccabees 2: 32–8).

Nor can we find in the Hebrew scriptures any perception that the justice of God might require a more humane treatment of their enemies than that which was taken for granted in the warfare of the time. On the contrary, it was often seen as a condition of God's support of their army that the taking of any town to which the Israelites laid claim for future occupation should be followed by the total extermination of the inhabitants in order to avoid any possible contamination by pagan religious practices (Deuteronomy 20: 17; 2 Samuel 12: 31 and so on). Even when the campaign involved no territorial claim it was accepted that a successful siege might result in the death or enslavement of the vanquished and the plunder of their property. Indeed the treatment of Jerusalem by its pagan captors in 598 was arguably more humane than that which the Jews themselves were authorized by their scriptures to inflict on their defeated enemies (2 Kings 24: 14).

The apparent lack of concern for what we would now call the laws of war has created problems for the interpreters of these scriptures.

Even the Jewish historian Josephus, when summarizing the rules of military engagement contained in Deuteronomy chapter 20,[2] evidently found it necessary to make them appear more humane to his Greek and Roman readers. Whereas the biblical text simply commands the Israelites to parley before laying siege, offering the inhabitants of a city the option of safe conduct into slavery, Josephus represents all Jewish wars as essentially defensive and suggests that the parley was intended to be a serious offer of peace. Modern interpreters, recognizing the problem of having to attribute to God the authorization of such apparently uncivilized military tactics, have stressed the fact that at certain times the Israelites believed themselves to be engaged in a 'holy war'. According to this ideology, the conquest and possession of the land required the ruthless elimination of any possible source of pagan influence. Failure to extend the Kingdom of the God of Israel by allowing alien elements to persist within the borders of the promised land was seen as a serious sin which might be requited by divine punishment (1 Samuel 28: 18). In return, God might manifest his presence among them and his endorsement of their military enterprise by affording them victory in the face of overwhelming numbers, or even by causing them deliberately to reduce their own forces in order to demonstrate the supernatural power that was at work on their side (Judges 7). It was perhaps this instinctive reliance on divine resources which caused them to allow liberal exemptions from military service in the case of those starting a farm or building a house, those about to be married or newly married, or even those who suffered from fear and cowardice (Deuteronomy 20: 5–8; 24: 5).

But none of this affects the fact that such laws of war as can be inferred from the Hebrew scriptures and which are said to be derived from the commands of God explicitly sanction the massacre or the enslavement of prisoners and civilians. The few recorded instances of more humane treatment are exceptions to the rule: in each case it is clear that the normal procedure would have been to execute the prisoners (1 Kings 20: 34; 2 Kings 6: 23). Even the prophets, who were often enlisted to advise on whether a campaign should be undertaken, said nothing about the way it should be conducted – though Amos's condemnation of certain atrocities committed by heathen armies suggests that he recognized at least some limits to the legitimate conduct of war (Amos 1). On the other hand, it would be wrong to imagine that the people of Israel, when engaged in war, were any less subject to the demands of God's justice than in the conduct of their civilian life. The sufferings entailed by warfare were not seen (as they might be today) as the consequences of unredeemed human nature going temporarily out of control. They were sanctioned by a God the very nature of whose justice was to ensure that immoral action was followed by just retribution. At first this was held to justify acts of total war carried out against Israel's enemies; but it was not long before it was seen to apply equally to Israel herself. Defeat, occupation and exile were all interpreted by the prophets as punishments visited by God on his disobedient people, or else as means by which that people might be disciplined and purified for the destiny which the same merciful God had prepared for them. God's justice, that is to say, might have benign consequences in the long term; but in the short term it was always understood to entail the threat, and at times the reality, of violent enforcement. The problem is that it was this same God whom Jesus called his Father and whose authority he invoked for his teaching.

One way of resolving the problem has been to claim that in this as in certain other matters (such as the commandments concerning the ritual of the Temple) Jesus simply made the Old Testament obsolete. He was a 'new Moses', and had authority to repeal the old law where necessary. But this is a dangerous simplification. There is little evidence that Jesus intended to repeal or reform the existing law, nor is it clear what practical means he could have adopted to do so. He consistently referred to scripture as possessing divine authority. His genius was to give it an interpretation that invested it with new moral force: its foundations he left undisturbed. Another approach has been to allow for some development in the Hebrews' understanding of God. The passages which authorize such inhumane military procedures are relatively early and belong to a period when such conduct was taken for granted. Later texts make no mention of them, and may, by implication, be thought to supersede them; indeed by the time of Jesus the whole question had become academic. The Jewish population of Palestine was under Roman occupation and was forbidden to carry arms unless under the orders of Roman officers. In these circumstances Jesus may well have had no occasion to make any direct comment on the martial tradition found in the Hebrew scriptures. Nevertheless it remains true that Jesus nowhere explicitly condemns the institution of war, he converses with a Roman soldier without making any criticism of his profession (Matthew 8: 5–10), and he occasionally uses forms of speech (such as 'I came to bring, not peace, but a sword', Matthew 10: 34) which seem hardly compatible with a total abhorrence of everything to do with war.

Jesus's teaching

Context

A second reason for hesitating to draw pacifist conclusions from Jesus's teaching is the recognition that it does not consist of timeless axioms binding upon all his followers in all circumstances, but is often related to a specific context and is expressed in a distinctive style. With regard, first, to context, modern critical scholarship demands caution: it is likely that sayings of Jesus were remembered more accurately than the original occasion on which they were uttered, and the context provided for them in the gospels may be a later invention. Nevertheless, weight must be given to the fact that there is no record of Jesus having made judgements on questions of peace and war, or of having given his teaching in situations where the use of armed force was contemplated. His own refusal to resist arrest, and the restraint he imposed on a follower who attempted to intervene with a weapon (Matthew 26: 51–2), seem to have been motivated more by his acceptance of his own personal destiny than by a general doctrine of non-resistance – according to one account he even authorized his disciples to carry weapons (Luke 22: 38). The 'pacifist' command with which we began – 'Do not resist evil' – in so far as it has a context at all, seems to be directed towards occasions of personal insult and conflict which fall far short of armed combat: a blow on the cheek, a requisition by the occupying power, the theft of a coat, and so on (Matthew 5: 38–42). To the question whether one may risk causing injury or death in defence of the innocent against attack or whether it is permissible to wage war for a just cause Jesus seems to have given no attention, and such questions can hardly be settled by appealing to sayings which appear to have been directed to quite different situations.

Style

Second, with regard to style: one of the most distinctive features of Jesus's teaching is its tendency to sharpen a point by what may seem almost grotesque exaggeration. The notion of a camel attempting to pass through the eye of a needle (Mark 10: 25), or of having a plank of wood stuck in one's eye without noticing it (Matthew 7: 4), are only the most obvious examples: there are many more. It is at least arguable that a similar factor of exaggeration should be allowed for in the moral commands. Jesus tells us not only to love our enemies but to *hate* our father or wife or brother in order to follow him (Luke 14: 26); to give away *everything* we possess (Luke 14: 33); to neglect even the sacred duty of attending to the burial of a parent if the Christian mission seems more urgent (Matthew 8: 22). Are such radical and uncompromising directions to be complied with literally, or are they instances of Jesus giving force and memorability to his teaching by a touch of exaggeration? The question may reasonably be asked; indeed the more general question of how far this teaching can be taken literally at all has troubled Christians throughout the history of the Church. The precepts contained in the Sermon on the Mount are, strictly speaking, incapable of being carried out literally amidst the ordinary circumstances of life. One possible response has been to change those circumstances – to adopt a life of radical poverty like St Francis of Assisi – or to follow a monastic rule which makes possible a high degree of personal self-denial without evading normal social obligations. For such people, a total renunciation of the use of force could be practicable, and indeed they have often received state exemption from duties laid on other citizens. But this solution, which appears to create two classes of Christians – those who can conform fully to this teaching and those who cannot – has not been accepted by some Christian traditions (particularly those stemming from the Reformation). Jesus's teaching, it is said, must have been intended for everyone. In which case, since it is plainly impracticable, some measure of exaggeration must be allowed for. The commands must be taken as an ideal, a constant stimulus to greater moral effort, a model by which to shape one's intentions and dispositions, rather than a scale by which to measure the correctness of one's actions. Of course one should abjure the use of force *wherever possible*; but there may be circumstances where to do so would be unreasonable or irresponsible.

Application

There is the question, third, how far Jesus's teaching is in any case applicable to the very different circumstances of today. A radical answer to this question, first advanced a century ago and still occasionally accepted today, is that all Jesus's activity and teaching was coloured by his expectation of the imminent end of the world as we know it. He expected the Kingdom of God to be inaugurated within the generation of those who heard him (Mark 9: 1); his moral teaching, therefore, must be regarded as an 'interim ethic', applicable only to the period before the End. This period Jesus seems to have envisaged as of such short duration that all human institutions and customs could be thought of as provisional. But in this, it seems,

Jesus was wrong – or rather, since he was fully human, he could not have been expected to have supernatural knowledge of the future and he consequently misjudged the timescale of the events he foresaw. His teaching, therefore, may need to be drastically modified for use in a world which has continued to exist in much the same form for a further two thousand years and shows every sign of continuing to do so.

Modern critical scholarship has not, on the whole, endorsed this reconstruction of Jesus's world-view, and much of his teaching has a long-term flavour which is barely compatible with it. But, in a modified form, the same contention is widely held today: Jesus's teaching was so conditioned by the particular circumstances of his time that it cannot be directly applied to the very different circumstances of today. He belonged to a subject people under Roman occupation. There was constant political tension, frequent violence and sometimes even open revolt. He numbered a 'Zealot' among his followers and cannot have been without sympathy for movements of rebellion. This picture is of course in stark contrast to the predominantly peaceful scene depicted by the gospels and has less evidence to support it than some scholars are ready to admit. Nevertheless it holds great attraction for those who today are living under comparable conditions and has given rise to an interpretation of Jesus's teaching (particularly in Liberation Theology) which is very far from pacifist in tone.

Whether or not this interpretation is correct, the same point can be made in a more general form. The circumstances under which we live, at least in the First World, are so different from anything that could have been envisaged by Jesus that a great deal of interpretation and adaptation may be needed if we are to make serious use of his recorded sayings when we make our moral judgements and decisions. Human beings who have found means both to double the life expectancy of the population and to destroy all human life over a wide area, both to communicate instantaneously with people on the other side of the world and to influence their welfare by rapidly executed financial transactions, to identify disability in a child while still in the womb and to determine the genetic programming of plants and animals – such beings can hardly be guided only by moral rules which were formulated when none of these possibilities and threats was present. In the same way it may be said that the destructiveness of armed combat has increased so dramatically in modern times that even if a clear ruling on the matter could be extracted from Jesus's teaching it would fail to take account of what, since his time, has become the overriding priority: to prevent a major war at all costs, if necessary by the threat of the use of force. In this situation, it is argued, the simple pacifist reading of Jesus's words is inadequate.

But, in this as in other matters, Christians do not base their conduct only on recorded words of Jesus. The Ten Commandments contain the clause, Thou shalt not kill, and Christians have necessarily regarded this as binding as much upon themselves as upon the rest of humankind. In the Hebrew scriptures the commandment was clearly interpreted as applying to homicide and murder: killing in war, in self-defence, or by a capital penalty imposed by a competent court, was implicitly exempted from the prohibition. In this, of course, the Jewish legal tradition was at one with others in the ancient world, and the theory of the just war itself (some forms of which are older than Christianity) is sometimes described as a systematic argument for exemption, under certain circumstances, from the prohibition to kill. Christians, that is to say, found themselves from the start in a world where the use of force was taken for granted as a necessity for state powers, but was sternly regulated in the case of individuals. It is clear that nothing in their new faith caused them to challenge the legitimate use of the sword by public authorities: St Paul could even write that they exercise this power 'in the service of God' (Romans 13: 4), and Christians are exhorted by the author of 1 Peter to be subject to 'every human institution' (1 Peter 2: 13), including, as is clear from the context, those to which was delegated the authority of the Emperor, an authority which was necessarily sustained by the presence of the Roman army. Whether they felt it possible to enlist in such services themselves we do not know. We have no evidence that Christians served in the army before the end of the second century, though we cannot be certain that they did not do so. On the other hand, by the fourth century things had changed so much that the entire Roman army consisted of Christians.

Conclusion

In general terms, therefore, one may say that Christians have based their thinking on issues of war and peace on the prohibition of homicide and the necessary exemptions from it which are found in the Hebrew scriptures[3] (and reflected in a number of texts in the New Testament) and from a philosophical tradition that was widespread in the ancient world. This has enabled them both to participate in the maintenance of law and order, in resistance to aggression and sometimes in the prosecution of wars perceived to be waged for just aims and by legitimate means, and to engage in debate with others on the permissibility of certain kinds of military action. But at the same time they have been constantly challenged by sayings of Jesus which enjoin non-violence, non-resistance and non-retaliation, and by a gospel which has at its heart the absolute priority of love towards one's fellow human beings. Their response to these two apparently contrary influences has varied from total pacifism on the one hand to promoting crusades on the other, the majority having always taken the view that the use of force will always be necessary to some extent to maintain order within and between civilized nations, and that Christians are not exempt from the obligation to play their part in it. Most Christians would accept that there is an inevitable tension between these two impulses, a tension which is felt in the individual conscience but which has seldom erupted in the form of denominational differences; but few would argue that any of these positions involves unfaithfulness to scripture, which bears witness to a God who requires us both to exercise justice within a framework of law and order and to model our lives on the infinite love shown in the life and death of Jesus Christ.

WAR AND PEACE IN CHRISTENDOM – WEST AND EAST

Ancient Christianity and St Augustine

Until not very long ago the story of how early Christians thought about warfare would have been simple. It would have run something like this: Christianity was from the start opposed to all killing and violence. At first Christians felt their calling was to withdraw into their own communities separated from the world and to prepare for the new age about to dawn. This obviously involved rejecting the very idea of warfare. Not until the second century could they even begin to come to grips with the realities of secular society, and then they remained faithful to their pacifist tradition. The scattered examples of Christians known to have been soldiers in Roman armies were – in this view – failed Christians who betrayed the gospel. Their betrayal was followed by the Church at large in the fourth century, with the Christianization of the Roman Empire. Then, with the advent of the first Christian Emperor, it turned its back on its essentially pacifist heritage. It adapted itself to the Roman establishment, along with its ideology, its social set-up, its armies and its wars. Finally, so this story would have run, around 400, Augustine gave intellectual form and sanction to Christian endorsement of warfare – albeit in a carefully qualified form – in his 'just war theory', which remained the foundation of Christian thought on this subject through most of the Middle Ages.

Modern scholarship has undermined this simple picture in several ways. From the older view just sketched, we may accept that there were few Christians to be found in Roman armies, at any rate before about 200. Was this because Christians were opposed to the bearing of arms, or, as has been argued, because to be a soldier meant being involved in a deeply and, from a Christian point of view, explicitly idolatrous religious system? The answer to this is by no means clear, and both attitudes are likely to have played their part.[4] It is clear, however, that there was a strong current of opposition among Christians to violence as such. Although some Christian writers were prepared to concede that wars could be just, we have no evidence before the age of Constantine that any of them would have approved of a Christian fighting, or enlisting as a soldier. Some, such as Tertullian and Origen in the third century, certainly thought bloodshed unlawful. The Christian response to injustice was not force, but the armoury of the spirit and prayer. What we cannot be sure about is how far such writers may be taken as representative of Christian public opinion at large. By the middle of the third century Christians were beginning to come to terms with Roman society; they were now far more numerous in all social classes; they followed all the secular pursuits and had fewer inhibitions about taking part in the activities of their non-Christian fellow Romans. These included soldiering. A career in the army, growing in prestige in the third century, attracted many Christians. It is evident that even before Constantine there were different voices within the Christian community. The tradition was ambiguous.

The advent of the first Christian Emperor transformed the situation for Christians. They had to adjust to the revolution which had turned them, almost overnight, from a persecuted and unpopular minority into a prestigious and powerful group in society, soon to become a dominant majority. They were spiritually and intellectually not well prepared for the experience. Within a few years, Christian clergy and intellectuals had come to see the Emperor as God's representative on earth, his rule as divinely sanctioned, and the Empire as the image of God's Kingdom. Most Christians, except only those regarded as heretical or schismatic in official circles, and eventually Augustine, accepted the Roman establishment uncritically and almost wholesale. It was to be expected that the Roman army and the profession of the soldier would not be exempt from this, and we do indeed find them being sanctioned by Christian writers and preachers.

This was the situation in which Augustine came to write about warfare. We should begin by noting that what he wrote on this subject was in the way of remarks made in passing, in the context of dealing with other themes: there is no attempt anywhere in his work at systematic analysis of the issues involved. Moreover, Augustine was not a thinker immune to intellectual challenge; on the contrary his mind never ceased to be on the move, and the manner in which he regarded war and killing naturally was deeply embedded in his thought about human sin and justice, about the nature of secular society and Roman order.

The most important shift in his thought concerns the nature of human society, and of the Roman Empire in particular. In his last thirty years or so, Augustine became increasingly conscious of the power of sin over human lives, and of the irresolvable tensions and conflicts it generates within human groups. More and more he distanced himself from the view that the Roman state and secular power were divinely sanctioned. He came to see political power as necessary to keep conflict in check, to control the disorder and chaos which were always threatening the fragile order in the societies of sinful human beings. War also belonged to these tragic 'necessities' required as a last resort to check the savagery, disorder and injustices which were always liable to break out between, as well as within, societies. It could be justly resorted to in order to right wrongs, and a duty when it was demanded by justice. It must be waged without the savagery and the lust for power which are the almost inevitable companions of violence. Augustine did not systematically set out to define either the conditions in which war could justly be waged, the purposes it could serve, or the means permissible in its pursuit. Indeed, he was content, for much of this sort of detail, to quote the views Cicero had propounded on these subjects. To credit him with a 'theory' of the just war is to impose an artificial simplicity on an evolving body of thought, and semblance of system on what are in fact scraps he never elaborated.

Augustine, far from checking the pacifist tendencies in early Christianity, as he is often said to have done, checked the uncritical way in which most of his Christian contemporaries were prepared to identify Christianity with the Roman state and all its works. What he asserted about war and violence was not much more than the central truth that to be legitimate they must always remain subject to the moral norms of justice and decency that apply to human actions in general.

War and peace in the Western and Eastern Churches after Augustine

So far as violence, warfare and killing were concerned, the limits imposed by humanity, justice and decency on which Augustine insisted were apt to be ignored in practice, especially in Western Europe. Here, in the new Germanic kingdoms that took the place of the Roman Empire, Christianity became the religion of a warrior society, dominated by a warrior aristocracy. Religious sanction was frequently claimed for warfare, especially when it was seen as undertaken in defence of Christian orthodoxy. Restraints such as those Augustine wished to be observed could not realistically be expected to be obeyed. Churchmen sometimes opposed wars waged on religious pretexts that rulers such as, for instance, Charlemagne used for military enterprises. But wars were, nevertheless, often waged in the name of religion.

It was not, however, until the second half of the eleventh century that Christian opinion swung behind the idea of a 'holy war', and then only in the orbit of Western Christendom. That God could command war – as he did in the Old Testament – was a commonplace since Augustine's time. Several things went into the making of what has been called the 'crusading idea', not least the conflation of penitential discipline with fighting for God. The papal reform movement of the eleventh century gave new impetus to warfare conceived in religious terms: warfare undertaken for a religious purpose, blessed by the Church, and often carried out under ecclesiastical direction. This was wholly in line with the central aims of the reform movement: to establish the supremacy of clerical (and especially papal) authority and leadership over all lay activity, especially that of bearing arms, and to direct lay action to spiritual ends.

This revolutionary new order, too, had its critics, as did the crusading movement, its most notorious outcome – and not only in the Byzantine East, where Christian opinion always remained more reserved about unrestrained 'holy war'. The early Middle Ages, like early Christianity, embraced a diversity of traditions. It was not until the thirteenth century that the morality of entering and waging war was again to be subjected to rational and discriminating moral evaluation. In the brief, but measured, discussion of the problem by

Thomas Aquinas the tradition of thought inaugurated by Augustine once again came to set the tone for thinkers, writers and preachers in the Western part of Christendom. Sometimes it could even influence the lay people called on to fight.

The Christian East had no concept of the 'just war' theory as it has developed in Western Christian thought, although a case can be made for a generalized sense of 'justified war' as a 'necessary evil' conducted out of the need to repel aggressors and to protect the innocent. Also absent from the East, generally speaking, is a 'crusading' mentality. War is evil, though sometimes necessary, so it can perhaps be 'justified' but it can never be 'just'. The focus in the Eastern Christian patristic tradition has not been on war and its problems. Rather the impetus for any thought about the issue is from a strong and focused stance regarding peace, not war. The proper approach, therefore, for a contemporary Eastern Christian approach to the issue of war is to start with peace. Then we can approach the issue of the exercise of military power in general terms.

The approach of the Eastern Orthodox Christian tradition is quite broad, for peace is used as one of several metaphors of the whole Christian experience and world view. Space allows only two examples from the authoritative tradition to support this observation.

First, in the New Testament we find a gathering of these concepts: salvation, concord among people, and the inner, personal condition. *Eirene* summarizes the whole eschatological vision of the salvation and divinization of humanity. Peace is the normal state of things under God. The opposite of God's peace is disorder. 'God is not a God of confusion but of peace', St Paul says in 1 Corinthians 14: 33. The New Testament relates the concept of *eirene* closely to the dynamic salvific concept of *zoe*, that is life, which is one of the summary words for the consequence of the saving work of Christ, the radical opposite of *thanatos*, that is death. Most significantly, Christ calls blessed those who are 'peacemakers'.

Second, this inclusive approach to peace is continued in the patristic tradition. St Basil makes a personal confession regarding the importance of peace: 'I cannot persuade myself that without love to others, and without, as far as rests with me, peaceableness towards all, I can be called a worthy servant of Christ.' These examples illustrate the centrality of peace as a value in the tradition which Eastern Orthodox Christians call authoritative.

Beginning with the position that peace is a central Christian value, the effort of the Church to address concrete socio-historical situations, and wherever possible to incarnate its vision of life in them, is an exercise in contextualization. Modern scholars recognize that the maintenance of order and the exercise of military activity by the state for purposes of enforcing justice and protecting the body politic from external attack were also accepted values in the pre-Constantinian Church. The acceptance of a 'Christian' army for defence against enemy nations and barbarian tribes, with scarcely a second thought, by Church Councils or Church Fathers is not, as some pacifists contend, a massive abandonment of pristine Christian pacifism, but an acknowledgement that with the recognition of Christianity by the Empire a radical change had taken place in the context in which the Church was living and had an opportunity to work. Byzantine culture was now focused on an effort to incarnate the Christian faith into the life of the Empire.

Because neither idolatry nor militarism stood in the way, the idea of a Christian soldier was possible. But this was far from a celebration of war. Evidence from canon law on the readmission of soldiers to Holy Communion, the prohibition of military involvement by the clergy, the general absence of a crusade mentality, the development of Byzantine military tactics which sought to avoid battle wherever possible, with preference for negotiations or tribute or ruse and deceit to avoid military engagement, all point to the development of a tolerance of military activity as a necessary, rather than as a positive good. The absence of a 'just war theory' in the East is a continuing witness to the Church's strong bias for peace as a central Christian value.

THE LAWS AND ETHICS OF WAR IN THE MIDDLE AGES

In the twelfth and thirteenth centuries the political scene in Western Europe was turbulent, and the crusade to recover the Holy Places for Christendom was being preached and pursued. At the same time universities and law schools were springing up in some profusion. It is therefore not surprising that many scholars sought to establish definitive principles governing the permissibility of going to war.

At Bologna in 1140 the monk Gratian completed a massive compilation of canon law generally known as the *Decretum*. In addressing the legitimacy of using force, Gratian starts from those passages of scripture that appear to forbid it, but goes on to interpret them in the light of natural law and of the Augustinian tradition, including Augustine's contention that war, itself a consequence of sin, may also constitute a just punishment for sin and indeed, by requiring

atonement for his sin, be an act of charity towards the sinner. Gratian
finds resort to war licit in defence against attack or in seeking redress
of wrong, provided always that the underlying intention is limited to
these ends and is directed towards the restoration of peace and the
correction of the aggressor or wrong-doer. In addition, he attaches
great importance to the authority on which war is waged.

During the century or so following the *Decretum* many jurists and
scholars, known as Decretists or Decretalists, addressed these questions
within the conceptual structure that Gratian had developed from the
Augustinian legacy. Some appear concerned primarily to justify war
against infidels and hence to legitimize the crusades. Many concentrated
upon the question of authority – who can embark upon war without
seeking higher authority or authorize others to go to war? The Pope?
The Holy Roman Emperor? The rulers of emerging nation-states like
England or France, or of city-states as in Italy? Different answers
emerged in different quarters, but the framework of discourse was
usually legal and constitutional rather than theological or scriptural.

Saint Thomas Aquinas addressed the subject of war in the second
part of his unfinished masterpiece *Summa Theologiae* (IIa IIae, Question 40).[5] In this great work he sought a synthesis of Aristotelian
reason and Christian revelation analogous to the synthesis of Aristotle
with Islam which Muslim philosophers had already attempted.[6] However, his conclusions generally conform to those of his predecessors
from Gratian onwards. Aquinas's contribution is directed principally
to discussion of conflicts between Christian princes: he mostly leaves
the issue of the crusades to his Decretalist colleagues.[7] He did not
attempt to say anything new, but was content to synthesize ideas
already current in writings drawn from the past.

On the subject of war, Aquinas asks first whether some wars are
permissible, and second whether it is always a sin to wage war. His
presumption is that war is evil: his question is whether there may
nevertheless be occasions on which it is not sinful. He begins by
quoting from scripture – on the one hand the teaching of Jesus against
offering resistance to the wicked and his warning that those who draw
the sword will die by the sword, on the other hand the advice of John
the Baptist to soldiers that they should simply do violence to no man
and be content with their pay.

He then proceeds to his own analysis and lays down three requirements which any war must satisfy if it is to be deemed just. His three
criteria still figure large among the seven or so that constitute current
interpretation of the just war tradition – frequently summarized as

lawful authority, just cause, right intention, last resort, reasonable prospect of success, discrimination (immunity of non-combatants) and proportion.

Lawful authority

Aquinas's first requirement is lawful authority, that is to say 'the authority of the sovereign on whose command war is waged'. He asserts that a private person has no business declaring war because he can seek redress by appealing to the judgement of his superiors. The context in which Aquinas is writing is the near anarchy of the Middle Ages in which the governments of city-states or emerging nation-states had to struggle to maintain their sovereignty against powerful barons or *condottieri*, and in which the Pope and the Holy Roman Emperor were engaged in a continuing contest over 'turf' with each other and with other rulers. Nevertheless, the subsequent development of the nation-state, still embryonic in Aquinas's time, has not completely resolved the identity of the 'sovereign' on whose command war is waged.[8]

Just cause

The second requirement postulated by Aquinas is just cause, where those are attacked 'because they deserve it on account of some wrong they have done'. He goes on to cite Augustine to the effect that 'we usually describe the just war as one that avenges wrongs, that is, when a nation or state has to be punished for refusing either to make amends for outrages done by its subjects or to restore what it has seized injuriously'. He does not confine his attribution of justness to self-defence against armed attack: the word *impugnatio* (attack) carries a strong connotation of 'getting one's retaliation in first', if not of actual aggression. He would not, however, allow justness to an *impugnatio* that was unprovoked or designed solely to further the purposes of its agent. Subsequent development of the just war tradition would add that the force used must not be disproportionate to the wrong that it is intended to avenge; the seeds of a criterion of proportion can indeed, as we shall see, be found in Aquinas's own writings.

Right intention

The third requirement is right intention: those who wage war must intend to promote a good and to avoid evil. Moreover, while lawful authority and just cause are necessary conditions for a war to be just, they are not sufficient if the intention is perverse. Right intention is made more specific in that 'those who wage a just war intend peace'. Aquinas expands this maxim with quotations from Gratian and Augustine – the latter condemning 'the craving to hurt people, the cruel thirst for revenge, the unappeased and unrelenting spirit, the savageness of fighting on, the lust to dominate and suchlike'. He picks up a further Augustinian thought that resort to force may be necessary for the good of the offender who must be punished 'with a kind of benign severity'.

Discrimination, double effect and proportion

In the Middle Ages discussion of discrimination centred around what was generally known as the Peace of God. In this context Gratian cited several canons, promulgated by synods or councils, that prohibited violent attacks upon clerics, peasants, or other unarmed non-combatants. Aquinas touched upon the *quid pro quo* for clerical immunity when he ruled that 'it is altogether wrong for clerics to fight in a war'.[9] He based this prohibition essentially upon the sacramental role of the priest at the eucharist – 'their office is not to kill nor to shed blood, but rather to be ready to shed their own blood for Christ, to do in deed what they portray at the altar'. More broadly, in a later question concerned with homicide in an individual context, he enunciates as a general principle that there is no justification for taking the life of an innocent person.[10]

In this same discussion of homicide Aquinas goes on to consider whether it is legitimate for a man to kill another in self-defence.[11] In a formulation sometimes described as the doctrine of double effect, he distinguishes between two effects of a single act, of which one alone is intended, while the other is incidental to that intention.[12]

> The way a moral act is to be classified depends on what is intended, not on what goes beyond such an intention since this is merely incidental thereto...an act of self-defence may have two effects: the saving of one's own life, and the killing of the attacker. Now such an act of self-defence is not illegitimate just because the agent intends to save his own life, because it is natural for anything to want to preserve itself in being as far as it can. An act that is properly motivated may nevertheless become vitiated if it is not proportionate to the end intended...[quoting

from the *Decretals* of Gregory IX, 1234] it is legitimate to answer force with force provided it goes no further than due defence requires... it remains nevertheless that it is not legitimate for a man actually to intend to kill another in self-defence.

Three points may be noted from this passage. First, the clear distinction between the intended and the incidental effects of an action.[13] Second, the assertion of the right of an individual to attach higher priority to preserving his or her own life than that of another – the difference of emphasis from St Augustine's argument in *De Libero Arbitrio* (P.L. 32, 1227–8) that to kill another person in self-defence is a sign of sinful attachment to something transitory, namely bodily life – demonstrates how far Aquinas was prepared to go in bringing natural law into a synthesis with Christian faith. Third, the requirement that the amount of force used even in self-defence should be no more than is necessary to achieve the intended effect: this echoes a passage in his earlier commentary (*c.* 1254–6) on the Sentences of Peter the Lombard in which, discussing whether we are obliged to show marks of charity to our enemies, he wrote that we are bound not to do them harm except to the extent that is necessary for the prevention of a greater evil or the promotion of a greater good.[14]

Conclusion

With an analysis more systematic than any that had gone before, Aquinas takes his place in the historical development of the just war tradition, not only by picking up and codifying points made by Augustine in the theological and by the Decretists and Decretalists in the legal tradition, but also by pointing forward to the importance which the criterion of proportion has assumed in subsequent discussion. Indeed, this nuance is implicit in his approach to the question: Is it always a sin to wage war? If we answer in the affirmative, the question of maintaining due proportion does not arise. If, however, we follow Aquinas in answering 'not if certain conditions are observed', the proportion between the harm done by going to war, or inherent in specific actions of war, and the good thereby achieved or the evil thereby averted can hardly fail to be one of those conditions. Perhaps if Aquinas had lived to complete and revise the *Summa* he would have brought this point into his discussion of war as well as his discussion of homicide.[15]

THE LAWS AND ETHICS OF WAR IN THE ERA OF EARLY IMPERIALISM

War and the Spanish Empire

Mediaeval scholars such as Aquinas were fully aware of their debt to the Spanish Moors and other Muslims, who had brought Aristotle's work into Western Europe after centuries of comparative neglect. But two hundred years later, in a Spain restored to Catholic dominion, their followers found it necessary to rethink much of what Aquinas had laid down concerning the waging of war. For the mediaeval moralists, crusading apart, war had signified first of all fighting between sovereign Christian princes, or between them and their feudal vassals, who often boasted private armies of their own. But now, in the recently discovered Central American colonies, a new kind of aggressive war was being waged by Spanish adventurers seeking to enrich themselves, with the connivance of the Crown, against relatively defenceless pagan inhabitants. What should the conscientious Christian say and do about this? At Salamanca university Franciscus de Vitoria (1480–1546), a contemporary of Bartholemy de Las Casas ('Apostle of the Indians'), found himself during the 1530s lecturing, often to future missionaries, on the justice or otherwise of the wars against the American 'Indians'. Nor did his work long remain strictly academic: his advice was soon being sought by Charles V, whose *New Laws for the Indies* (1542) were based on Vitoria's work.

Vitoria's treatises, *De Indiis* and *De jure belli Hispanorum in barbaros*, contain the seeds of a new discipline: international law. It is this fact which gives them a permanent place in the history of political ideas. Vitoria follows Aquinas in combining natural with revealed truth. But he was also a man of his own time who acknowledged the political, as well as spiritual, role of the Church and the Papacy. However, his gaze is focused primarily on the places where the Church's power impinges for the first time upon people who have had no contact with it.

The two most striking positions which Vitoria adopts are: (a) that, *pace* Augustine, difference of religion is no justification for going to war[16] and (b) that, *pace* Alexander VI's 1493 Bull 'giving' America to the Spaniards, neither the Spanish Crown nor the Papacy, notwithstanding its universality of spiritual jurisdiction, has any rightful dominion over the Indians. As to (a), faith cannot be propagated by force.[17] Indeed, such a suggestion leads to paradox, since if it is licit for the Spaniards to force the faith on the Indians, it is equally licit for the Indians to defend themselves against attack. Thus both sides are fighting a just war, in which case it is wrong to fight at all, since both belligerents are innocent (that is intend no harm) and are therefore immune from deliberate attack.[18]

As to (b), it was argued by some that, whether because they were slaves by nature, or mentally incompetent, or in mortal sin or heresy, the Indians had no true title to their land or property. It was therefore licit to appropriate these by force. Vitoria refutes these arguments too, citing many precedents and scriptural texts.[19] He also refutes further claims: (a) that the Holy Roman Emperor is lord of the whole world (and thus of the Indians), and (b) (more subtly) that the Pope, in order to exercise his universal spiritual jurisdiction, is also temporal monarch of the whole world and in that role has (in effect) devolved his jurisdiction over the Indians to the Spanish.[20] It is in this discussion of jurisdiction that Vitoria can be said to have laid the foundations of international law. Claim (a) is dismissed as baseless, since dominion must be founded either on natural, divine or human law: but none of these warrants the thesis.[21] Claim (b) proves equally false, particularly because it rests on a misunderstanding of the Pope's powers.[22]

These are somewhat dated and recherché arguments. More modern-seeming are three positive claims. First, while the Spaniards have no business waging war on the Indians, they may go freely among them for peaceful purposes, such as missionary work or trade. If they are attacked during the course of such peaceful activity, they are entitled (once reason and persuasion have been tried and failed) to use force to defend themselves.[23] Second, the citizen may conscientiously refuse to serve his prince in a particular war. Indeed, if the war is unjust because it involves killing the innocent then he must do so, because 'it is not lawful to kill innocent citizens at the Prince's command' and 'no one can authorize the killing of an innocent person'. Here Vitoria goes further than modern states do, for he not only allows the citizen to refuse participation in particular wars; he insists that this is a duty if the war will involve intentional killing of the innocent.[24] On the other hand, he argues that foreseen collateral killing of innocents, for example women and children, in a siege is licit if abjuring such killing would lead to the justice of the just belligerents being balked. This concession rests on the *proportionality* principle (we must ensure that greater evils do not arise out of the war than the war would avert) rather than upon the *discrimination* criterion, which of course forbids deliberate slaughter of the innocent.[25]

Vitoria's position here seems to point simultaneously in two opposing directions, both relevant to modern predicaments. On the one hand, he anticipates modern positions on non-combatant immunity by insisting that the intentional killing of the innocent is always unlawful, and nobody can authorize it.[26] On the other hand, in licensing consent to the killing of innocents in sieges for the sake of justice and the deterrence of future wrong-doing, he opens moral floodgates which have subsequently proved very hard to close.

War and the Dutch Empire

In 1625 a Dutch Calvinist, Hugo Grotius, published a book which was to have a permanent influence on later Christian thinking about war: *De Jure Belli ac Pacis*.[27] Grotius's earliest work (1604) was a study of the Law of Prize in the context of the maritime rivalry between the Netherlands and Portugal in the East Indies. In this his instinctive feeling for natural law coincided with the mercantile interest of the Netherlands in leading him to advocate freedom of the seas for all nations against the restrictions which the Portuguese wished to place upon the maritime trade of other powers. In his later work he rejected *raison d'état* as a just cause for war and sought, on a basis of natural law, to impose restraint upon sovereign governments and to establish legal limits upon the modes of violence that might be employed in war. He thus went beyond consideration of the circumstances in which it may be legitimate to go to war (*jus ad bellum*) to embrace the means by which it may be legitimate to wage it (*jus in bello*).

Grotius rooted his thinking firmly in the sayings and acts of Jesus as recorded in the gospels. He was equally familiar with the history of the early Church, the writings of the Fathers, Augustine, the mediaeval scholastics (notably Aquinas) and the Spanish Catholic writers Vitoria and Suarez. He thus placed himself firmly in the Christian just war tradition. But he developed this tradition in practical ways which provided a bridge into international humanitarian law as we know it today. Thus he devoted much attention to the immunity of the 'innocent', which he takes to include not only women, children and the elderly but all whose manner of life is 'opposed to war' such as religious or literary persons, farmers, merchants, artisans and workmen. He adds to this list prisoners of war and neutrals. Military commanders are, he says, to forbid plundering and the violent sack of cities (pillage) which cannot take place without harming many innocent people. He follows

Aquinas in accepting the law of double effect – 'many things follow indirectly and beyond the purpose of the doer' – but warns against overstepping the mark. His test is that we must take careful stock of what occurs beyond our purpose unless 'the good which our action has in view is much greater than the evil which is feared, or unless the good and evil balance' (the principle of proportion).

Grotius expressly forbids the use of poison, the use of falsehood or deception (except to save innocent life), terrorism and attacks on things which have artistic value or are devoted to sacred uses. Also forbidden is the harming or killing of hostages. He comments that, according to the law of nations, prisoners of war become slaves. By contrast, he asserts that both Christians and Muslims 'among themselves' have agreed that prisoners shall be exchanged or freed in return for suitable ransom. He rules that innocent prisoners are not to be killed, punished with undue severity or have excessively heavy tasks imposed upon them. He considers that those who go to war without a just cause deserve punishment. But responsibility for any war crime is widely spread, including those who consented or helped or advised, or failed to forbid it, or failed to help the injured, or concealed facts which ought to have been made known. He follows the schoolmen in attaching importance to the intention behind an act as well as to its intrinsic nature and likely consequences: his own contribution in this area is perhaps most significant in the weight that he places upon the supreme authority of the individual conscience.

Accepting the sovereign state as the basic unit of international law, Grotius enunciated a concept of the equality of sovereign states, between whom he thought it a rule of natural law that agreements should be honoured. He was prepared to extend just cause to permit 'getting your retaliation in first' on the strict understanding that there must be concrete evidence that the adversary is about to attack. He nevertheless stressed the dangers in reckless recourse to force even in a just cause, foreshadowing what is now accepted as a just war criterion of reasonable prospect of success. While generally respectful of authority, he enjoined conscientious objection where the objector is convinced that a particular war is unjust.

Even though he was writing during the Thirty Years' War, Grotius derived the normative character of natural law from a view of man's innate propensities as intrinsically good – a perception different from that of his near contemporary, Thomas Hobbes. He did, however, perceive charity as a perfection of nature and distinguished between natural law, which binds all men, and the requirements of charity which are binding only upon Christians.

MODERN APPLICATIONS

Some nineteenth-century developments

By the middle of the nineteenth-century war had become far more destructive than Grotius could have foreseen, prompting many new Christian-inspired initiatives on behalf of its victims by concerned individuals. Jean Henry Dunant (1828–1910) was a native of Geneva. Coming from a patrician family, he went into banking, but was a natural reformer who increasingly devoted himself to philanthropy and international good causes. At the age of 30, having witnessed the appalling suffering of the wounded at the battle of Solferino (1859), he became seized of the need to humanize conflict, in the sense of urging proper treatment for the victims. There were not enough ambulance workers, and those who did exist had no conventional protection from being fired on, obstructed or captured. Dunant regarded this as a scandal. He wrote a book and lobbied tirelessly (not unlike Florence Nightingale) among the 'top people' of Europe. His work led quickly to the convening of the first Geneva conference in 1863, and so to the inauguration by five Swiss citizens of an International Committee for Succouring the Wounded, with himself as secretary. A 15-nation conference was arranged for the following year, from which emerged the first Geneva Convention for bettering the condition of wounded soldiers. The Committee developed into what is now known as the International Committee of the Red Cross (ICRC). Despite a chequered later history, Dunant eventually became joint winner of the first ever Nobel peace prize.

A number of bad episodes in the early stages of the American civil war led President Lincoln's government to seek some codification of the law of war for the guidance of the Union army. US Army General Order No. 100 of 24 April 1863 set out Instructions for the Government of the Armies of the United States in the field. Produced by a board of officers, it was the work of Francis Lieber (1800–72), a veteran of the Napoleonic wars and of the Greek War of Independence, who had emigrated to America in the 1820s. It became known as Lieber's Code. It was so good and comprehensive that it was widely copied and indeed became the model for the

1899 Hague Convention. Its crucial move was to oppose the previous notion of prisoners as some type of criminal or bargaining counter. 'A prisoner of war is subject to no punishment for being a public enemy, nor is any revenge wreaked upon him by the intentional infliction of any suffering, or disgrace, by cruel imprisonment, by want of food, by mutilation, death or any barbarity.' He is to be 'fed upon plain and wholesome food whenever practicable, and treated with humanity'. This established the prisoner of war as a distinct category, alongside the wounded, deserving to be treated as 'innocent' and meriting special protection.

It is a paradox that from the mid-1860s for nearly 50 years it was Russia – whose public face was often imperial and militaristic – which figured also as the great power most concerned with peace, disarmament and the law of war. Certainly it was on initiative from the Czars that conferences were convened in 1868 (St Petersburg), 1874 (Brussels), 1899 and 1907 (The Hague). The St Petersburg International Military Convention was notable for taking a first step towards qualitative arms control under the rubric that 'the necessities of war ought to yield to the requirements of humanity' and for saying that states should forgo the type of weapons 'which uselessly aggravate the sufferings of disabled men or render their death inevitable'. Its aim was to harness the progress of civilization (that is to say technology) in order to alleviate as much as possible the calamities of war. The proposed method was to seek agreement on technical limits beyond which weapons would produce more suffering than was necessary to put men and women *hors de combat*. The Brussels Declaration reinforced this point: 'the laws of war do not recognise in belligerents an unlimited power in the adoption of means of injuring the enemy'. It also declared as especially forbidden the use of poison or poisoned weapons. These points were picked up 25 years later in the two Hague Conventions.

A notable figure linking the Brussels conference with the Hague Conventions was Fedor Fedorvitch Martens (1845–1908), a jurist in the service of the Czar and Russia's principal active expert of that time in international law. He was born in Estonia of a poor Lutheran family, migrated to Russia, took a law degree, and while in his twenties entered the Imperial Foreign Ministry, took a Russian name, joined the Orthodox Church, and became a professor of international law at St Petersburg and a privy councillor. Widely honoured academically as a prolific author and editor, he was also a staunch Russian patriot. He chaired commissions in both the Hague

Conferences and made an indelible mark there by promoting the amendment clause still known as 'the Martens Clause'. The stated motive of this was striking, if highly idealistic:

> it is our unanimous desire that the armies of civilised nations be not simply provided with the most murderous and perfected weapons, but that they shall also be imbued with a notion of right, justice and humanity, binding even in invaded territory and even in regard to the enemy.

Recognizing that the law of war as codified could never go so far, but not wanting to leave cases hanging loose at the arbitrary discretion of military commanders, he wrote as follows:

> Until a perfectly complete code of the laws of war is issued the Conference thinks it right to declare that in cases not included in the present arrangement, populations and belligerents remain under the protection and empire of the principles of international law, as they result from the usages established between civilised nations, from the laws of humanity and the requirements of the public conscience'.[28]

This can only have been, for him, a second best. Nevertheless the clause, with unimportant alterations, found its way into the preamble of the two Hague Conventions, the Geneva Convention and Protocols and many other humanitarian instruments. Martens died soon after the second Hague Conference on a train homebound from Estonia.

Finally it is worth noting the little known fact that a group which included Cardinal Manning attempted to introduce some 'postulata' about modern warfare into the proceedings of the first Vatican Council (1869–70). These would have condemned the burden of mass-conscription, borne largely by the poor. They would also have condemned 'illegal and unjust wars' – or rather 'hideous massacres spreading far and wide' consequent on the mass-manufacture of ever more destructive weapons. Finally they demanded a conciliar pronouncement about 'the principles which determine whether war is a duty or a crime'. Unfortunately their 'postulata' were never debated, the Council being prematurely halted by the threat of war.

Varieties of pacifism

Until the nineteenth century the refusal to fight was mainly a matter of personal choice. It was not until the second half of the century that population records were kept by such means as censuses (the first British census was taken in 1801) and it was then possible to introduce military conscription on a reasonably fair basis. It was this military conscription that made conscientious objection inevitable. The massive disillusionment after World War I gave a great boost to pacifism in Europe. Conscientious objection, both from religious and humanitarian motives, became a socially significant movement. Between the two world wars, pacifism became a mass movement under such inspired leaders as the Reverend Dick Sheppard of the Peace Pledge Union. But from the time of the Spanish Civil War onwards, as the storm clouds of Fascism darkened, support for pacifism drained away, leaving a much smaller core of conscientious objectors who refused to serve in World War II. In theological circles, the critique of Reinhold Niebuhr – himself a pacifist until the early 1930s – and the involvement of Dietrich Bonhoeffer in the plot to kill Hitler provided a theological rationale for military action and the right of resistance to dictatorship respectively.

There were three main categories of objectors. First were those who objected to the principle of compulsion. During World War II a well-known Quaker scientist, Kathleen Lonsdale, who was willing to do fire-watching as a voluntary act, refused to do it when it became compulsory. She was fined in 1943, refused to pay the fine, and spent a month in Holloway gaol.

Second were those who were prepared to serve in a non-combatant role. Various options were available to conscientious objector tribunals during World War II: non-combatant service in the armed forces, non-combatant service under civilian control, or unconditional exemption from military service. There were also those Christians who objected on grounds of conscience to using particular weapons (such as nuclear weapons) or to the aims of particular conflicts (such as to defend *apartheid*) or to oppress Jews or gypsies. There were also those just war pacifist Christians who applied just war criteria so rigorously that no war ever passed all the tests.

Finally, some Christians think of pacifism as a vocation, comparable to the vocation of celibacy for clergy. They do not maintain that all Christians must refuse to undertake military service, any more than that all Christians should be celibate even though it is a vocation for some. For us, they say, the vocation of celibacy or pacifism is authentic and unconditional; we are to love our enemies in all circumstances, to take literally and consistently the strenuous commands of Jesus. You may have a different vocation, they say, such as to uphold the secular order so that justice may prevail, and that requires some modification of the full pacifist position.

There is no single Christian position that is always right so that all other positions are always wrong. We have the lives and teachings of saints and prophets to help us to choose rightly. Even so, being only human, we will make mistakes.

Nuclear weapons and the East–West divide

The advent of the nuclear era has made a profound difference to the traditional arguments between pacifists and adherents of the just war theory. Since World War II, with peaks in the late 1950s to early 1960s and late 1970s to early 1980s, major 'ban the bomb' movements developed with strong Christian and Christian-pacifist involvement. There was a growing convergence between pacifists and nuclear-pacifists, and indeed those who argued that a strict application of just war criteria excluded the possibility of using nuclear weapons and other indiscriminate weapons of mass destruction in accordance with those criteria. But other Christians advocated nuclear *deterrence*, arguing that this was theologically legitimate since the threat of use of nuclear weapons actually prevented war, both nuclear and conventional, for it dissuaded the other side from activities which could lead to war, such as intimidation or blackmail. Views from both sides of this debate can be discerned in the Pastoral Letter of the American Catholic Bishops, *The Challenge of Peace* (1983).[29] The World Council of Churches' Hearing on Nuclear Weapons (1981) dealt with the issue as follows:

Advocates of the strategy of nuclear deterrence, who might endorse . . . condemnation of nuclear war, argue that the strategy is ethically justified precisely because its aim is to prevent war . . . the ethical point at issue is whether the possession of, preparation for the use of, and readiness to use nuclear weapons fall under the same moral condemnation as their actual use. There is, of course, a profound difference between intentions and deeds, not least in terms of their possible consequences. There is also an element of ambiguity in threats, especially when part of their effectiveness lies in the uncertainty about whether they will actually be carried out. But we cannot escape the conclusion that the readiness to do something wrong shares in the wrongness of the action itself.[30]

The advocates of nuclear deterrence naturally contested this position
– drawing attention to the distinction between an 'intention' and
'readiness' to do something, on the one hand, and the threat or
conditional intention which actually prevents it ever being necessary
to do so, on the other.

The final document of the European Ecumenical Assembly *Peace
With Justice*, (Basel, 1989) states that deterrence based on weapons of
mass destruction should be overcome. This would be recognized
within the European churches as a goal towards which to strive.
Whereas the major churches as institutions could hardly be seen as
having been part of the peace movement of the late 1970s and early
1980s, there was very strong representation of individual Christians
and Christian groups in the peace movement, whether in secular or
specifically Christian anti-nuclear movements. Compared with its
impact in the rest of society, the Christian voice was over-represented
in the peace movement in almost every country.[31]

For the first time, Catholics were well represented in it, following
the conclusion of the Second Vatican Council and the Vietnam War.
The Council had absolutely ruled out nuclear attacks on cities. This
anathema posed a dilemma for Catholics in the nuclear states, in so
far as it condemned absolutely actions which the operational strat-
egies of the nuclear powers seemed to require them to be willing in
certain circumstances to carry out.[32]

However, with the end of the cold war, and therefore the disap-
pearance of the conditions under which, in the early 1980s, deterrence
still seemed to some people (including the Pope) morally acceptable,
the opportunity has arisen for a reassessment. Some Bishops' Conferences produced fresh statements. The Americans, for example,
insisted in a statement of 1993[33] that the eventual elimination
of nuclear weapons was more than a moral ideal: it should be a policy
goal. They insisted on a genuine commitment by the USA to Article
VI of the Nuclear Non-Proliferation Treaty. But perhaps the
most remarkable reassessment has come from the Holy See's permanent UN Representative. In October 1993 he told the UN General
Assembly that there is no longer any case for retaining, let
alone further developing, 'such cataclysmic firepower...security
lies in the abolition of nuclear weapons and the strengthening
of international law'.[34] In short, the need to restrain, and if possible
to reverse the potential for worldwide proliferation of nuclear
weapons, trumps any case for deterrence that has been accepted
until now.

Non-violence as a weapon of the oppressed and for liberation

In the twentieth century it may seem strange that the Sermon on the Mount was most effectively returned as practical politics by a Hindu, Mahatma Gandhi (1869–1948). He had been inspired by an American, Henry David Thoreau (1817–62), and an unorthodox Russian Orthodox, Leo Tolstoy (1828–1910). He used pacifist methods of *satyagraha*, including civil disobedience to unjust laws, in the movement to liberate India from British colonialism. From Gandhi the lineage of influence passes through the Civil Rights movement led by Martin Luther King, Jr, and the black opposition to *apartheid* with such non-violent leaders as Albert Luthuli, Allan Boesak, Frank Chikane and Desmond Tutu.

At the same time, pacifism has been challenged by those upholding the rights of resistance. Much of a decolonization process of the 1950s and early 1960s proceeded surprisingly peacefully, although there have been situations of appalling violence both during and after the colonial period. The issues are complex. Even Kenneth Kaunda of Zambia, who waged a non-violent struggle for his own country's independence, was reluctantly forced to see that violence was necessary for the liberation of Zimbabwe. In many countries armed liberation movements developed in order to achieve their independence. The decision of the World Council of Churches (WCC) to support the humanitarian projects of armed liberation movements in Southern Africa created controversy within the member churches. Rejection was strongest in churches not known for a predominantly pacifist tradition, particularly in West Germany and Great Britain.

In Latin America, figures such as Camilo Torres (the priest killed fighting with the Colombian guerillas) and Ernesto Cardenal (who became a prominent advocate of the Sandanista revolution and one of four priests in the Sandanista government) were examples of those who felt that Christian advocacy of violent resistance could not be excluded in situations of extreme oppression. Others, such as Helder Camara, argued that both in terms of principle and practice, active non-violence was the better way to break the 'spiral of violence'.

Non-violence can be a costly method, as many of its leaders including King and Gandhi have emphasized – in life and death. Nor is it guaranteed to succeed because of its moral superiority, as events in China (Tiananmen Square) show. History is not so clear-cut or inherently moral as that, and political change can also occur as a result of a mix of non-violent and violent forms of resistance, as in South Africa.

What can be stated with clarity is that the growing body of historical examples shows that massive levels of state violence in war or repression have a severely declining utility and that mass non-violent action is increasingly seen as both a more moral and a more effective approach.[35]

The ecumenical debate

The World Convocation on Justice, Peace and the Integrity of Creation (Seoul, 1900) speaks of the need to overcome the institution of war, and continues the clear denunciation of the possession as well as the use of weapons of mass destruction. The emerging ecumenical consensus rejects war, but does not preclude resistance to tyranny or oppressive government. At the WCC Assembly in Canberra (1991) some British delegates were among the minority who spoke in favour of armed force as a last resort in the Gulf (Kuwait) War. The 1994 WCC Central Committee in South Africa spoke in terms even more utopian, not just about overcoming the institution of war, but even about the overcoming of violence itself.

Some might see as equally utopian Pope John XXIII's pronouncement that 'in this age which boasts of its atomic power, it no longer makes sense to maintain that war is a fit instrument with which to repair the violation of justice'.[36] The Second Vatican Council took up John XXIII's theme in different words, noting that 'war threatens to lead the combatants to a savagery far surpassing that of the past', and that consequently 'it is our clear duty...to strain every muscle in working for the time when all war can be completely outlawed by international consent'.[37]

Yet in the absence of an effective system of international peace enforcement, the Council – in line with Article 51 of the UN Charter – granted the right of a nation to defend itself.[38] But even this admission was qualified by two provisos. The first was pronounced during the Council, in its one and only explicit anathema, condemning absolutely 'any act of war aimed indiscriminately at the destruction of entire cities or extensive areas along with their population' as 'a crime against God and man himself'.[39] Second, the Council insisted on the need for a universal public authority with the power to safeguard everybody's rights so that the institution of war could be outlawed.[40] This plea for a global authority to be created by consent to guarantee the common security of all has been heard ever more strongly in papal and other pronouncements since then. It has certainly taken the form of consistent support for the United Nations; but beyond this the Council also, for the first time in the modern era, acknowledged the legitimacy, for Catholics, of personal pacifism, praising those 'who renounce the use of violence in the vindication of their rights'.[41]

Since the Council ended in 1965 the bishops, and especially the Holy See, have become increasingly sceptical about the justice of any wars, even those clearly waged for national self-defence. The principal reason is the disproportionate and indiscriminate destruction and misery caused by modern warfare, especially to civilians. Since the dawn of the nuclear age, this consideration has been redoubled by the fear that war may escalate towards uncontrolled devastation.

John Paul II, unlike some bishops in the belligerent states, was profoundly sceptical about the justice of the war over Kuwait because of its likely disproportionality.[42] Since then, an unsigned article in a journal often associated with the thought of the Holy See has gone even further, condemning the concept of 'just war' itself as no longer tenable, and claiming that all modern war is 'in effect total'.[43] Not all Catholic scholars have accepted this argument,[44] and certainly bishops in countries involved in recent wars have not always been as downright in their condemnation of war as the spokesmen for the Holy See, who doubtless view things from a more independent, global perspective.

An Eastern Orthodox approach to peace in the nuclear age

The response within the Orthodox Church, and of course outside it as well, has been not to deny the need for the defence and protection of the innocent, but rather to raise the issue of nuclear war up to the level of global concern. Arguments about consequences reach their apogee in this concern.

This is most evident in the effort to contextualize the Christian concern for peace in an age of nuclear weaponry. The protection of the whole of humanity from the threat of nuclear conflagration has led to fearsome warnings against the proliferation of nuclear weapons, for reasoned and balanced reductions of nuclear arms, and for the re-emphasis of the Christian call to a ministry of peace-making – all this in the name of the Christian value of peace. Witness the following two statements, whose source will remain unidentified for the moment:

> The proper understanding of Christian commandments can justify
> the moral conditions that were applied to waging a just war in the

past...Nevertheless, the living spirit of Holy Scriptures and Tradition does not allow us to make our conclusions from the church's tradition of the past absolute and dead. A nuclear age is an age of such radical changes in the outer life of humanity that we have no right to be uncritical in applying yesterday's evaluation to today. This concerns first of all our new perception of war. Since 1945, when nuclear weapons appeared, humanity has entered a basically new period of its history – a nuclear age...The consequences of a possible nuclear war are not only terrifying because an unpredictable number of people will be killed. They will be no less terrible for survivors...proceeding from the above, we resolutely declare: today's reality demands that such measures should be taken immediately as to completely deliver humanity from the nuclear threat.

The second passage, also from an orthodox source, is as follows:

It is a fundamental Christian axiom that there is only one war which a Christian can fight: that 'against the principalities, against the powers, against the rulers of the darkness of the world, against spiritual wickedness in high places' (Ephesians 14.9)...Christ blesses the peacemakers and calls them the children of God (Matthew 5.9) and the Bible further exhorts us to 'follow after those things which make for peace' (Romans 14.19)...Peace is the goal and hope of mankind...(we resolve to) dedicate ourselves anew to the cause of peace and condemn and abhor all armed aggression ...[in order] to prevent the ultimate destruction of mankind we call upon the leaders of all nations to exert every effort to de- escalate the arms race, and work ceaselessly toward the goal of peace...[We call for] meaningful and substantive negotiations to stop the increase of nuclear weaponry, to reduce nuclear armaments, to resume serious negotiations to eliminate their use.

Both of these statements are part of larger and more nuanced documents. Both, however, acknowledge a changed situation, a new context for thinking about war and peace. Both writers are concerned, as Christians speaking out of the fundamental commitment to peace, to acknowledge that the new nuclear context demands a new approach to war, which is essentially a position of nuclear pacifism and all that it implies. The first statement above is excerpted from the 7 February 1986 'Message of the Holy Synod of the Russian Orthodox Church in a nuclear age'. The second statement is from the documents of the

1984 clergy–laity congress of the Greek Orthodox Archdiocese of North and South America.

Behind each of the applications of the Christian value of peace in the public sphere as it relates to military activity is an assessment of the context within which the Church seeks practically and realistically to incarnate its value system. Part of the input in determining what that specific embodiment should be is a concern with consequences. As the Church faced the pagan Roman military system, and in Byzantium, the assessment of consequences, which valued military activity for the protection of life, culture, justice, and the innocent, was a major contributing factor to the position of the Church toward war-making, which permitted a qualified support for military activity. But in the present context of the nuclear arms race and the possible nuclear destruction of the world, the interests of peace clearly have led Orthodox people to once again revise their perspective.

Consequences have always had a place in Orthodox moral reasoning, as an examination of any major issue of concern in the Biblical and Patristic tradition will show. The assessment of the consequences of a nuclear holocaust demands that the central affirmation to peace in the Christian teaching and vision expresses itself today as a rejection of nuclear weaponry. This is an appropriate stance for the Church to take in the light of its central commitment to peace.

NOTES

1.   John Macquarrie, *Principles of Christian Theology* (London: SCM Press, 1966), p. 13.
2.   Josephus, *Antiquities* 4: 296–7 (Loeb, vol. 4, pp. 618–19)
3.   It is often assumed that a further principle can be inferred from 'an eye for an eye' (Exodus 21: 24 and elsewhere), authorizing acts of retaliation. But this is a misapplication: in the Jewish legal tradition it was interpreted as a principle governing damages or compensation. Indeed one text runs, 'you shall *give* an eye for an eye'.
4.   Stanley Harakas points out that two factors made it impossible for the ante-Nicene church to encourage Christian participation in the Roman military. The first was the intimate relationship of pagan religious rites with army life, and the second was the 'death culture' of Roman society, embodied in the army's involvement in the gladiatorial games.
5.   Quotations from the *Summa Theologiae* are taken from the translation in the Blackfriars edition (London: Eyre and Spottiswode; New York:

McGraw Hill), Vol. 35 (1972), pp. 81–9, for IIa IIae, Q. 40, Arts. 1 and 2; Vol. 38 (1975), pp. 38–45, for IIa IIae, Q. 64, Arts. 6 and 7.

6. His thinking took account of theirs to the extent that, in some of the metaphysical discussions in the *Summa* though not in his treatment of war, he cites Ibn Sina and Ibn Rushd by name and challenges some of their interpretations of Aristotle.

7. Professor Jonathan Riley Smith, of Cambridge, points out in a letter to the editors of this book that crusade theory had been fairly comprehensively dealt with by Pope Innocent IV (1243–54) and by his contemporary Decretalist Hostiensis, and that Aquinas's discussion of the relations between Christians and infidels (*Summa Theologiae*, IIa IIae, Q. 10) largely follows their ideas.

8. In recent years the mediaeval arguments about the authority of the Pope or the Emperor have found an echo in discussion of the place of the United Nations in the definition of Lawful Authority.

9. *Summa Theologiae*, IIa IIae, Q. 40, Art. 2. Professor Riley Smith has drawn attention to IIa IIae, Q. 188, Art. 3., in which Aquinas permits a military function to religious institutes (such as the orders of Hospitallers and Templars, founded in the time of the crusades), provided that it is exercised not for worldly motives but to defend the worship of God or the public good or the poor and oppressed. Military service in obedience to God is here permitted to clerics, and service in the Holy Land is expressly mentioned as an example of obedience to God imposed as an act of penitence. But for clerical members of the orders, Q. 40, Art. 2 would limit this service to the 'chaplaincy duties' enjoined upon them in that article.

10. *Summa Theologiae*, IIa IIae, Q. 64, Art. 6.

11. *Ibid.*, Art. 7.

12. See Chapter 4 below, section on 'Discrimination'.

13. However, G. E. M. Anscombe points out, in *Intention* (Oxford: Basil Blackwell, 2nd ed., 1979) p. 89, that while the incidental effects of an action may be 'unintended', they are nevertheless 'voluntary' if they are clearly foreseen and could be avoided if the agent chose not to do the action.

14. *Scriptum in Tertium Petri Lombardi Sententiarum Librum*, Dist. XXX, Q. 1, Art. 2.

15. Brian Wicker, in his essay 'When Is a War Not a War?' in Roger Williamson, (ed.) *Some Corner of a Foreign Field: Intervention and World Order*, (London: Macmillan, 1997) has suggested that one reason why Aquinas does not find it necessary to allude directly to the requirement of proportion in his treatment of war is that the commonplace mediaeval economic doctrine of the 'just price' would have led any mediaeval thinker to take proportionality for granted, since maintaining proportion in warfare amounts to nothing more than paying the just price for its waging, and no more.

16. Franciscus de Vitoria, *De Jure Belli*, 10. See *De Indis et De Jure Belli Relectiones*, ed. Ernest Nys (Washington: Carnegie Institute, 1917).

17. Vitoria, *De Indis*, II, 15; Aquinas, *Summa Theologiae*, IIa IIae, Q. 10, Art. 8.

18. Compare James Turner Johnson, *Ideology, Reason and the Limitation of War* (Princeton University Press, 1975), p. 155.
19. Vitoria, *De Indis, passim.*
20. *Ibid.,* II *passim.*
21. *Ibid.,* II, 1–2.
22. *Ibid.,* II, 3–7.
23. *Ibid.,* III, 6.
24. Vitoria, *De Jure Belli,* 22 and 23. The concept of 'innocence' in war here takes on a new meaning. Vitoria is not discussing the use of violence against clerics and others, under the old 'Peace of God' laws, but people caught up in war yet not doing their attackers any harm (the literal Latin meaning of 'in-nocent'). The Spanish invaders had encountered 'Indians' who were neither heretics, apostates nor 'pagans' of the sort familiar to Aquinas, who 'hardly envisages cultures in which Christ has not explicitly been preached at all' (Timothy MacDermott, *Summa Theologiae: A Concise Translation* (London: Eyre and Spottiswode, 1989), p. 328). Vitoria clearly thinks that the sorts of treatment meted out to unbelievers living in the known world including the ecclesiastical and secular punishments such as Aquinas condoned (*Summa Theologiae*, IIa IIae, Q. 10), are simply not relevant to the Indians of central America, who are 'innocent' in a sense hitherto hardly envisaged in the Christian theory of just war.
25. Vitoria, *De Jure Belli,* 37. See James Turner Johnson, *Just War Tradition and the Restraint of War* (Princeton: Princeton University Press, 1981), pp. 200 ff.
26. see Rosalyn Higgins, 'Dissenting Opinion', No. 12, p. 2, in International Court of Justice, *Legality of the Threat or Use of Nuclear Weapons* (The Hague, 8 July 1996).
27. Translated into English by Francis W. Kelsay as *The Law of War and Peace* (Indianapolis, no date).
28. Quoted in Geoffrey Best, *Humanity in Warfare* (London: Methuen, 1980), p. 166.
29. United States Catholic Conference, *The Challenge of Peace: God's Promise and Our Response* (London: Catholic Truth Society, 1983).
30. *Report of the Public Hearing,* in P. Albrecht and N. Koshy (eds.), *Before It's Too Late: The Challenge of Nuclear Disarmament: The Complete Record of the Public Hearing on Nuclear Weapons and Disarmament Organised by the World Council of Churches* (Geneva: WCC, 1963), pp. 3–34. Quotation from p. 29.
31. For the official record see: CEC/CCEE, *Peace With Justice: The Official Documentation of the European Ecumenical Assembly,* held in Basel, 15–21 May 1989 (Geneva: CEC, 1989), frequently referred to as the Basel Report. In East Germany the Church's peace activity became a focal point for the wider movement of social reform and democratization which led to the overturning of the system at the end of 1989. Compare T. Garton Ash, *We The People: The Revolution of '89 Witnessed in Warsaw, Budapest, Berlin and Prague* (London: Granta and Penguin, 1990), pp. 61–77.

32. Pastoral Constitution on *The Church in the Modern World*, hereinafter referred to by its Latin title, *Gaudium et Spes*, in *The Documents of Vatican II* (London and Dublin: Geoffrey Chapman, 1966), para. 80.
33. US Bishops, 'The Harvest of Justice is Sown in Peace', in *Origins*, (Washington, DC), Vol. 23, 9 December 1993, para. IIE, p. 459. More recently, the Dutch bishops, in a new Pastoral Letter, *Can the World Make Peace?* (1996), have said that nuclear weapons 'still present a danger not sufficiently eliminated' and that they pose 'a moral problem that will be solved only when all countries accept, verifiably, the obligation to abandon possession and use of these weapons'.
34. Archbishop R. Martino, 25 October 1993 speech to the UN General Assembly. Further pressure for the elimination of nuclear weapons has since come with the publication of the Pugwash Conferences book on *A Nuclear Weapon Free World* (Boulder, San Francisco and Oxford: Westview Press, 1993), the report of the Canberra Commission of international experts on the elimination of nuclear weapons (Canberra: Australia, Department of Foreign Affairs, 1996), and the judgement of the International Court of Justice on *The Use and Threat of Use of Nuclear Weapons* (The Hague, 8 July 1996).
35. Gene Sharp has done monumental work in cataloguing the range of techniques below the threshold of violence, which are available to populations. Compare G. Sharp, *The Politics of Non-Violent Action* (Boston: Porter Sargent, 1973), and G. Sharp, *Making Europe Unconquerable: The Potential of Civilian-based Deterrence and Defence* (London: Taylor and Francis, 1985).
36. Encyclical letter of John XXIII, *Pacem in Terris*, 1963, para. 127, translated by H. E. Winstone as *Peace on Earth* (London: Catholic Truth Society, 1963).
37. *Gaudium et Spes*, para. 82.
38. *Ibid.*, para. 79.
39. *Ibid.*, para. 80.
40. *Ibid.*, para. 82.
41. *Ibid.*, para. 79.
42. Quoted Chapter 6, below, p. 160 and Note 37 on p. 173.
43. *Conscienza Cristiana e Guerra Moderna*, in *Civilta Cattolica*, Vol. 142 (Rome, 6 July 1991), pp. 3–16. For an English translation, see William Shannon, in *Origins* (Washington, DC), Vol. 21, 19 December 1991), pp. 450–5.
44. John Langan SJ, 'The Just War Theory After the Gulf War', in *Theological Studies*, Vol. 53 (1992), pp. 1–18.

3 War and Peace in Islamic Law

SCRIPTURAL AND JURIDICAL AUTHORITY IN ISLAM

Islam, as a formalized and institutionalized belief system, has its origins in seventh-century Arabia, with the revelations to the Prophet Muhammad, which we know as the Qur'an. The Qur'an states, however, that it confirms the earlier scriptures and prophets of God (Q. 3: 3, 5: 48, and so on). Muhammad was a prophet who also, in his later life, became a statesman. Fleeing persecution in his native Makkah (Mecca), he was invited, with his followers, to Madinah (Medina), where he founded a plural state, based on a constitution known as the Covenant of Madinah. Thus, unlike Christianity, Islam had immediately to grapple with the application of scripture to political life.

The Qur'an is the supreme authority in Islam and the first source for Islamic Law, including the law regulating war and peace. Muslims believe that it is the actual word of God, revealed over 23 years to the Prophet Muhammad, recorded accurately and memorized, in its intended order, during the lifetime of the Prophet and brought together in one volume shortly after he died. There is only one written version of the text, although there are slight variations in the way certain verses are read.

In addition to the text, there are numerous commentaries on the Qur'an (*tafsir*), by scholars of all periods and cultures, but all these are regarded by scholars as human opinion alone, and as such, although worthy of great respect, they are not beyond disagreement or refutation by other scholars.

The second source of authority is the Hadith, the records of the words and deeds of the Prophet, which confirm, explain or elaborate Qur'anic teachings, but may not contradict the Qur'an, since they derive their authority from the Qur'an itself. Some of these were recorded in writing at the time of the Prophet; the largest collections were made in the second and third centuries after the Prophet, and sifted according to the validity of their chains of transmission (*isnad*) by the compilers of such works as the *Sahih* (authentic traditions) of al-Bukhari and Muslim. These collections are accepted by all Sunni Muslims, and most of them also appear in the collections of Shi'ah

Muslims (those who believe in a hereditary spiritual and temporal leadership of the Muslims by descendants of the Prophet). The Shi'ah also have their own collections, believed to have been transmitted through the *imams* who descend from the Prophet.

Muslims try to memorize both the text of the Qur'an and as many of the *hadiths* as possible to guide them in their lives. Translations of the Qur'an into languages other than Arabic abound, although it is still preferable for Muslims to learn as much Arabic as possible to be able to understand the original text, as translation inevitably involves interpretation. However the science of Hadith – which ones are strong and weak, reliable and unreliable – is one undertaken only by dedicated scholars in Qur'an and Hadith. In Islam, especially Shi'i Islam, it is therefore only the most erudite and pious of such scholars who are recognized as qualified to use their own judgement (*ijtihad*) in coming to an authoritative conclusion on the basis of these texts.

Ijtihad

Ijtihad is encouraged by the Qur'an's frequent exhortations to think, use human reason and reflect, and by a *hadith* in which the Prophet applauded one of his followers for using *ijtihad*. Sources of law such as *ijma* (consensus of Muslim scholars on an opinion regarding any given subject), or *qiyas* (reasoning by analogy) are forms of *ijtihad*. These and others are methods to reach decisions on the basis of the texts and the spirit of the Qur'an and *Sunnah* (the practice of the Prophet). There are several other sources such as custom (*urf*) and laws of previous religions which do not contradict Qur'an and Hadith, and consideration of the public good (*maslahah*). In addition there are numerous general juristic rules, derived from the spirit and objectives of the religion, which guide those formulating laws. Some of these are:

- protection of life, honour, property, mind and religion;
- a harm must be removed, but should not be removed by a greater harm; and
- removing harm comes before acquiring benefit.

Early scholars and ijtihad
Abu Hanifah (702–72), the earliest of the classical scholars, and his followers, in the frontier town of Kufa in Iraq, where there was Greek influence, took a rationalistic approach, supported by the Umayyad rulers, using few *hadiths* or texts from the Qur'an, and much personal

opinion (*ra'y*). Malik (716–95), Ibn Hanbal (780–855) and al-Shafi'i (768–820) insisted on proper textual evidence from the revealed scripture and the divinely guided sayings of the Prophet, so as to avoid straying from the path shown by God (the *shari'ah*).

The founders of the classical schools of Islamic law never invited people to follow them, nor did it occur to them that they would be followed for generations to come. In fact Malik, who compiled a collection of *hadiths* under various topic headings called *Al-Muwatta*, refused to allow the Caliph Ja'afar Mansur to have his work copied and sent to provincial governors as an authority for them to rely on. He said that there were many other companions of the Prophet whose opinions were also valuable. The school of thought that was based on his work followed the practice of the people of Madinah, since Malik thought they embodied the practice they had witnessed from the Prophet.

Ibn Hanbal memorized and recorded more *hadiths* than any of the others[1] and said, 'Draw your knowledge from whence the *Imams* drew theirs, and do not content yourself with following others, for that is certainly blindness of sight.'[2] He was persecuted by the Caliph al-Mu'atasim, who was trying to enforce a rationalist philosophy on the Islamic state, but was reaffirmed by his successor, al-Mutawakkil. Al-Shafi'i tried to systematize legal thinking in his book *al-Risala*, devising new methods of *ijtihad* to help reconcile apparent contradictions between texts. The varying methods used by these and other scholars gave rise to differing opinions on the less obvious points and details of Islamic law, and these differences are manifest in the works of the various schools of law (*madhhabs*) that developed, the most prominent being the Hanafi, Maliki, Shafi'i and Hanbali.[3] The *Shi'is* follow the school of *Imam* Ja'afar, the sixth *imam* descended from Ali, who studied with Abu Hanifah.

In the eleventh century the Islamic state began to fragment and one of the Caliphs, seeing the dangers of certain sects gaining undue prominence, and legal opinions being given by people not equipped with the necessary knowledge and qualifications,[4] announced that 'the door of *ijtihad* was closed' and that only the existing legal writings of the four juristic schools were to be followed from then on. This gave rise to a period in which innovative thinking dwindled, and *taqlid* (blind imitation) of earlier thinkers was the norm. In any case, since the society itself stagnated, there was no cause for new thinking as people found solutions to their problems in existing works. Some Muslims still favour this mode of thinking, seeing themselves as less well qualified to use *ijtihad* than their predecessors, and in some circles the very act of speculation and acknowledgement of the fallibility of historically privileged interpretations of scripture and tradition are regarded as a political challenge which may be met with varying penalties.

However, the 'closing of the door of *ijtihad*' did not stop some great thinkers from taking their own path: Al-Ghazali (d. 1111), abandoned his distinguished legal studies to study Sufism (Islamic mysticism and asceticism). He wrote a refutation of rational philosophy in favour of mystical inner knowledge, and thereafter Sufism gradually became the prevailing mode of thought, rather than jurisprudence.

Ibn Rushd (Averroes) was a judge in al-Andalus (Muslim Spain), and was also known in Europe as 'the commentator' on the philosophy of Aristotle. He opposed Ghazali's viewpoint, preferring the rationalist approach of the philosophers, and this approach gained him a reputation for departing from Islam. His chief legal work, necessarily rather conservative in the face of these accusations, was *Bidayat al-Mujtahid wa Nihayat al-Muqtasid*, a primer for jurists in using *ijtihad*. In it, he contents himself mainly with summarizing the views of all the earlier scholars on a large compendium of subjects, including *jihad* (The Book of Jihad is one of the shorter sections), and only occasionally expresses his own choice of opinion. Ibn Taymiyyah (1263–1328), writing shortly after the Mongol invasions, was similarly cautious in expressing a preference for a view that it is only those who stand in the way of making 'the religion God's entirely' who should be killed in battle, while the view that women, children, monks, and so on could be killed because they were unbelievers, was contrary to the Qur'anic verses which say that 'God loves not aggressors'.[5]

The nineteenth century colonial expansion of European power in the Islamic world brought not only the fruits of the rational sciences it had largely taken over from the Muslims[6] in the Middle Ages and continued to develop, but also the seeds of a growing hostility to Christianity and religious faith in general, alien to Muslim piety. Muhammad Abduh (Grand Mufti of Egypt, d. 1905) in his writings argued, in a bid to counteract excessive Westernization and secularization of the law, for a revival in the use of *ijtihad*, as well as faith in Islamic teachings, and in all the rational sciences, encouraging eclecticism between the existing schools of law, and return to the textual sources, in order to find the interpretations that were most appropriate to the needs of the time.

Mahmud Shaltut (see below, pp. 84–7) subsequently felt free to condemn[7] the excessive use, by some classical jurists, of *naskh* (abrogation of one Qur'anic verse by another), and M. al-Ghunaimi (1968) explains that this use of *naskh* was based on a misinterpretation of the Qur'anic verses: *naskh* was meant, in the Qur'an, to apply only to earlier scriptures, which had been superseded by the Qur'an itself, not to different verses within the Qur'an.

Any conclusions arrived at by individual scholars or schools of Islamic law, including the recognized four Sunni schools, are understood to be human opinions, and the very fact of their difference shows that they are not infallible. The Prophet said:

> Verily my *ummah*, or the *ummah* of Muhammad, will not agree on error and the hand of Allah is upon the community; he who sets himself apart from it will be set apart in Hell Fire.
>
> (Hadith: *Mishkat al-Masabih*)

This is an essentially democratic concept of orthodoxy by consensus (*ijma*), rather than one imposed by an ecclesiastical central authority, although some governments have tried at different times to impose one interpretation or another. The word 'heresy' has no equivalent in Islam, though *bid'a* (innovation) comes close to it. Within the classical body of scholarly opinion, there is so much variety that it is possible to find support for most points of view, without resorting to outside sources or personal opinion.

Fiqh and shari'ah law

The body of interpretation of the scriptures for the formation of laws is called *fiqh*, and the laws so arrived at are *al-shari'ah* (the path). *Shari'ah*, however, encompasses both social laws with penal sanctions, and moral guidance whose sanction lies only with God, the ultimate Lawgiver. Its general purposes are justice, equality, the welfare of the individual and of the community. These are constant, whereas the implementation of the *shari'ah* through concrete, specific laws depends on the circumstances.

Pre-modern *shari'ah* law still forms the basis of some sections of the law governing the various Muslim countries, and some governments claim that the *shari'ah* is the basis for all their laws, but it has been much diluted, and sometimes replaced altogether, with laws from other sources such as European law, socialism, or earlier traditions. Borrowing from *urf* (customs) and other outside sources which do not contradict the Qur'an and Hadith is a practice sanctioned by historical precedent from the very beginning, but Muslims are becoming increasingly aware that many of their current laws do not conform to the *shari'ah*, either in spirit or in detail, and are seeking means to change them to conform more closely with the guidance in the Qur'an and Hadith, often returning to pre-modern interpretations to achieve this.

Western writers often take the views of one or other classical or modern Muslim writer as 'the Islamic view'. In the Christian tradition, people like Augustine or Aquinas are often taken as authorities, but in Islam, for any view of any scholar to obtain credibility, it must show its textual basis in the Qur'an and authentic Hadith, and must also show that the derivation has been based on sound linguistic understanding of the texts. The Qur'an and Hadith are thus the only sources of Islamic law known and recognized by all Muslims. Nothing is acceptable if it contradicts the text or the spirit of these two sources.

WAR AND PEACE IN THE QUR'AN AND HADITH

Islam is a religion that governs all aspects of life, and there are rulings in the Qur'an and Hadith on war and peace. In the Qur'an, the relationship intended by God between people and nations is one of peace. War is a contingency that becomes necessary at certain times and under certain conditions. Muslims learn from the Qur'an that the objective of God in creating the human race in different communities was a relationship of peace:

> O mankind, We have created you from a male and a female and made you into nations and tribes so that you may get to know one another. (49: 13)

The objective of the family unit is affection and mercy, and that of creating a foetus in its mother's womb is to form bonds of blood and marriage between people:

> It is He Who created the human being from fluid, making relationships of blood and marriage. (25: 54)

Sowing enmity and hatred amongst people is the work of Satan:

> Satan wishes to sow enmity and hatred between you with intoxicants and gambling. (5: 91)

Division into warring factions is seen as a punishment which God brings on people who do wrong:

He has power to...divide you into discordant factions and make
you taste the might of each other...   (6: 65)

War is hateful (2: 216), and changing fear into a sense of safety is a
reward for those who believe and do good deeds (24: 55). Sanctuary is
a blessing people should be thankful for (29: 67). Paradise is the Land
of Peace – *Dar al-Salam* – (5: 127). War becomes a necessity to stop
evil from triumphing in a way that would corrupt the earth (2: 251).
There is no other justification for war.

For Muslims to participate in war there must be valid justification
and strict conditions. A thorough survey of the Qur'an shows that
these rulings on the justifications of war, its conduct, termination, and
consequences are consistent throughout.

All the battles that took place during the Prophet's lifetime, under
the guidance of the Qur'an and the Prophet, have been surveyed; and
it has been shown that they were for no other justification than for
self-defence or pre-empting an imminent attack.[8] For more than ten
years in Makkah, Muslims were persecuted, but before permission
was given to fight they were instructed to restrain themselves (4: 77)
and endure with patience and fortitude:

Pardon and forgive them until God gives his command.
                              (2: 109; see also 29: 59, 16: 42)

After the Muslims were forced out of their homes and their town, and
those who remained behind were subjected to even more abuse, God
gave His permission to fight:

Permission is given to those who fight because they have
been wronged, and Allah is indeed able to give them victory;
those who have been driven from their homes unjustly only because
they said, 'Our Lord is Allah' – for had it not been for Allah's
repelling some people by means of others, monasteries, churches,
synagogues and mosques, in which the name of Allah is much
mentioned, would certainly have been destroyed. Verily Allah
helps those that help Him – Lo! Allah is Strong, Almighty – those
who, if they are given power in the land, establish worship and
pay the poor-due and enjoin kindness and forbid iniquity.
                              (22: 39–41)

War was thus seen as justifiable and necessary to defend people's right
to their own beliefs. When the believers have been given victory, they
should not become triumphant or arrogant or have a sense of being a

superpower, because the rewards are for those who do not seek to exalt themselves on earth or spread corruption (28: 83).

Right intention is an essential condition. When fighting takes place, it should be *fi sabil illah* – in the way of God – as is often repeated in the Qur'an, and His way is prescribed in the Qur'an as the right way within the teaching it gives on the justifications and the conditions for the conduct of war and peace. The Prophet was asked about those who fight for booty, and those who fight out of self-aggrandizement or to be seen as a hero. He said that none of these was in the way of Allah, only someone who fights so that the word of God is uppermost (Hadith: Bukhari). This expression of the word of God being 'uppermost' was misunderstood by some to mean that Islam should rule over other religions, whereas, according to the principle that different parts of the Qur'an interpret each other, we find (9: 40) that by simply concealing the Prophet in the cave from his trackers, after he had narrowly escaped an attempt to murder him, God made His word 'uppermost', and the word of the wrongdoers 'lowered'.

Where there is both just cause and righteous intention, war becomes an obligation for self-defence (2: 190) and defending those who are oppressed, men, women and children who cry for help (4: 75). It is the duty of the Muslims to help them, except against a people with whom the Muslims have a treaty (8: 72).

Jihad – meaning of the term

The theme of warring Islam as instigated by the Qur'an and Hadith has given rise to many distortions by Western scholars and even by some Muslim writers. These arise from misconceptions about terminology and, above all, from distortion by taking quotations out of context.[9] *Jihad* (for example 25: 52) does not mean 'Holy War'. That term does not exist in Arabic and its translation into Arabic sounds quite alien. *Jihad* is always described in the Qur'an as *fi sabil illah*. It can mean argumentation, financial help or actual fighting. The term which is specifically used for fighting is *qital*.

The Qur'an gives a clear instruction that there is no compulsion in religion (2: 256). It states that people will remain different (11: 118), they will always have different religions and ways and this is an unalterable fact (5: 48). God tells the Prophet that most people will not believe 'even if you are eager that they should' (12: 103).

Who can call for a jihad?

The Qur'an does not limit *jihad* to the state. The word *jihad* means struggle, or striving, and in this sense it is an obligation on every Muslim at all times, inwardly and outwardly to struggle against evil. However, when this struggle requires force to subdue a tyrannical and actively hostile person or group of people, it becomes necessary for the Muslims to act in a co-ordinated way under a leader, or *imam*,[10] who should be chosen for his qualities of justice and piety, in order to enforce justice on the offending party. The Prophet was the first *imam* to lead such a struggle. After him came the recognized leaders of the Islamic community, although some of these fell well short of the ideal. In the Shi'ah community, the only recognized *imam* had to be a descendant of the Prophet, and after the twelfth (or sixth) of these went into 'occultation' in the tenth century, there was no successor (although this did not stop the Shi'i Safavi dynasty establishing Shi'ism as the national religion of Iran in the sixteenth century). The Sunnis, for their part, maintained some semblance of unity under the nominal leadership of one or sometimes two Caliphs (*khalifahs*) until the beginning of the twentieth century.

There is no 'conscription' in the Qur'an. The Prophet is instructed only to 'urge on the believers' (4: 64). The Qur'an – and the Hadith at greater length – encourage the Muslim fighters (those who are defending themselves or the oppressed) in the strongest way, by showing the just cause, showing the bad conduct of the enemy, and promising great rewards in the afterlife for those who make such sacrifices.[11]

Who should be fought?

When fighting takes place the object of the fighting is clearly defined:

> Fight in the way of God those who fight against you, but do not transgress. God does not love the transgressor. (2: 190)

'Those who fight against you' means actual fighters – civilians are protected. The Prophet and his successors, when they sent an army, gave them clear instructions not to attack civilians – women, old people, religious people engaged in their worship – nor to poison or destroy crops or animals. Discrimination and proportionality should strictly be observed. Thus wars and weapons of destruction that destroy civilians and their towns are excluded by the Qur'an and the word and deed of the Prophet, these being the only binding authority in Islamic law.

Although the Prophet did attempt to use catapults against the town of Ta'if, it was only to break down the fortifications, not to bombard the inhabitants.[12]

The prohibition against bombarding civilians is regularly reinforced by: 'Do not transgress, God does not love the transgressor'. Transgression has been explained by Qur'anic exegetes as meaning:

> initiation of fighting, fighting those with whom a treaty has been concluded, surprising the enemy without first inviting them to make peace, destroying crops or killing those who should be protected.
> (Baydawi on Q. 2: 190)

It is clear that the orders are always couched in emotive language:

> Whoever attacks you, attack him just as he has attacked you. Be conscious of Allah and know that He is with those who are conscious of Him.
> (2: 194)

And we note the repetition of 'do not transgress', 'God does not love the transgressors' and 'He loves those who are conscious of Him'. These instructions are given to people who, from the beginning, should have the intention of acting 'in the way of Allah'. Linguistically we notice that the verses, although emotive, always restrict actions in a legalistic way, with 'ifs' and 'buts' and 'except' and 'as long as'.[13] It should be noted that the Qur'an, in treating the theme of war, as with many other themes, regularly gives the reasons and justifications for any action it demands.

There came a time when the *fitnah* (persecution) (2: 193, 8: 39) of the Muslims grew and 'bitter enmity' came to such a point that the unbelievers were out to convert the Muslims back to paganism or finish them off.

> They would persist in fighting you until they turn you back from your religion, if they could.
> (2: 217)

It is such hardened polytheists[14] as these in Arabia, whose aim was to expel the Muslims or convert them back to paganism and who would accept nothing other than this, and kept breaking their treaties repeatedly, whom the Muslims were ordered to treat in the same way – to expel them or accept nothing from them except Islam:

> Kill [those who fight you] wherever you find them [whether in the sanctuary or outside it – the Muslims having been hesitant to fight

in the sanctuary as they thought it was forbidden]. Expel them from where they expelled you: seeking to convert you [*fitna* – persecution] is worse than killing [them].   (2: 191)

It is also this category of people that is referred to in the *hadith*:

I have been ordered to fight the people until they say 'There is no god but Allah.'

The general rule is, 'There is no compulsion in religion' (2: 256), but the central sanctuary of Islam was to be reserved for *tawhid*, the oneness of God, and it was thus declared:

Believers, the polytheists are indeed impure, so let them not after this year approach the sacred mosque.   (9: 27)

Reasonable prospects of success

The Qur'an mentions that a few well-motivated Muslims can defeat a greater number of unbelievers with God's help:

O Apostle! rouse the Believers to the fight. If there are twenty amongst you, patient and persevering, they will vanquish two hundred: if a hundred, they will vanquish a thousand of the Unbelievers: for these are a people without understanding.   (8: 65)

And this statement was proved at the Battle of Badr, the first fought between the Madinan Muslims and their Makkan enemies, when 300 young, inexperienced and poorly armed Muslims defeated a well-equipped, experienced army of 1000 from Makkah.

However, the following verse makes things easier for the Muslims, reducing the odds:

For the present, God hath lightened your (task), for He knoweth that there is a weak spot in you: But (even so), if there are a hundred of you, patient and persevering, they will vanquish two hundred, and if a thousand, they will vanquish two thousand, with the leave of God: for God is with those who patiently persevere.   (8: 66)

Cessation of hostilities and making treaties

Once the hostility of the enemy ceases, the Muslims must stop fighting (2: 121–93, 8: 39):

And if they incline to peace, do likewise, and put your trust in Allah. Even if they intend to deceive you, remember that Allah is sufficient for you.   (8: 61–2)

When the war is over, the Qur'an and Hadith have set instructions as to the treatment of prisoners of war and the new relationship with the non-Muslims. The war is certainly not a means in Islam of converting other people from their religions.

The often quoted division of the world into *Dar al-Harb* (home of war) and *Dar al-Islam* (home of Islam) is seen nowhere in the Qur'an or in the Hadith, the only authoritative sources of Islam. The *Dar al-Islam* included all peoples who were not hostile to Muslims, and in whose lands the Muslims could practise their religion in safety. Some jurists made subdivisions within this to show those peoples who had treaties and agreements with Muslims but were not themselves Muslim (*Dar al-Sulh* and *Dar al-Aqd*). The *Dar al-Harb* (home of war) described those peoples and lands in which Muslims could not feel safe from attack. The word *harb* signifies destructive warmongering, as distinct from *jihad* which is striving 'in the way of Allah' to bring order and justice in place of savagery. *Dar al-Harb* did not include those lands further afield who have not yet heard the call of Islam, as is stated quite clearly by al-Mawardi.[15]

The Qur'an and Hadith talk about the different situations that exist between a Muslim state and a neighbouring warring enemy. They mention a state of defensive war, within the prescriptions specified above; the state of peace through a treaty for a limited or unlimited period; the state of truce; and the state where a member of a hostile camp can come into a Muslim land for special purposes, under safe conduct.

The Prophet and his companions did make treaties, such as that of Hudaybiyah in the sixth year after the migration to Madinah, the permanent one with the Christians of Najran, and the one made by the second Caliph Umar with the people of Jerusalem. Faithfulness to a treaty is a most serious obligation which the Qur'an and Hadith incessantly emphasize:

Believers, fulfil your bonds.   (5: 1)

Keep the agreements of Allah when you have made them and do not break your oaths after you have made them with Allah as your bond ...

Covenants should not be broken because one community feels stronger than another. (8: 91–2)

Breaking treaties puts the culprit in a state lower than animals (8: 55). As stated above, even defending a Muslim minority is not allowed when there is a treaty with the camp they are in. Only when the other side breaks a treaty are the Muslims allowed to rescind it, publicly, giving plenty of warning before hostilities resume (9: 3–4).

Prisoners of war

There is nothing in the Qur'an to say that prisoners of war must be held captive, but as this was the practice of the time and there was no international body to oversee exchanges of prisoners, the Qur'an deals with the subject. There are only two cases where it mentions their treatment:

> O Prophet! Tell the captives you have, 'If Allah knows goodness in your heart He will give you better rewards than have been taken from you and forgive you. He is forgiving, merciful.' And if they intend to be treacherous to you, they have been treacherous to Allah in the past and He has put them into your hands. (8: 70–1)

> When you have fully overcome the enemy in the battle, then tighten their bonds, but thereafter set them free either by an act of grace or against ransom.   (47: 4)

Grace is suggested first, before ransom. Even when some were not set free, for one reason or another, they must, according to the Qur'an and Hadith, be treated in a most humane way. There is nothing in the Qur'an or Hadith to prevent the Muslims following the present international humanitarian conventions on war or prisoners of war.

Non-Muslims under Islamic rule

When the Muslim army is victorious over the enemy, whoever wishes to remain in the land can do so with safety for himself and his religion and his freedom, and if they wish to leave they can do so with safe conduct. If they choose to stay among the Muslims, they can become members of the Muslim community. If they wish to continue in their faith they have the right to do so and are offered security. The only obligation on them was to pay *jizyah*, an exemption tax which exempts the person from military service and from paying *zakah* which the Muslims have to pay – a tax considerably heavier than the *jizyah*. Neither has the option of refusing to pay, but in return the non-Muslims are given the protection of the state.

Jizyah was not a poll tax, and it was not charged on old or poor people or women or children. Initially it applied only to those Christians and Jews who were recognized as 'People of the Book' in the Qur'an, but this became extended to other religions which had books, like the Zoroastrians (under the second Caliph, Umar) and Hindus, under the Mughal rulers. There was no question of forcing people to convert to Islam, only to allow it to be practised and propagated in safety. In fact, the early Umayyad Caliphs were quite displeased when some of their subjects did convert to Islam, as they could no longer regard them as inferior non-Arabs.

Are the Muslims allowed to co-operate with non-Muslims?

Yes, under the injunction to:

> Co-operate in what is good and pious and do not co-operate in what is sinful and aggression: (5: 2)

In the sphere of war and peace, there is nothing in the Qur'an or Hadith to make Muslims feel unable to sign and act according to the modern international conventions, and there is much in the Qur'an and Hadith from which modern international law can benefit. The Prophet Muhammad remembered an alliance he witnessed before his call to prophethood that was contracted between the chiefs of Makkah to protect the poor and weak against oppression, and said:

> I have witnessed in the house of Ibn Jud'an an alliance which I would not exchange for the best of red camels, and if it were to be called for now that Islam is here, I would respond readily.

(Red camels were proverbial in Arabic for the best one can have.) There is nothing in Islam that prevents the Muslims from having peaceful, amicable and good relations with other nations when they read and hear regularly the Qur'anic injunction, referring to members of other faiths:

> God does not forbid you from being kind and equitable to those who have neither made war on you on account of your religion nor driven you from your homes. God loves those who are equitable.   (60: 8)

Such co-operation includes participation in international peace-making and peace-keeping efforts. The rule of arbitration in violent disputes between groups of Muslims, which is given in the Qur'an (49: 9)[16] could, in agreement with rules of Islamic jurisprudence, be applied more generally to disputes within the international community. Therefore Muslims should and do participate in arbitration of disputes by international bodies such as the United Nations.

Modern international organizations and easy travel should make it easier for different people to get to know one another, co-operate in what is good and live in peace.

> There is no virtue in much of their counsels: only in his who enjoins charity, kindness and peace among people...   (4: 114)

SOME CLASSICAL LEGAL INTERPRETATIONS

Most early works of Islamic law consist of *hadiths* arranged under convenient topic headings: the only intellectual exercise applied by the compiler was in which ones he chose and which he left out. In *Al-Muwatta* of Malik, for example, the section called the Book of *Jihad* contains subsections such as 'the stimulation of the desire for *Jihad*, the prohibition against killing women and children in military expeditions, fulfilling safe conduct, booty, martyrs, horses, acquisition of land, and burial'. There is no analysis or interpretation of these *hadiths*, of which only 51 are quoted in the entire Book of *Jihad*, all applying to military *jihad* only. This set a precedent for scholars of law to define *jihad* narrowly within the area of military action.

Al-Shaybani[17] (d. 804), a follower of the rationalist Abu Hanifah, structures his work (*Kitab al-Siyar*) differently, as a dialogue, in which one person asks a question about a point of law, starting, 'What do you think about...?' and the scholar replies, 'I think that...'. Only rarely does the questioner ask, 'Is there a *hadith* to support this opinion?', and then one is given. Thus the scholar bases most of his conclusions on personal opinion (*ra'y*) and human reasoning alone, according to expediency. This gives rise to some opinions starkly contrasting with the Qur'an and Hadith. For example, whereas the Qur'an does not mention killing of captives as an option, Al-Shaybani allows it as a way of disposing of surplus male captives when there is not enough transport to take them away from the battlefield. The areas covered do not include the aims of *jihad*, but seem mainly to be concerned with the disposal of property and persons. Again, non-violent forms of *jihad* are not mentioned, and military action remains the focus of the discussion.

Al-Shafi'i (768–820), founder of one of the classical schools of law, deals with the subject of *jihad* in his book *Kitab al-Umm* (The Mother of Books), where he examines the progression of the revelation from the first *jihad* – the *hijra* or migration to Madinah (a non-violent *jihad*) – to the first permission to fight (to right a wrong done) and then to the *fard* or obligatory duty to fight:

> Fighting is prescribed for you, and ye dislike it. But it is possible that ye dislike a thing which is good for you, and that ye love a thing which is bad for you. But God knoweth, and ye know not.
> (2: 216)

According to his theory of abrogation (*naskh*) this last stage abrogates the previous two. 'Abrogation' is not really an accurate translation of the word *naskh* as, according to some interpretations, an abrogating verse does not actually cancel out an abrogated one, but 'supersedes' it. The Qur'anic verses used to justify the use of *naskh* actually refer to the revelations of the successive religions.[18] What God says in the Qur'an is:

> None of Our revelations do We abrogate or cause to be forgotten, but We substitute something better or similar ... (2: 106)

Thus, although the Qur'an 'supersedes' previous revelations, it also endorses them (2: 97 and so on)[19] and although Islam (submission to God) is the only religion that will be accepted of people by God (3: 85), those who sincerely follow earlier religions of the one God will still get their reward from Him (2: 62).

The context of the above verse 'prescribing' fighting gives it a very different meaning from the one that resulted from Shafi'i's explanation. Two verses earlier there is the question:

> Did you suppose that you would go to Paradise untouched by the suffering which was endured by those before you? Affliction and adversity befell them; and so battered were they that they cried out: 'When will the help of Allah come?' His help is ever near. (2: 214)

and after it come the verses encouraging the Muslims who were reluctant to fight in the sacred month, even though they had been attacked in the sacred month. Although the wording of the verse of obligation (2: 216) is the same as for the prescription of fasting (*kutiba alaykum*) the meaning here seems to be quite different: this is an 'affliction', common to the followers of earlier prophets, which cannot be avoided, and so must be faced up to, not a positive religious duty like fasting. The duty of *qital* (fighting), if it is a 'duty', is here only in self-defence, as Shafi'i himself probably realized. Since the Arabic word *qital* is reciprocal – meaning both fighting and being fought – *kutiba alaykum al-qital* could also mean that the fate of the Muslims was to *endure* attack. In fact 'endurance and steadfastness' (*sabr*) is what is prescribed in the Qur'an, whether in battle:

> Did ye think that ye would enter Heaven without God testing those of you who fought hard (in His cause) and remained steadfast?
>   (3: 142; see also 2: 249, 3: 185, 8: 65)

or in prayer, or in repelling evil with good (at least 40 other references). In the passage in question (2: 213–18), which excuses fighting in the sacred month on the ground that 'persecution is worse than fighting', the main point is to emphasize that, whatever their enemies do to them, the Muslims should not recant and die as unbelievers (2: 218).[20] Some later writers misunderstood the meaning of *naskh* and missed this distinction between the two meanings of *kutiba alaykum*, and in this way the notion of fighting/*jihad* as a *fard* (obligatory duty) subtly became an institution in Islamic law, and was even included by some as a sixth 'pillar' of Islam[21] alongside faith, prayer, charity, fasting and pilgrimage.

Shafi'i goes on to consider who should be fought. He equates the *kafirun* (disbelievers) with the *mushrikun* (polytheists), and it is clear that he is referring to the polytheists fought by the Prophet within Arabia, who were fighting him. He does not even consider the question of exceptions for non-combatants as he is only dealing with those who actually persecuted the first Muslims. Shafi'i did not see any exceptions.[22] However, this does not necessarily mean that Shafi'i thought non-combatants could be killed.[23] Ibn Rushd therefore was later able to state that being a *mushrik* was the main reason for being fought.

Shafi'i then covers the people who are under obligation to fight, and those who are excused, and the prohibition of desertion in battle (without stipulating any earthly punishment). There follows an unusual section on *Idh-har din Allah* (manifestation of God's religion) which explores the meaning of the verses about making *din Allah*, the way of God, 'predominant' over other religions. First he mentions one in which it is 'force of argument' which makes the *din* predominate:

It is He Who hath sent His Apostle with guidance and the Religion of Truth, to proclaim it over all religion, even though the Pagans may detest (it). (9: 33)

Then he goes on to explain how, in his own lifetime, the Prophet saw most of the polytheists and many people of other religions within Arabia and in Syria and Yemen accept Islam, and predicted that, in the great Byzantine and Persian Empires which bordered Arabia, Islam would again triumph, after the demise of the incumbent rulers.

The next section deals with such subjects as the *jizyah* or payment to the Muslims by people who cease to fight them but wish to retain their own religion within an Islamic state. This payment, Shafi'i explains from the Qur'anic verse, is a sign that they concede rule to the Muslims. He restricts this option to the People of the Book (Jews and Christians). Polytheists must be fought until they accept Islam or are killed. This conclusion is based on Qur'an 9: 7–13 which relate only to one particular group of polytheists who broke their promises and were out to exterminate the Muslims. Shafi'i here confused the general command with the particular one, ignoring the *hadith* that specifically allows polytheists to pay *jizyah*:

When you meet enemies who are polytheists, invite them to three courses of action. If they respond to any one of these, you also accept it and restrain yourself from doing them any harm. Invite them to (accept) Islam; if they respond to you, accept it from them and desist from fighting against them.... If they refuse to accept Islam, demand from them the *jizyah*. If they agree to pay, accept it from them and hold your hand. If they refuse to pay the tax, seek Allah's help and fight them. (Hadith: *Muslim*)

Following this, he considers other kinds of agreements and treaties stressing the obligation to keep treaties and vows, supported by numerous verses from the Qur'an, and deals with the status of land under various forms of treaties, when and how treaties may be broken, when a truce can be made (depending on the power ratio between the Muslims and the enemy), and finally with internal (civil) war, in which he follows the Qur'anic verse on peacemaking mentioned above.

Al-Mawardi (d. 1072), a Shafi'i jurist,[24] in his book *Al-ahkam al-sultaniyya* (The Laws of Islamic Governance),[25] goes into warfare in more detail, from the point of view of the duties of the ruler. He defines those to be fought as 'Those whom the call of Islam has reached, but they have refused it and have taken up arms.' As to those who have not heard the call:

> It is forbidden to kill them, use fire against them or begin an attack before explaining the invitation to Islam to them, informing them of the miracles of the Prophet and making plain the proofs so as to encourage acceptance on their part.[26]

Although admitting that there is disagreement as to whether old men can be killed in battle, he states that it is not permitted to kill women, children or young slaves, because the Prophet forbade it, but if they fight then they can be fought. If the enemy use Muslims as human shields, then the Muslims must make every effort to avoid killing them, even if it means the Muslims will be encircled, and find other ways to escape 'as best they can'. If any Muslim is killed by accident, then compensation must be paid.

In this handbook for Muslim rulers, Mawardi also deals with the qualifications of the commander, the rights and duties of the commander and the fighters, and devotes a whole chapter (5) to the 'Command of Wars waged for the Public Good' which deals with the treatment of hostile apostates and rebels within the Islamic polity.

In the case of rebels, he again quotes the 'peacemaking' verse and explores its interpretations, but again insists that due warning and opportunity to offer excuses be given to the rebels before fighting them. Although forms of damage to be inflicted on Muslim rebels are restricted, since 'they are in *Dar al-Islam* and everything in it is protected', when a Muslim is forced to defend his life, even against another Muslim, 'he may defend his life by killing the person who is threatening it, *as long as there is no other way of defence*'.[27]

As mentioned earlier, the opinions of the many earlier jurists are summarized in *Bidayat al-Mujtahid* by Ibn Rushd,[28] in the Book of *Jihad*, one of the shorter sections. Since Ibn Rushd also holds that philosophy may justify religious imperatives, *jihad* implies a set of religious, philosophical and social considerations. In *Bidayat al-Mujtahid*, Ibn Rushd intends to present the religio-social authority which the four main schools of Islamic law ascribe to *jihad*, and he wants to mediate between them where there is conflict. In the process he also clarifies their common ground.

He covers the legal status of *jihad* as an obligation (*fard*) and those who are obliged to take part in it (that is only a section of the community); the enemy; damage allowed to be inflicted on the different categories of enemies; the prerequisites for warfare; the maximum number of enemies against which one is obliged to stand one's ground; truce; and the aims of warfare.

Ibn Rushd sees *jihad* as an obligation the Qur'an imposes on Muslims actively to promote Islam. The obligation to *jihad* is collective, not personal. Ibn Rushd explains this by resolving apparently contradictory injunctions in the Qur'an. On the one hand the Book allows that 'it is not for the believers to march out all together, so why should not a party from each section of them march out, in order that they may gain some understanding in religion, and that they may warn their people when they return to them, mayhap they will beware?' (9: 122). Since the Qur'an praises those who strive and contrasts them with the ones who 'sit still' (4: 94), we would expect it to reward the former and condemn the latter. But, on the other hand, although only some of them go out to 'gain understanding in religion', nonetheless the Qur'an promises a reward for *all* the members of the community (4: 94). The obligation to *jihad*, therefore, while addressed to all the individual members of the Muslim community, is not an obligation for each individual in the following sense: if its aim can be achieved by a limited number of individuals, then it will be satisfied for the whole of that community. There are a number of other such communal obligations in Islam, which are called *fard kifayah*. However, obligation is not the same as compulsion. There is no conscription or earthly penalty specified for non-compliance, or even for desertion.

The obligation to *jihad* applies first of all to free Muslim men generally and excludes those of other religions within the Islamic state. Others excused from duty include the frail, the sick, the blind, the lame and those whose parents refuse them permission. At the other extreme, in conditions of dire need, such as an attack by the enemy on Islamic territory, the obligation extends to all free Muslim men and to women and slaves as well.

'The Muslims are agreed', Ibn Rushd says 'that the aim of warfare against the People of the Book is ... either conversion to Islam or payment of the *jizyah* (tax).' He says that there is disagreement about whether polytheists who are not People of the Book are allowed to pay *jizyah* or not, and mentions the conflict between the general and the particular rule, based on the *hadith* allowing polytheists to pay *jizyah*, saying that some disallow this since it dates from an earlier period, before the migration to Madinah, and was subsequently abrogated by the general command to fight polytheists. Others, he says, 'maintain that general rules should always be interpreted in association with the particular rules, no matter whether the one is more recent than the other or whether this is unknown', and therefore accept *jizyah* from polytheists

Ibn Rushd proposes elsewhere that a consistent and coherent set of beliefs and practices, a common sense of conscience, autonomy, and action such as the Qur'an implies, is necessary to a just social order.[29] By contrast, polytheist religions have diverse gods presumably making distinct and potentially competing demands, each based on its own authority, without affording any common measure through which to resolve disputes. Such diversity has its natural end in contradiction and conflict, and therefore cannot co-exist with Muslim, Christian and Jewish societies.

Ibn Rushd points out that this school of thought contrasts with another tradition within Islam, which questions whether such absolute intolerance towards polytheists is acceptable in a just state. He frames the issue in terms of taxation. Muslims have an obligation to *jihad*, to defend the state in times of war and to participate in numerous duties to the community. Since the People of the Book are free of these obligations, membership of the Islamic state imposes other duties on them: they are expected to pay a tax towards defending and developing the state in which they may pursue their own practice. This tax (*jizyah*) signifies that they accept Muslim rule; it exempts them from military service, and entitles them to the protection of the Islamic state and to its welfare benefits. This tradition proposes that it is permissible to expect tax from polytheists also; and therefore the implication is that the latter may live within the civil society of an Islamic state. Justice makes room for polytheists in the society.

This controversy over whether or not to accept tax from polytheists, and therefore to include them within the social order, does not deny the more important common ground, that the structures of the Islamic State make provision for other religions and practices. Such tolerance is part of the just social order; and the need to act justly towards Muslims and other religious groups that is an important part of the obligation to *jihad* also structures its operation in other contexts, such as warfare.

War is not to be entered into lightly. A 'prerequisite for war' is that 'the enemy must have heard the summons to Islam'. The intention behind this prerequisite is that the community should fight only where negotiations have been unsuccessful. The Muslim army must seek the enemy's consent to the principles of Islam and to its commitment to justice, or to living within such a community, which offers the best chance of justice; it is when the enemy refuse such compromise that it is permissible to attack them.

In other words, the principal basis for *jihad* remains the validity of the Qur'an as the word of Allah and the just social order it promulgates. Actions under this obligation, even when they take the form of warfare, must not offend against the requirements of justice. The tolerance that *jihad* permits is not open-ended. The Muslim community will not have to accept any and every alternative mode of life and behaviour even when it is antithetical to justice.

Ibn Taymiyah, (1263–1328), seeing *jihad* as a punishment for those who disobey God and His Messenger, concurs that anyone 'who has heard the call of the Messenger of God, peace be upon him, and has shown active hostility to it should be fought *"until there is no persecution and the religion is God's entirely"* '.[30] He considers the opinion that all unbelievers can be killed to be wrong since:

we may only fight those who fight us when we want to make God's religion victorious. God, Who is exalted, has said in this respect: '*And fight in the way of God with those who fight you, but aggress not: God loves not the aggressors.*' (Q. 2: 190) ... Now the unbelief of those who do not hinder the Muslims from establishing God's religion is only prejudicial to themselves.[31]

He goes more than his predecessors into the religious benefits of performing *jihad*, and explains that:

jihad implies all kinds of worship, both in its inner and outer forms. More than any other act, it implies love and devotion for God ...

(that is that doing military *jihad* involves all the above), but he still does not go so far as to extend the term beyond the purely military meaning.

SOME MODERN INTERPRETATIONS

The differing interpretations of *jihad* continue to form a tension in modern Islamic thinking. In classical times the rise of 'military' *jihad* thinking coincided with a period of great political power and success, and may well have been motivated by political influence, and even influence from other non-Muslim sources.[32] Ibn Taymiyah was writing at the time of the Mongol invasions of the Muslim world, when the need for self-defence was uppermost. In the nineteenth and early twentieth centuries, when the political power of the Islamic state was about to collapse, the thinking became even more focused on defensive *jihad*.

Under colonial invasion, *jihad* was tried by various groups of people, often led by Sufis (Muslims taking the path of spiritual purification) like Abdul Qadir in Algeria and Umar Mukhtar in Libya. It was crushed by the superior technology of the European forces. Sayyid Ahmad Barelwi, too (a follower of the eighteenth-century mystic, Shah Wali Allah, of Delhi), argued that the encroachments of the Sikhs and the British into the Muslim Mughal empire could only be resisted by *jihad*. Barelwi maintained the *jihad* tradition against the British Raj until he was killed in battle in 1831.

Writing in 1871 in India, under established European rule, various Muslim thinkers, like Sayyid Ahmad Khan, tried to persuade the Muslims that, in order to fight non-Muslims, there must be '*positive* oppression or obstruction to the Moslems in the exercise of their faith; not merely want of countenance, negative withholding of support, or absence of profession of the faith'. Hussein, in 1887, thought that, if the Muslims gave up their idea that it was 'their religious duty to wage war against another people solely because that people is opposed to Islam', they could be 'saved for ever from rebellion' and 'peace and security may be established for ever in this country'.[33]

Maulana Abu'l-A'la Mawdudi and others

Against this same background, but in the more unstable times following the Russian revolution and preceding World War II, the Pakistani thinker Mawdudi (1903–79) took a more radical, less defeatist, view. Mawdudi places the concept of *jihad* at the heart of his religious and political beliefs, arguing that the inherent revolutionary nature of Islam requires it 'to alter the social order of the world and rebuild it in conformity with its own tenets and ideals'.[34] This programme is to be carried out by Muslims who form 'that International Revolutionary Party organized by Islam to carry into effect its revolutionary programme', and this, in turn, means that '*jihad* refers to that revolutionary struggle and utmost exertion which the Islamic party brings into play to achieve this objective'.

However, it is clear that his understanding of *jihad* is not limited to its military form, but also encompasses non-violent means of campaigning and persuasion, occupying the same ground as the communist term 'struggle'. He defines *jihad* to mean 'to exert one's utmost endeavour in promoting a cause', 'To change the outlook of the people and initiate a revolution among them through speech or writing is a form of *jihad*. To alter the old tyrannical social system and establish a new just order of life by the power of the sword is also *jihad*, and to expend goods and exert oneself physically for this cause is *jihad* too.' The 'sole aim' of the *jihad* of the early Muslims against the 'ruling classes' of the neighbouring peoples, was that of:

> establishing a just system; their real purpose was to annihilate the tyrannical classes who had assumed 'divine' powers and were trampling their subjects under the patronage of despotic rulers and kings. When they realized all this, the sympathies of these downtrodden people turned towards the Party of Islam...[35]

Islamic *jihad*, he says, is a striving for justice, to create a 'just and equitable order for human beings' and 'God's just order'. It is at that level that Islam is inherently revolutionary, he claims, since for Muslims to suffer the rule of an unjust state is for them to deny Islam itself. *Jihad*, then, has as its objective the installation of an 'Islamic system of state rule', by eliminating an 'un-Islamic system'.

Islamic *jihad*, he considers, is both offensive and defensive, if the terms can be applied at all to a movement which 'strives to replace an opposing ideology and replace it with a system of government based on its own ideology' rather than a matter of attack and defence of territory:

> It is offensive because the Muslim Party attacks the rule of an opposing ideology, and it is defensive because the Muslim Party is constrained to capture state power in order to protect the principles of Islam in space–time forces. As a party it has no home to defend: it upholds certain principles which it must protect. Similarly, this party does not attack the home of the opposing party, but launches an assault on the principles of the opponent. The objective of this attack is not to coerce the opponent to relinquish his principles, but to abolish the government which sustains them.[36]

Mawdudi also makes it clear that non-Muslim minorities in this Islamic state must abide by Muslim precepts:

> The Islamic government, with a view to securing the general welfare of the public and for reasons of self-defence, will not permit such

cultural activities, as may be permissible in non-Muslim systems but which Islam regards as detrimental and even fatal to moral fibre.[37]

Yet, for Mawdudi, this is not intolerance; on the contrary,

> Islam provides full opportunity for self-advancement to the peoples of other faiths under conditions of peace and tranquillity and displays such magnanimity towards them that the world has yet to show a parallel example of tolerance.

He explains the difference between fighting to establish personal rule, or to turn people into slaves, or 'build an earthly Paradise by appropriating the hard-earned wealth of the people', and the 'hard labour' of *jihad*. 'Islam regards only that war as *jihad* which is fought in the service of Allah – a war to fulfil the Will of God.' 'The governing class of an Islamic state offers service without any thought of personal benefits.'[38]

In a passage he wrote in 1932 he argues that *jihad* is primarily total individual exertion 'in the way of Allah' but, according to *shari'ah*, is reserved for war against those who perpetrate oppression as 'enemies of Islam'. Mawdudi also argued that there were two forms of *jihad*, the classic concept of defensive *jihad* and an additional form which he described as 'corrective *jihad* – the need to correct the behaviour of corrupt and un-Islamic regimes ruling over Muslims'. It was soon after World War II that India gained its independence from Britain, and the Muslims were able to set up their own 'Islamic' state of Pakistan.

Mahmud Shaltut (1923–63), Shaykh of al-Azhar University 1958–63

After World War II, Shaltut, a great authority on *shari'ah*, unlike most of the other popular modern writers mentioned here, and honoured as the head of the most august Egyptian religious scholarly establishment, deals with *jihad* in his book *al-Qur'an wa al-Qital* (The Qur'an and Fighting), published in 1948.[39] His interpretation stresses the defensive nature of *jihad*, and its peaceful forms. He rejects the reasoning of earlier scholars:

> which consists in explaining the verses and chapters of the Qur'an, in their traditional order. This may be done from different points of view: grammatical, historical, stylistic, legal and philosophical. However, all these trends in interpretation obscure the Divine Guidance. Often verses are explained in ways completely opposed

to their real meanings or purposes and sometimes they are even considered to have been abrogated. According to this traditional method, verses are interpreted on the basis of certain extra-Qur'anic assumptions or principles. One can see the result e.g. in the exegesis of the verses concerning fighting: about 70 verses are considered to have been abrogated, since they are incompatible with the legitimacy of fighting. Therefore this method of interpretation does scant justice to the fact that the Qur'an is the primary source of Islam. Moreover, the numerous different interpretations, which were the consequence of this method, created an intellectual anarchy and an aversion against the Qur'an and its interpreters.

Shaltut prefers a second method:

which consists in collecting all the verses concerning a certain topic and analysing them in their interrelation. Thus the purpose of these verses, and the rules that can be derived from them, become clear. There is no need to squeeze any verse into an unsuitable interpretation. Thus, justice is done to all the merits of the Divine Formulation... It can promote the guidance of humanity as it shows that the Qur'anic topics are not merely theoretical, but that they also contain realistic examples that are directly relevant to everyday life...

He emphasizes the general call to Islam in the Qur'an and the reasons people have for accepting it: that it is a simple and easy truth, not complicated or unnatural – a clear truth that speaks for itself and does not require any further means to enlist adherents. This is something also emphasized by Muhammad Abduh before him, and the whole subsequent movement of returning to the basics of Islam, to the simplicity of the original 'call' which was understood by the first Muslims without the need for exegesis or scholarship. He explains that

The Qur'an instructs us clearly that God did not wish people to become believers by way of force and compulsion, but only by way of study, reflection and contemplation,

and that if He had wished to compel them, He could have done so, but He left them free to choose.

There is 'no power but reason, and no coercion except force of argument' to make people accept Islam, not even miracles after the fashion of earlier prophets (another modernist emphasis). Neither belief nor repentance can be obtained by coercion, but must be 'freely and peacefully accepted by the heart'. 'There is absolutely no justification for anybody, whoever it may be, to hold or profess that one of the ways in which the call to Islam has been propagated, has been conversion by means of the sword or by fighting.'

He then proceeds to synthesize, rather than analyse, the 'verses of fighting' in the Qur'an, emphasizing first the responsibility for making peace between disputing parties, where, although fighting is permitted, it is only to bring the oppressive party back to 'what is right' and 'each party must have its due'. He explains that the Qur'an deals comprehensively with fighting between Muslims and non-Muslims, going into:

> the causes which may lead to it, its aim, upon the attainment of which fighting must stop, the obligatory preparations for it by the Muslims and the necessary caution against an unexpected outbreak of it. It treats of many provisions and regulations and enters upon connected subjects like armistices or treaties.

The first 'verses of fighting', he explains,

> are very clear and do not contain even the slightest evidence of religious compulsion. On the contrary, they confirm that the practice that people ward each other off is one of God's principles of creation, inevitable for the preservation of order and for the continuation of righteousness and civilisation.

Continuing to the verses in Surah 2: 190–4 he concludes that:

> there is not a single trace to be found of any idea of conversion by force in them ... the aim upon the attainment of which Muslims must cease fighting is the termination of the aggression and the establishment of religious liberty devoted to God and free from any pressure of force.

With regard to the verse in *Surat al-Tawba* (9: 29) which had previously been interpreted[40] to legitimize fighting *all* the People of the Book (and others) until they accept Islam or pay the *jizyah*, Shaltut points out that it only applies to a *group* of the People of the Book, 'which is characterized by the fact that "*they do not believe in God etc*"'. so that 'there was nothing to hold them back from breaking pledges, and violating rights, and they were not inclined to desist from aggression and tyranny'.[41]

On the basis of his exhaustive examination of the Qur'anic verses, something not even attempted by the classical scholars, Shaltut concludes that 'there is not a single verse in the Qur'an which could support the opinion that the aim of fighting in Islam is conversion'.

Jihad as an all-comprehensive war: Sayyid Qutb (1907–66)

The most noted modern advocate of the interpretation of *jihad* as an all-encompassing war is the late Egyptian scholar, Sayyid Qutb,[42] a member of the Muslim Brotherhood.[43] Qutb was born and brought up at a time when his own country (Egypt) was colonized by the British. Coming from a good educational and religious background, he clearly understood the damage that colonization had brought to his country and to his people in terms of religion. Hence came the need to free and liberate the Muslim lands (Egypt, in his case) from the disbelieving forces and bring it back into the realm of Islam. Although he started his career as a proponent of Westernization, he became totally disenchanted with the West after the establishment of the state of Israel in 1948. His disillusionment with the West was further accentuated during his stay in the United States, when he realized the American bias against the Arabs. Hence, he abandoned his early career and started to write and comment on Islamic topics and became the editor of a magazine published by the Muslim Brotherhood. Nasser's disagreement with the Muslim Brotherhood led to the arrest and imprisonment of members of that society, including Sayyid Qutb. The combination of these factors led to the radicalization of his thought. For him, it becomes imperative to awaken his fellow Muslim brothers to fight not only the external powers and their influences, but also their agents in a manner that befitted the situation. Hence, it was very natural for him to put emphasis on the *qital* (fighting) aspect of *jihad* rather than its peaceful forms.[44]

Qutb's treatment of *jihad* is based on the view that Islam is the last ordained religion which sets standards for all time and in all places. Its truth is grounded in its divine origin. God has chosen Islam as the religion for humankind: 'This day I have perfected your religion for you and completed My favour to you. I have chosen Islam to be your faith' (5: 3) and elected those who accept its truth, practise its tenets and encourage others to embrace it, as leaders (*ummah*) to guide society and liberate humanity from oppressive rulers. 'You are the best nation that has ever been raised up for mankind. You enjoin justice and forbid evil. You believe in Allah' (3: 110). The fulfilment of this mission can be achieved through the assumption of political power so as to lead the transformation process or the redemption of society. Its success is secured by Divine promise: 'We wrote in the scripture after the Message had been given: The righteous among My servants shall inherit the earth. Verily in this is a message to those who serve Us' (21: 104).

For Qutb, Islam, as the last revealed guidance for humankind, supersedes all other human systems with its superb social, political and economic order. Muslims, therefore, are urged not to accept any norms and values of other cultures, since they have their own superior ones. It follows that Muslims are obliged to keep the moral standards of social behaviour as they are decreed in the Qur'an and denounce oppression and evil practices, so that human society can be elevated to the perfect one (God's order). According to Qutb, the nature of Islam is that it emphasizes establishing the rule of God on earth and bringing back humanity from the worship of lords to the worship of God alone.[45] It is within this context that Islam, according to Qutb, has a divine imperative and natural duty to establish its system on earth so that all people – Muslims and non-Muslims – may benefit from its just and humane laws as well as enjoy freedom of expression and belief.[46] Since Islam is a universal message, the whole of the world should embrace or make peace with it. No particular groups or political forces should impede the progress of preaching Islam; people should be allowed to choose freely between accepting Islam or rejecting it. And if someone threatens the practice of the *din* (religion), then it becomes obligatory on Islam to challenge him until he is killed or announces his submission (which implies that the doors for preaching Islam would be opened without any obstacles).[47] This religion, Qutb says,

> is a universal declaration of the freedom of man from servitude to other men ... it is a declaration that the sovereignty belongs to God alone and that He is the Lord of all the worlds. It means a challenge to all kinds and forms of systems which are based on the concept of sovereignty of man ... to proclaim the authority and sovereignty of God means to eliminate all human kingship. [However] those who have usurped the authority of God and are oppressing God's creatures are not going to give up (their power easily). (Hence) it becomes incumbent upon Islam to strike hard

against them in order to establish its own system. Once it achieves its goal Islam would then allow people to choose freely between accepting or rejecting it.[48]

It would be foolish to believe that a divine mission declared to free humankind throughout the earth could be fulfilled without employing *jihad. Jihad*, therefore, must be used irrespective of whether the house of Islam is secure or otherwise. It is an eternal process that never ends until the religion of God is established throughout the earth. Qutb holds that when Islam demands peace, the aim is not to ensure that only *Dar al-Islam* is secure, rather it desires that the religion is purified for God and that the submission of all humankind be to God alone. Also, some people should not be lords over others.[49]

It is the nature of this message that makes the co-existence between truth and falsehood impossible, and the struggle between the Divine system and others (Qutb calls them *jahiliyyah* systems[50] – a term used to refer to the age of ignorance before the advent of Islam) an eternal struggle, until the way prescribed by Allah prevails. There will always be those (the usurpers) who would oppose Islam and strike fiercely against it. Hence, it becomes a duty on Muslims to use force to free people throughout the earth from the enemies of Islam. From his perspective, 'the reason for *jihad* lies in the nature of the message of Islam and in the actual conditions it finds in human societies, and not merely in the necessity for defence, which may be temporary and of limited extent'.[51]

Qutb rejects the concept of *jihad* as a defensive war and accuses Muslim scholars who interpret *jihad* as such of being defeatist and apologetic, influenced by Western orientalists' works. He writes: 'Those who say that Islamic *jihad* was merely for the defence of the homeland of Islam diminish the greatness of the Islamic way of life'; 'Those who look for causes of a defensive nature in the history of the expansion of Islam are caught by the aggressive attacks of the orientalists at a time when Muslims possess neither glory nor do they possess Islam.'[52] He asserts that *jihad* is not defensive; rather it must be understood according to the dynamic character of Islam which aims from its inception to bring people to the worship of God in their individual life and in the state constitution.[53] The fact that Muslims were restrained from fighting during the early stages of the Islamic mission was a matter of strategy and not of principle. They were not in a position to do so because of the circumstances surrounding them. But once those conditions were changed the whole concept of *jihad* became transformed from defence into a movement to free humankind throughout the earth. Thus Islamic *jihad* is not a temporary phase; it is a continuous struggle and as long as *jahiliyyah* systems exist on earth the Muslims are commissioned to enter into the battlefield, take control of the political power and establish God's rule on earth.[54]

In dealing with the issue of *jihad*, Qutb rejected the concept of *naskh*
(abrogating) and *mansukh* (abrogated). He divided *jihad* into many
stages corresponding to the revelation at different situations. For him,
the verses on *jihad* were all revealed according to different circumstances and must be treated as such indefinitely. Therefore, he holds
that the revelation of *Surat al-Tawbah* – Repentance – (which contains
the 'final' directives on *jihad*) did not abrogate other previous verses
on *jihad*; hence those verses which preceded *Surat al-Tawbah* should
remain viable so as to be utilized in future cases similar to those which
occurred during the early Islamic era. On this basis Qutb insists that
there should be no attempt to misinterpret the text and confuse the
issue in order to justify peace with the polytheists while the task to free
humankind is not yet accomplished. Thus, for him, *jihad* is a practical
matter and it should not be abandoned until the religion is purified
for God.[55]

Qutb asserts that the Qur'an (8: 37–9) contains a clear-cut message
to fight persecution:

> Make war on them until persecution is no more and Allah's religion
> reigns supreme,

as there will always be a group of people who will stand against
the practice of Islam; hence Muslims are required to strike back in
order to open the way for the practice of the religion. He also quotes
(9: 26–30):

> Fight against such of those, to whom the Book was given, as believe
> neither in Allah nor the Last Day ...

This verse was revealed after disposing of the polytheist problem – an
order sent to break down the power of the Jews and the Christians to
stop them from impeding the expansion of Islam. Qutb holds that
there is an eternal struggle between the ideology of the Muslim nation
and that of the People of the Book. This struggle has not eased off
since the emergence of Islam, and it aims at destroying Muslims and
Islam through changing its social, political and economic structure
under the name of liberal progressive reform. Therefore, it is incumbent on Muslims not to be deceived by their treachery and to continue
to strive until the religion is purified for God.[56]

Qutb's writing on *jihad* seems to be out of touch with current
reality. Indeed, his interpretation of the subject goes against the very
essence of the Divine message: that is to establish peace, justice and
tranquillity on earth through co-operation, mutual understanding and

toleration. The Quran says 'Believers (the Muslims), Jews, Christians, and Sabaeans – whoever believes in God and the last Day and does what is right – shall be rewarded by their Lord; they have nothing to fear or to regret' (2: 62).

'Help one another in what is good and pious, not in what is wicked and sinful' (5:1). Followers of other religions have been here since time immemorial and will continue to be here until the Day of Judgement. It is probably the will of God to have diversity of faith-beliefs and faith-practices. Hence we do not need to intervene and arrogate to ourselves the power and authority that belong to God alone. Observe what the Qur'an says, 'Had your Lord pleased, all the people of the earth would have believed in Him' (10: 96). 'You cannot guide whom you please: it is Allah who guides whom He will. He best knows those who yield to guidance' (28: 54). 'It is not for you (O Muhammad) to guide them. Allah gives guidance to whom He will' (2: 272). Qutb's view of *jihad* certainly means that Muslims would have to spend their lives fighting others with devastating consequences not only on Muslims themselves, but also on humanity as a whole, and the outcome would be sheer ruin and destruction. Indeed, his writing has already had a disastrous impact on the stability of some Muslim countries including his own country (Egypt), as it has paved the way for the emergence of splinter and extremist groups which have used his rhetoric on *jihad* for their own purposes, therefore projecting an ugly and alien image of Islam which is in its essence a peace-loving religion.[57]

Qutb's interpretation of *jihad* moreover runs contrary to the history of the expansion of Islam, which was based on 'Call men to the path of your Lord with wisdom and mild exhortation. Reason with them in the most courteous manner' (16: 123). 'There shall be no compulsion in religion. True guidance is now distinct from error' (2: 256). 'Let him who will, believe in it, and him who will, deny it' (18: 29). Islam certainly did not establish itself in Malaysia, Indonesia or other parts of the world by the use of the sword; indeed it was by peaceful means. And nowadays, more than any other time before, Islam needs to assert itself internationally not via force and violence, but rather through dialogue, trust and mutual cooperation. It is, therefore, logical to conclude that Qutb's interpretation of *jihad* does more harm than good to his fellow Muslims who are striving to find common ground with followers of other faiths in an attempt to live in peace and harmony in a world with countless people of different faiths and beliefs.

Ayatollah Khomeini (1900–89)

The only one of these writers on *jihad* to have himself led a successful popular revolution[58] to rid his country of a corrupt, unIslamic ruler, was Ayatollah Khomeini. In one of his lectures in Najaf (Iraq) in 1972, titled *Mubaraza ba Nafs ya Jihad-i Akbar* (The struggle against the Appetitive Soul or the Supreme *Jihad*), he mentioned the spiritual side of *jihad* as a precursor to the military outer struggle. He said that Truth is obscured by successive veils – lust, vainglory, arrogance, love of power, selfishness – and once these veils are removed, the light of God will shine within the soul of a believer. The act of removing these veils, or deadly sins, is called the greater *jihad*. Its consummation opens the way for a fruitful engagement in worldly affairs. This engagement consists of cleansing society of decadence, corruption and tyrannical governments. The performance of these and similar tasks constitutes the lesser *jihad*.[59] Through his doctrine of *wilayat al-faqih* – responsibility for action by the scholars of law, since they are 'the heirs of the prophets' according to a *hadith* – he overcame Shi'i resistance to political action in the absence of the rightful *imam* (descended from the Prophet Muhammad).[60]

As with Mawdudi and Qutb, the emphasis has shifted from fighting the external or internal attacker, to removing the unjust ruler. The distinction between communist and Islamic terminology in the Iranian revolution is less blurred than in earlier Muslim independence struggles in India, Algeria and Libya.[61]

Shaykh Omar Abdul Rahman

Notorious for his alleged involvement in the bombing of the International Trade Center Building in New York, the Egyptian Shaykh Omar Abdul Rahman explains in his book *The Present Rulers and Islam. Are they Muslims or Not?*[62] the aspects of *jihad* theory related to the removal of unjust rulers, and the justifications for rebellion against them. Again the current political situation dictates the emphasis of the writings. In Muslim countries like Egypt, the rulers are supported by Western neo-colonial power and are seen to be imposed on the Muslims, and to perpetuate Western hegemony, laws and ways of thinking inimical to Islam.

Most of Shaykh Omar's book is very conventional, and fully based on the Qur'an and numerous *hadiths*, and opinions of earlier scholars, most of which urge patience and discourage rebellion against the ruler if it will cause harm and conflict (*fitnah*) greater than the good achieved (that is, there is proportionality) and unless the ruler shows clear signs of unbelief and hostility towards Islam, preferring attempts to reform the ruler if at all possible. Al-Zarqani, for example, a Hanbali scholar, is quoted as saying:

> Patience before oppression comes before revolt against it since in revolt we expect the exchange of security for fear and bloodshed, for the spread of evil and violence and this is weightier than patience under oppression. From the sources of religion and tradition it is clear that of these two evils, the first, patience under the oppressor is to be preferred.

Shaykh Omar sums up, saying that:

> The guiding principle is that the *ummah* should remove the *imam* when there is just cause and whenever this would not lead to *fitnah*. The majority concurs that this is the correct response to corruption, oppression and abuse of the law. When the conduct of the *imam* is detrimental to the condition of the Muslims and undermines religion, then it is for the *ummah* to overthrow him since the reason for his appointment was in fact the ordering and improvement of the affairs of the *ummah*. Some within this body of opinion still hold that where his removal would lead to *fitnah* the course is determined by the lesser of the two evils.[63]

However, in two paragraphs,[64] Shaykh Omar expresses his preference for an opinion of 'some scholars' that 'the Khalifah should be overthrown whenever there is a justification for doing so even though it may lead to *fitnah* (civil strife)', which he sees rather as:

> a struggle for reform since its ultimate aim would be the elevation of Truth, the uprooting of corruption and the reaffirmation of Islam. The very existence of a threat to the social order is in itself justification for the overthrow of the regime. This is because the most serious of threats is ultimately that which comes from within the regime, the responsibility to preserve and establish Islam remains with every Muslim.

The last part of the book attempts to explain what would count as clear signs of *kufr* (unbelief) such as to justify rebellion against the ruler, distinguishing between mere occasional disobedience to the 'divine writ' and outright rejection of it, imposing a 'secular legal code' on the people 'in substitution of the Divine *Shari'ah*'. He quotes the verse:

If any do fail to judge by (the light of) what God hath revealed, they
are (no better than) Unbelievers.   (5: 44)

Abandoning the prayer and 'changing the *shari'ah*' are some of the
'clear signs' of *kufr*. The Shaykh puts forward some very obvious
examples, like that of the Mongols under Genghis Khan who imposed
the death penalty for offences carrying lesser punishments in Islamic
shari'ah or not considered offences at all; and 'calling into question
the *haram* nature' of sexual intercourse outside marriage. This would
be equivalent to *shirk*, or associating partners with God, according to
the Qur'anic verse:

> Or have they partners (of Allah) who have made lawful for them in
> religion that which Allah allowed not?   (42: 21)

However, it is not made clear how to decide exactly what changes to
the *shari'ah* would disqualify the ruler to an extent which would
justify the *fitnah* that would be caused by removing him.

HOW DOES ISLAMIC LAW APPLY TO MODERN WARFARE?

The basic rules of Islamic law remain the same in modern times, except
that the scale of the warfare has become greater and more devastating
with modern weapons and equipment. Islamic law still does not permit
Muslims to fight people who are not fighting them, or to use fire (a
prerogative of God), and non-combatants should not be involved, as
they are in modern warfare that uses weapons of mass destruction.
    In the face of the overwhelming military superiority of the non-
Muslim world, alliances with non-Muslims have been the main form
of self-defence possible to Muslim countries since the decline of Muslim military power in the eighteenth and nineteenth centuries. However, some Muslim scholars protested when Saudi Arabia was
reluctantly persuaded by the US to allow non-Muslim forces into
their country, the cradle of Islam, ostensibly as a temporary measure[65]
to defend them against Iraq during the Kuwait war, on the grounds
that the Qur'an commands believers not to make the unbelievers their
friends and protectors:

> O ye who believe! take not for friends and protectors those who
> take your religion for a mockery or sport, whether among those
> who received the Scripture before you, or among those who reject
> Faith; but fear ye God, if ye have faith (indeed).   (5: 57)

and that the Land of Arabia was specially holy and should be kept free of unbelievers (2: 191, see pp. 108–9).

Iran has been accused of trying to obtain nuclear weapons, although the Iranian government has publicly condemned them as a means of self-defence because they employ disproportionate use of force,[66] and Pakistan is suspected of having acquired 'an Islamic bomb'. However, the Muslim world still lags behind, both in high tech weaponry and in the skill, or will, to use it. Muslim countries like Egypt and Pakistan appear more concerned to divest Israel and India of their nuclear arsenals, which they see as a threat, than to acquire the technology themselves, and Egypt initially expressed reservations about signing a recent non-proliferation treaty as a lever to achieve this. Though one modern Muslim writer[67] opines that nuclear weapons can legitimately be produced as a deterrent, on the strength of the verse:

Make ready for them whatever force and strings of horses you can, to terrify thereby the enemy of God and your enemy. (8: 60)

and that retaliation would be allowed with nuclear weapons if attacked, the use of nuclear, or indeed other modern chemical or biological weapons, even in such circumstances, would still cause untold 'mischief on the earth':

When it is said to them: 'Make not mischief on the earth,' they say: 'Why, we only Want to make peace!' (2: 11)

and destroy, with fire and by radiation, poisoning and so on, innumerable non-combatants, possibly even the Muslims themselves in their own lands, none of which effects are permissible in Islamic law.

Ayatollah Taleqani, one of the most eminent thinkers behind the Iranian revolution of 1979, included the arms trade as one of the harmful forms of trade forbidden (*haram*) to Muslims,[68] but there are few leaders of Muslim countries who can avoid being bribed, pressurized or frightened into spending large proportions of their sometimes meagre national budgets on expensive foreign arms, in return for whatever aid and trade the developed nations are willing to offer.

In this context of military weakness and subservience to non-Muslims, little reference to Islamic law is made by modern Muslim rulers when the prospect of war is mentioned, although Saddam Hussein, originally leader of a secular party, was quick to call for *jihad*, and to be seen praying, when under attack. One notable exception during the run-up to the 1990–1 Kuwait war was King Hussein of Jordan, who, without actually mentioning Islamic law, showed that he understood and upheld its principles. After repeated, energetic attempts at peace-making between the 'brotherly Arab countries' of Iraq and Kuwait, he pleaded against the war on humanitarian and ecological grounds:

> A war in the Gulf would not only result in devastating human death and injury and tremendous economic loss and prolonged political confrontation between Orient and Occident, it could also lead to an environmental catastrophe that would be swift, severe, and devastating.[69]

In such conflicts as the one in Bosnia, and Palestine, Muslims are torn between their obligations under international laws and agreements, to which they are party, and their obligation under Islamic law to supply military and other aid to Muslims, wherever they are, who are being oppressed and even exterminated because they are Muslims. This accounts for the indignation felt by Egyptian Muslims at the Camp David agreement, which effectively debarred the Egyptian govern-ment from calling for a *jihad* against the Zionist state that oppresses Muslim Palestinians. Officially, Muslim governments have chosen to act within the framework of the United Nations, rather than provoke antagonism by supporting military action.

The most obvious application of Islamic teachings to modern war-fare is in the verse quoted above:

> If there are twenty amongst you, patient and persevering, they will vanquish two hundred: if a hundred, they will vanquish a thousand of the Unbelievers: for these are a people without understanding.

Faith in such teachings, along with the belief that anyone killed 'in the way of Allah' (that is in self defence, or defence of the Muslims, or of Islam) will go straight to Paradise, with all its rewards as mentioned in the Qur'an and Hadith, gives Muslim fighters a courage which Wes-tern writers and journalists marvel at, in a bemused way, as a kind of admirable insanity.

TERRORISM

However, where this courage is applied in a way which is counter-productive, harms innocent people, and causes needless destruction, it is condemned by Islamic law as extremism. The Muslims are praised in the Qur'an as a people who take the middle course and keep the balance of justice between right and wrong. Terrorism and extremism are alike foreign to Islam. The very concept of 'terrorism' has no expression in the Arabic language, but is imported from the West.

The methods used by irregular, militant groups are mostly gleaned from a number of non-Islamic sources, and show little more respect for Islamic, or any other, law than do those used by modern states. The Qur'an, for example, says:

> Make not your own hands contribute to (your) destruction; but do good; for God loveth those who do good. (2: 19)

which should outlaw suicide bombings, and 'no soul shall bear another's burden' (35: 17), which should outlaw the harming of innocent non-combatants. The prohibitions on using fire as a weapon should also prevent such terrorist atrocities involving civilians; so should the need to invite the enemies to Islam before attacking them. The terrorist works completely outside the law of Islam, setting himself up as plaintiff, judge and executioner, and executes people who have committed no crime, while leaving the criminals unharmed. He also works in secrecy, often without stating the reason for the attack, which is condemned in the Qur'an (4: 81, 58: 9) and contrary to the main purpose of *jihad*, which is to establish religious principles and justice. Terrorism, in the sense of frightening people, is also contrary to the Hadith. The Prophet said:

> 'By Allah, he does not believe! By Allah, he does not believe! By Allah, he does not believe!' It was said, 'Who is that, O Allah's Messenger?' He said, 'That person whose neighbour does not feel safe from his evil.' (Bukhari)

However, occasionally some justification is apparently sought by terrorists through reference to Islamic sources. In late 1996, for example, Algerian extremists have allegedly expressed a preference for cutting throats rather than using other forms of killing, as it is more practical (requiring no supplies of ammunition) and more Islamic, being mentioned in the Qur'an: 'smite their necks' (8: 12, 47: 4). It is not clear, however, to what extent the practical considerations outweigh the religious ones; nor is it clear, indeed, what is the purpose of these killings that are going on, or who is actually behind them.

The Prophet said:

Fighting is of two kinds: The one who seeks Allah's favour, obeys the leader, gives the property he values, treats his associates gently and avoids doing mischief, will have the reward for all the time whether he is asleep or awake; but the one who fights in a boasting spirit, for the sake of display and to gain a reputation, who disobeys the leader and does mischief in the earth will not return with credit or without blame.   (Hadith: *Abu Dawud*)

This can apply equally to all kinds of terrorism, by states as well as groups of rebels. Some recent and current governments of Islamic states have made a great show of the expensive weaponry they have bought with state funds from the West, and never tire of trumpeting their military victories. Wasting state money on unnecessary arms was one of the main charges levelled at the Shah of Iran.

In Islam the end does not justify the means; the means are the end. Fighting in the way of Allah is like living in the way of Allah. Both should exemplify the spirit of truth, justice and goodness, whether or not they meet with worldly success.

CONCLUSION

In his farewell sermon, the Prophet urged his people to hold on to two things he was leaving them which would prevent them going astray – the Qur'an and Hadith. The body of Islamic law is a monumental and constantly developing human attempt to put the word of God into practice and follow the Prophet's good example, as the Qur'an recommends (33: 21), and so establish peace, truth, justice and mercy in all human dealings.

The Qur'an describes how Allah set up the balance of justice between good and evil (55: 7–9), and one of the ways in which this is maintained is that one group of people check another (22: 40) by struggling against them, in the same way that the balance of nature is maintained by constant competition. The verses of fighting in the Qur'an constantly check and balance one another, first urging struggle against evil, and then restraining and limiting the means to this end so as to ensure that they remain good, and this is why confusion arose in the minds of some who wanted clear yes or no answers to whether fighting was allowed. The Prophet said:

Verily Allah has enjoined goodness to everything; so when you kill, kill in a good way...   (Hadith: *Muslim*)

Whether in war or peace, in military or non-violent campaigns, the watchwords in the Qur'an are *sabr* (steadfastness) and *sakina* (tranquillity, sent by Allah into the hearts of the believers). Islamic law sustained a vast, international Islamic civilization over twelve centuries. Even now, without a state to enforce it, Islam rules the lives of millions of Muslims worldwide and without an army it is still spreading fast. A chapter like this can only skim the surface of the many volumes devoted to it. Points of law can be endlessly interpreted, misinterpreted and reinterpreted, but always there is the Qur'an and the example of the Prophet Muhammad to return to.

NOTES

1. His collection is so vast that it has still defied translation into English.
2. T. Hughes, *The Dictionary of Islam* (Lahore: The Book House 1885), under 'Ibn Hanbal'.
3. Adherents to the school (*madhhab*) of Abu Hanifah eventually became the most numerous since the Ottoman Turkish rulers adopted this school of law to help them run their extensive empire, for example Malikis mostly to be found in North Africa, Shafi'is in Egypt and Hanbalis in Saudi Arabia. The four founding imams were so close in time that they learned from one another.
4. See the entry on *ijtihad* in Hughes, *The Dictionary of Islam*, for a full explanation of the 'almost impossible' quantity of knowledge and quality of personal piety required.
5. *Shaybani: The Islamic Law of Nations* trans. M. Khadduri (Johns Hopkins Press, 1966), Introduction, p. 56; and R. Peters, *Jihad in Classical and Modern Islam* (Princeton: Markus Wiener Publishers, 1996), p. 49 for Ibn Taymiyya's argument.
6. See George Sarton, *An Introduction to the History of Science*, Baltimore, 1931.
7. Mahmud Shaltut, *The Muslim Conception of International Law and the Western Approach* (The Hague: Martinus Nijhof, 1968).
8. See Abbas Mahmoud al-Aqqad, *Haqa'iq al-Islam wa abatil khusumih* (Cairo: Dar al-Hilal, 1957), pp. 187–91, quoting a survey by Ahmad Zaki Pasha.
9. James J. Busuttil, 'Slay them wherever you find them: Humanitarian Law in Islam', in *Revue de Droit Penal Militaire et de Droit de la Guerre* (Oxford: Linacre College, 1991), pp. 113–40.
10. See Ibn Naqib al-Misri, *Reliance of the Traveller*, trans. Nuh Ha Mim Keller (Evanston: Sunna Books, 1994); and Abu'l-Hasan al-Mawardi,

al-Ahkam as-Sultaniyyah: The Laws of Islamic Governance, trans. A. Yate (London: Ta Ha Publishers, 1996).

11.   See for example 3: 169–72, 9: 120–1 and many *hadiths* in the chapters on *jihad* in the various collections of *hadiths*.

12.   See Ibn Ishaq, *Life of Prophet Muhammad*, trans. A. Guillaume (Oxford University Press, 1955, repr. 1968, 1970). Use of catapults gave rise to an argument about whether such weapons should be used if they might harm non-combatants accidentally. The arguments are summarized in Ibn Rushd, *Bidayat al-Mujtahid*, Book of Jihad 1:3, who says there is a consensus against using such weapons if such harm might occur. Scholars generally accepted the idea of ramming fortifications with catapults because the Prophet did so at Tarif. If there were women and children behind such fortifications some scholars called for stopping using the catapult while others disapproved it in accordance with the *ayah*:

> If they had been apart, we should certainly have punished the unbelievers among them with a grievous punishment...   (18: 25).

13.   See for instance 2: 190–4, 9: 2–32.

14.   *Mushrikun* and *kafirun*. *Mushrikun* comes from the word *shirk*, from the verb *sharaka* (to share) and means 'associating partners with God' or worshipping anything other than God, even alongside God, and is explained in the Qur'an as meaning even following one's own whims and desires instead of the Will of God. This is the one unforgivable sin in Islam. To be a true Muslim, one must put Allah at the centre of one's life and dedicate all one's actions to serving Him, with no other intention. Deeds are judged by intention. *Kafirun* (disbelievers) are those who close their eyes and ears and hearts to the truth of God's message, and refuse to believe in it, who try to cover it and repress it, and are ungrateful to God, and so behave oppressively towards those who believe.

15.   Al-Mawardi, *al-Ahkam as-Sultaniyyah*, p. 60.

16.   See the following chapter.

17.   *Shaybani: The Islamic Law of Nations*, trans. Khadduri.

18.   See M. T. Ghunaimi, *The Muslim Conception of International Law and the Western Approach* (The Hague: Martinus Nijhof, 1968). See also M. Shaltat, p. 84–7 above.

19.   Muhammad is thus described in the Qur'an as *khatam*, the 'seal' of the prophets (33: 40)

20.   Steadfastness and patience (*sabr* means both) are qualities which are equally valuable in peace and in war. In *Surat al-Fat-h* (the Opening-Up/Victory/Triumph), and in some other places, God is praised for sending His *sakina* (tranquillity) into the hearts of the believers, enabling them, without violence, to triumph over their enemies at Hudaybiyah. If Shafi'i had continued his explanation of *naskh* as far as this, he might have said that this kind of *sabr* supersedes military resistance as the 'something better' ordained by God! It certainly fulfils other Qur'anic exhortations to repel evil with something better, and to forgive injury.

21. Most recently by Abd'al-Salam Faraj, *al-Farida al- Gaiba* (Egypt, 1981) in Peters, *Jihad in Classical and Modern Islam*, pp. 161 ff.
22. Ibn Rushd, *Bidayat al-Mujtahid*, Book of Jihad 1:3.
23. It is in such subtle ways that the word of the Qur'an came gradually to be misunderstood and used to justify actions far from its spirit. Thankfully, the words are still there and can be seen afresh and reinterpreted by each generation, and Muslims do not have to rely on the interpretations of scholars. On the whole, the true spirit of the Qur'an has usually predominated over such misunderstandings.
24. His work is closely mirrored in that of Abu Ya'la, a writer of the same period, in the Hanbali school. He differs, however, in that he does not allow the use of fire against an enemy.
25. Al-Mawardi, *al-Ahkam as-Sultaniyyah*. For details of English translation, see note 10 above.
26. In some cases the reaction was swift and violent, in others it resulted in dialogue and the exchange of deputations and teachers, resulting either in conversion of the people to Islam or a permanent treaty of friendship, with reciprocal obligations, like the one made by the Prophet with the Christians of Najran. Even time-limited treaties could be renewed as desirable.
27. Al-Mawardi, *al-Alkam as-Sultaniyyah*, p. 91. This restriction preceded Aquinas's discussion on self-defence by more than a century.
28. *Bidayat al-Mujtahid wa Nihayat al-Muqtasid*, The Book of Jihad.
29. See for example his references to the community in Ibn Rushd, *The Harmony between Philosophy and Religion*, trans. and ed. G. Hourani (London, 1976).
30. Peters, *Jihad in Classical and Modern Islam*, p. 44. The meaning of this verse is debated by scholars, who translate it variously as 'the religion is purified for Allah', 'until God's religion is victorious', and so on, implying that Islam triumphs over other religions. We think it means 'until all religion is worship of God' – a prerequisite for obeying His laws.
31. Peters, *Jihad in Classical and Modern Islam*, pp. 49–50.
32. The Christian Byzantine Emperors justified war as 'just, meritorious and even holy so long as it serves the interests of the state. Constantine VII justified that belief on the ground that his majesty is not anticipating gain but aiming uniquely at the security, liberty and prosperity of his subjects' (Ghunaimi, *op. cit.*, p. 77).
33. Peters, *Jihad in Classical and Modern Islam*, pp. 123–4.
34. Speech delivered on Iqbal Day (April 13) in 1939 at Lahore Town Hall, Pakistan.
35. Sayyid Abu'-A'la Mawdudi, *Jihad fi Sabilillah* (Jihad in Islam), trans. K. Ahmad (UK Islamic Mission, 1997), p. 13.
36. *Ibid.*, p. 14.
37. *Ibid.*
38. *Ibid.*, p. 15.
39. *Ibid.*, pp. 59–101.
40. Ibn Rushd, Book of Jihad, 1: 7.
41. Peters, *Jihad in Classical and Modern Islam*, p. 77.

42.   A similar view is also championed by the Indian scholar Mawdudi. See his book *Jihad in Islam* (IIFSO Kuwait, undated).

43.   A movement of Islamic revival developed by the followers of Muhammad Abduh, and established in 1926.

44.   Y. Y. Haddad, 'The Quranic justification for an Islamic revolution: The view of Sayyid Qutb', in *Middle East Journal*, **37**(1) (Winter 1983), pp. 17–18.

45.   *Ibid.*, pp. 19–20.

46.   Sayyid Qutb, *The Islamic Concept and its Characteristic* (Indianapolis: American Trust Publication, 1991), p. 12.

47.   Sayyid Qutb, *Milestones* (Lahore: Kazi Publications, undated), pp. 79–80. Also, see Sayyid Qutb, *Islam and Peace* (Cairo: Dar al-Shuruq, 1988), especially pp. 21–37.

48.   Qutb, *Islam and Peace*, pp. 80–5. Also see Sayyid Qutb, *Fi Zilal al-Quran* Beirut: Dar al-Shuruq, 1987), Vol. 3, pp. 1433–5.

49.   Qutb, *Milestones*, pp. 88–9.

50.   For more information on this point see Y. Y. Haddad, 'Sayyid Qutb: Ideologue of Islamic Revival', in John L. Esposito (ed.), *Voices of Resurgent Islam* (Oxford University Press, 1983), especially pp. 85–7. Also see Ronald Nettler, 'A modern Islamic confession of faith and conception of religion: Sayyid Qutb's introduction to the *tafsir, Fi Zilal al-Quran*', *British Journal of Middle Eastern Studies*, **21** (1) (1994), pp. 102–14.

51.   Nettler, 'A modern Islamic confession of faith', p. 101.

52.   *Ibid.*, pp. 98–102.

53.   S. M. Solihin, *Studies on Sayyid Qutb's Fi Zilal al-Quran* (Unpublished thesis, Department of Theology, Faculty of Arts, University of Birmingham, 1993), p. 284.

54.   Qutb, *Fi Zilal al-Quran*, Vol. 3, pp. 1437–44.

55.   Solihin, *Studies on Sayyid Qutb's Fi Zilal Al-Quran*, pp. 299–302.

56.   Qutb, *Fi Zilal al-Quran*, Vol. 1, p. 108.

57.   For more information on this point see Y. Al-Qaradawi, *Islamic Awakening Between Rejection And Extremism* (Hemdon, Virginia: American Trust Publications and International Institute of Islamic Thought, 1991).

58.   The Iranian Islamic Revolution, 1979.

59.   Y. Choueiri, *Islamic Fundamentalism* (London: Pinter, 1990), p. 159.

60.   Ayatollah Ruhollah Khomeini, 'Islamic Government', in *Islam and Revolution*, trans. H. Algar (California: Mizan Press, 1981; London: KPI, 1985).

61.   H. Ball, *Islamic and Socialist Thought in Revolutionary Iran* (MA dissertation, SOAS, 1989).

62.   Shaykh Omar Abdul Rahman, *The Present Rulers and Islam* (London: Al-Firdous, 1990).

63.   *Ibid.*, p. 23.

64.   *Ibid.*, p. 18.

65.   See Ramsey Clark (former US Attorney General), *The Fire This Time: US War Crimes in the Gulf* (New York: Thunder's Mouth Press, 1992), p. 27.

66. See the following chapter. Nuclear bombs could be condemned on a large number of counts under Islamic law, for example for 'causing mischief in the land', for killing indiscriminately, for being potentially suicidal, and so on.
67. Abd al-Muta'ali al-Saidi, *Fi maydan al-ijtihad* (Helwan: Jami'iyyat al-thaqafa al-Islamiyya, n.d.), in Peters, *Jihad in Classical and Modern Islam*, p. 146.
68. Sayyid Mahmud Taleqani, *Society and Economics in Islam: Features of Islamic Economics*, trans. R. Campbell (California: Mizan Press, 1982).
69. *Ibid.*, p. 95.

4 Common and Divergent Themes in the Two Traditions

From the preceding material this chapter first of all attempts to draw out theological, philosophical, legal and political principles which are common to both traditions. It then deals with principles which mark divergencies between them. Matters of practical judgement follow, including points which both traditions share as well as those where divergencies are apparent.

THEOLOGICAL/PHILOSOPHICAL/LEGAL/POLITICAL PRINCIPLES

God/Allah

Both traditions are rooted unambiguously in a monotheistic faith: God/Allah is one, eternal, immutable, omnipotent and omniscient. (Henceforth the term 'God' will be used to refer to the one divinity whom both traditions worship). God creates and sustains the universe. He is the author of the moral law by which human beings must live. Despite our failings He is loving and merciful to all who try to live according to His will and His teaching. He has chosen certain people to make known His will for us, at certain moments of history.

Creation

We human beings are created by God to act as trustees of all the earth. We do not possess creation as freeholders who can do what we like with it. We are but leaseholders (vicegerents) who have responsibilities to God for its care and protection.

Universalism

Each tradition claims that its teachings apply to the whole human family, living and dead. Just as the will of the one God holds sway over the whole human race, so too do the truths embodied in the teachings of the faith. Thus neither tradition can be identified as the religion of, or as belonging to, any particular culture, race or nation. Both claim to be valid for all humanity. Islam and Christianity both incorporate an eschatological vision of humanity united in one community under God, sharing a common faith expressed in a common adherence to divine commandments. Both therefore regard all merely human, political arrangements (for example the system of nation-states) as provisional and temporary: none is to be accepted as a permanent expression of the divine will (that way lies idolatry).

Scripture

Both traditions recognize the Hebrew scriptures as writings 'inspired' by God. Both hold, however, that these scriptures do not provide the definitive word about the divine will for us. Each tradition possesses definitive writings unique to itself (the New Testament, the Qur'an) by which it aspires to live. Each holds that all earlier sacred writings are to be interpreted in the light of these definitive writings. Each regards its scripture as embodying, in a special and irreplaceable sense, the divine word, and therefore as telling us, with divine authority, essential truths about God's will for us. For example, as the two previous chapters show, there are parallels between the two traditions' scriptural treatment of warfare in the ancient world. There are also parallels to be drawn between their methods of interpretation for the modern world.

Application of scripture for today

Both traditions recognize a need for the teachings of this scripture to be made available to, and thus have authority over, believers living in a very different, modern world. Somehow, scripture has to be given relevance to life today, so that it can offer help in answering modern questions. Each tradition has developed special procedures by which to do this. But these procedures have in turn led, in both traditions, to controversies and even conflicts about what sacred scripture commits its believers to.

Ethical fundamentals

The two traditions share many common ethical principles, but several are of special importance for the present study. Of course, there are

significant numbers of people within each group who would disagree
with some of the following claims. Nevertheless it is the consensus of
all those responsible for this book that the following claims are valid.

Both traditions regard peace, not conflict, as the condition under
which human beings can and should best live and flourish. The
'Hobbesian' belief, that we are naturally and irredeemably doomed
to a state of conflict containable only by some overwhelming political
authority, is not acceptable to either tradition. Definitive divine
revelation teaches us that, despite our failings, peace among people
is possible. Thus Stanley Harakas, from an Orthodox perspective,
quotes St Paul (1 Cor. 14: 33): 'God is not a God of confusion, but
of peace' – a text paralleled by Qur'anic texts, in which division into
warring factions is seen as a punishment which God brings on people
who do wrong (5: 65). Changing fear into a sense of safety is a reward
for those who believe and do good deeds (24: 55; see Luke 2: 14).
Paradise is the Land of Peace – *Dar al-Islam* (5: 127; see Isaiah 9: 6).
For believers in both traditions the presumption must therefore
always be against war. Fighting is, at best, a last resort. For Muslims
to participate in war there must be valid justifications and strict
conditions, as the Qur'an consistently emphasizes. These conditions
are comparable to those developed by Christian moralists from
Augustine's time onwards. Perhaps at root both traditions stem
from the Jewish inheritance: Hebrew respect for the sanctity of life
under God meant that war could at best be nothing more than a
necessary evil.[1] This comes out in the tradition which insists that iron,
the material of weaponry, must not touch the stones of any altar to be
raised to Yahweh, because it would profane the sacred (Exodus 20:
25, Deut. 27: 4–7, Joshua 8: 31). Similarly King David was forbidden
to build the Temple because his hands were stained with the blood of
his enemies in warfare. Its construction had to be handed over to his
son Solomon, because he was a man of peace (1 Chron. 22: 8–9).

Both traditions see faith as a wholly voluntary submission of the
human being to the divine will as revealed to us. Therefore there can
be no such thing as the forcible or compulsory imposition of faith
upon those who are for the time being unbelievers. True faith cannot
be attained by such means. Despite the sorry history of both faiths
sketched in Chapter 1, conversion by force or threat of force is wholly
and equally unacceptable to both.

In both traditions there is clearly recognized a constant need to
return, despite distractions of every kind, to the fundamentals, or
foundations of the faith. In both cases, this can only be done by

careful scholarly scrutiny of the texts of the scriptures and of the traditions of interpretation which have grown up subsequently.

While both traditions hold that the truths of faith are available universally to the whole of humankind, irrespective of race, gender, nationality or culture, both also currently recognize the *de facto* provisional legitimacy of the sovereign nation-state system of the modern world, enshrined in international laws which are binding mainly on governments. They see these laws as a regime under which the international community has to work for the present and foreseeable future, always bearing in mind the aspiration to an eschatological universal community of humanity which both traditions share. Hence both religions agree in principle that the 'sovereignty' of the nation-state is authoritative in its own domain only in so far as it recognizes the claims of international law and of the higher laws of God. It is difficult to reconcile this shared belief with the fact that today the international community treats state borders almost as sacred and that their violation becomes the one just cause for wars.

Despite the above-mentioned convergent themes there are many differences. At the theological/philosophical/legal/political level the following are the most relevant to this study.

Revelation and scripture

Islam teaches that divine revelation consists of authoritative, inspired *messages* given by God to successive prophets, including Moses and Jesus; the last of these is the Qur'an. God revealed the words to the Prophet Muhammad and made him memorize them. This definitive message was then written down, and memorized by his Companions and disseminated, because God wishes every human being to be given, to ponder on, and to live by it. The written Arabic text of the Qur'an is thus the definitive revelation that God has given to the world. The Qur'an possesses its own authority by virtue of this fact; not as the result of any process of 'authorization' or approval by the Muslim community. There is also a well-established and widely accepted body of early interpretative material (*tafsir*). Thus little dispute exists within Islam about the content of the Qur'an itself. For the Muslim there is a single, generally accepted Arabic text from which to begin, although some difficulties arise over its meaning. The second textual source is the collections of *hadiths* (reports of the sayings and deeds of the Prophet Muhammad) from which Muslims learn the *Sunnah* or model practice of the Prophet. Muslim scholars had to decide which *hadiths* were to be regarded as authoritative. The difficulties arise over their meaning.[2] Translations into other languages are merely approximations: they do not have any authority approaching that of the original text in Arabic.

Christianity, on the other hand, claims that divine revelation consists of God's revealing *Himself*. Without any compromise of his divinity or his oneness, God enters into history by being born a member of the human race in Jesus. But Jesus left no written account of his teaching; apart from a few words in the language he is assumed to have spoken, all that we possess has been at some stage translated into Greek and assembled, with varying degrees of editorial activity, by the writers of the gospels. These accounts, along with other writings that issued from the first two generations of the Christian Church, constitute the New Testament, which, by the end of the second century CE, was acknowledged by Christians as 'scripture' of equal, and soon of superior, authority in relation to the Old Testament. The Bible which resulted, containing both 'Testaments', may be likened not so much to a book as to a whole library, comprising many different genres of writing. The precise determination of the 'canon' of scripture (the question of which books should be admitted to the 'library') was the work of the early Church (in this sense the 'librarian'); with regard to a small number of writings its decisions have remained controversial to this day, and in the Old Testament a slightly different list of writings is accepted as authoritative by certain churches.

Extrapolation from scripture

The way in which each tradition 'extrapolates' from its ancient scriptural texts to the present day reflects the differences in concepts of divine revelation noted above.

Islam

The Qur'an is the supreme authority in Islam and the first source for Islamic Law, including the law regulating war and peace. The second source is the Hadith, the traditions of the Prophet's words and actions, which confirm, explain or elaborate Qur'anic teachings, but may not contradict the Qur'an, since they derive their authority from the Qur'an itself. These are the bases for all other sources of Islamic law such as the *ijma*, or consensus of Muslim scholars on an opinion regarding any given subject, or the *qiyas* which is reasoning by analogy. These are only procedures for arriving at decisions on the basis of the texts or the spirit of the Qur'an and Hadith. The Qur'an and Hadith are thus the principal sources of Islamic law. Although it is well known that elements of customary law from pre-Islamic Arabia have been used by Muslim lawyers from early on, nothing is acceptable if it contradicts the text or the spirit of these two sources. Opinions arrived at by individual scholars or schools of Islamic law are no more than opinions. In Islam, to give credibility to any view, a scholar must show its textual basis in the Qur'an and authentic Hadith, and must also show that the derivation has been based on sound linguistic understanding of the texts.

Western writers often take the views of some classic (or even modern) Muslim writer as 'the Islamic view'. But, while it is tempting to Western observers to think of 'Islam' as a more united and consistent body of doctrine and law than is the case with post-Reformation Christianity, this is not really so. Not only are there different schools of Muslim thought (*madhhabs*) in classical Islam, each to some extent followed by Muslims in different geographical areas of the Islamic world, but Muslims differ widely among themselves as to the extent to which classical Islam is, or can be, influenced by modern trends drawn from non-Islamic sources, including of course modern international law.

In the earliest phase of Islam the use of reason (*ijtihad*) to arrive at appropriate answers based on the Qur'an and Hadith (and often adapting the customary law inherited from pre-Islamic societies) was freely practised.[3]

But, as has already been said, in the eleventh century the Islamic state began to fragment and one of the Caliphs, seeing the dangers of the excessive variations in legal opinion that had arisen, announced that 'the door of *ijtihad* was closed' and that only the existing legal writings of the four juristic schools were to be followed from then on.

In the nineteenth century, with the advent of European power in the Islamic world, bringing the fruits of the rational sciences it had taken over from the Muslims and continued to develop, Muhammad Abduh (Grand Mufti of Egypt, d. 1905) in his writings argued for a revival in the use of *ijtihad*, as well as faith in Islamic teachings and in all the rational sciences.[4]

Today, following the complex history sketched in Chapter 3 above, Muslims can feel liberated from slavish limitation to one school of Muslim juridic thought (*madhhab*) or another, and welcome the possibility of some input from Islamic sources into lawmaking, replacing the blind imitation of European laws which prevailed during the colonial period. However, many Muslims hold that modernist *ijtihad* has tended, under European domination, to become so 'liberal' as to lose much of the virtue of Islamic law, for instance by giving legitimacy to such forbidden practices as usury, attempting to outlaw fasting in Ramadan (one of the basic 'pillars' of Islam), and ignoring Islamic business ethics, to give only a few glaring instances.

Some Western scholars and some conservative Muslims imagine that 'the door' is still closed to this day and that Islam has nothing to fall back on except what the schools of law and scholars of the classical period decided. But scholars in present-day Muslim countries not only reach their decisions on the basis of the Qur'an and Hadith, and the principles derived from them, without feeling necessarily bound by what any former school of law has decided; they also commonly adopt Western-derived legal principles, notably in the field of international law. Indeed Muslim states have mostly accepted for themselves as fully as any other states the international law regime of today.

Christianity

The legacy of Jesus – his life, death, and resurrection, teaching and example – as recorded in the New Testament and interpreted by those who first experienced his impact has to be appropriated afresh in each generation. In the Catholic tradition this task of appropriation and re-appropriation is made possible because of the understanding that the Church is itself the sacrament of Jesus's living presence in the world, and is thus authorised to give teaching which is binding on the faithful. On the other hand, some Christian communities, such as the Society of Friends (Quakers) refuse to accept any sacramental dimension to the structure of faith at all, let alone any sacramental concept of the Church as the body of Christ permanently alive in the world today. In other denominations the living word of God is discerned primarily in preaching that is authentically based on scripture, in the life of the Church as it witnesses corporately to the truth it has received, or in the interpretative or prophetic voice of individuals or groups who are seeking guidance in scripture or tradition to confront a new moral or religious challenge. It follows that when these churches meet in larger councils or assemblies, such as the General Synod of the Church of England or the World Council of Churches, the statements they issue may reflect a considerable variety of interpretation of the relevant texts and different Christian responses to the moral and intellectual challenges presented by the modern world.

In addition to the practical problems which arise from the necessity to apply ancient scriptural norms to the realities of life today there is a further theological consideration. Human beings are 'fallen', their understanding and their judgements are distorted by sin, and no religious statement, whatever authority is claimed for it, can be regarded as representing the whole truth for every time and every place. Moreover the continual growth of human knowledge and the constantly new conditions of life created by technological innovation make it necessary for doctrinal and moral principles to be reformulated in every generation. In this process scripture continues to exercise a determining influence; and Church tradition, with its roots in natural theology as well as the Bible, will continue to have whatever degree of authority is accorded to it in each denomination. In the Roman Catholic Church, it is believed that under certain conditions a general council of the bishops (such as the Second Vatican Council) or the Pope himself is able to formulate Christian truth 'infallibly' and that the Church can give fully authoritative teaching in the name of Christ. In Protestant churches, by contrast, individual believers, with the help of the Holy Spirit, have prime responsibility for discerning the guidance which scripture can offer for faith, devotion and action. Yet, despite these divergencies of application, the place of scripture as the ultimate source of divine revelation is an assured premise of Christian thought and action in all the main churches.

PRACTICAL JUDGEMENTS

Despite the differences in concepts of authority for arriving at theological or moral principles, there are many common themes in the two traditions, notably in their approaches to violent conflict and how to limit its harmful effects. At the same time, divergencies inevitably become apparent as well. Convergencies and divergencies are implicit in the first chapters of this study, but may be summarized as follows.

The first principle to insist upon is acceptance by both traditions of a presumption against war. Both emphasize the necessity of peace as a basis for human beings to flourish as they should. 'Thou shalt not kill' is a divine commandment that both share with Jewish tradition, even when they differ in its application to particular cases and circumstances (Deut. 5: 17, Mark 10: 19, Matt. 5: 18, Qur'an 5: 32). These fundamental ethical principles, together with the inevitable dilemmas that history presents us with, compel believers in both traditions to formulate precise conditions for the limited use of military force, as a necessary evil – always as a last resort.

Both traditions agree that there must be no forcible conversion and that there are binding conditions for limiting the use of violence and the waging of war. Unfortunately they also share a sorry history of departing from their own principles, as Chapter 1 reminds us. In more detail, comparisons can be made between mediaeval Christian wars against the 'infidels' and Muslim wars against polytheists. There are parallels in the respective codes for dealing with prisoners in ancient and mediaeval wars.[5] Today nation-states which regard themselves as of Christian provenance and states which regard themselves as of Muslim provenance equally accept the modern international laws which regulate conflict and the use of military force, including the humanitarian laws of war and the Charter of the United Nations discussed in Chapter 5 below.

The limitations on warfare to which both traditions subscribe, though in different ways and to different degrees, may be divided into those which apply to the initiation of war (the *ad bellum* conditions) and those which apply during the conduct of war (the *in bello* conditions):

Ad bellum conditions for a 'just war'

Just cause

There must be a 'just cause' for war between sovereign states, namely the righting of a wrong committed by an 'aggressor' or 'transgressor'. Thus, despite his many changes of mind during a long career, and despite his reservations at times about the legitimacy of killing at all, Augustine constantly maintained that a war in which soldiers acted in a public function in defence of others could be just.[6] A more developed teaching about the need for war to be waged only to right a wrong already committed, or about to be committed, became explicit in Christian teaching from Aquinas onwards. The fact that no prior wrong had been committed by the Indians was part of Vitoria's reason for condemning the sixteenth-century Spanish wars of conquest against them in Central America.[7] Today, the vast majority of Christians support the UN Charter in limiting just international war to the maintenance or restoration of international peace and security (Art. 42) or to self-defence against aggression, whether by a single state or by a group of states acting collectively (Art. 51).

An approach comparable to that of St Augustine is implicit in the Qur'anic teaching that the justification of war is to prevent evil from triumphing (2: 251). Even after ten years of persecution the Muslims of Makkah were permitted to fight only after they had been forced out of their homes (an application of the 'last resort' principle as well as that of just cause) (22: 39–41). It has been convincingly argued that the wars which took place during the lifetime of the Prophet were waged exclusively for self-defence of the Muslims, or in pre-emption against imminent attack against them.[8] Even in the case of fighting in self-defence, arrogance or a sense of triumphalism is forbidden to the Muslims because the reward is for those who do not exalt themselves or seek to spread corruption (28: 83). This Muslim teaching is paralleled by that of Augustine, later quoted by Aquinas, forbidding 'the unappeased and unrelenting spirit . . . the lust to dominate', and so on. Of course, exactly what 'self-defence' means in concrete circumstances is often controversial. But modern international law on the subject is officially accepted in principle by all states.

Right intention
War is justified only if waged with the right intention. For Augustine, Gratian and Aquinas (and the authentic subsequent Christian tradition) this means pursuing the good and avoiding evil, and in particular fighting to put right the wrong that has been done and for the sake of establishing genuine peace.[9] Islam agrees. After all, the territory in which Islam holds sway, the *Dar al-Islam*, is simultaneously the territory where people submit to God's will and the territory of justice and peace. The opposite of the *Dar al-Islam* is the *Dar al-Harb*, the territory of injustice and disorder, of conflict where people do not accept God's law. Hence, as the Qur'an says, changing fear into a sense of safety is a reward for those who believe and do good deeds (24: 55), for paradise is the land of peace (5: 127). War may be waged, if at all, only to keep 'the way of God' uppermost: that is not for unworthy motives like seeking booty or self-aggrandisement or a sense of heroism. Keeping 'the way of God uppermost' does not imply (*pace* some commentators) that Muslims can fight in order that Islam should rule over other religions. It simply implies following the divine will by not pursuing unworthy objectives.[10]

Lawful authority
War is just only if it is initiated by a lawful authority. Augustine had insisted that for an individual to kill his attacker, even in self-defence,

was contrary to the Christian teaching about the primacy of charity and the commandment forbidding killing. Only warfare conducted by a public authority could license any killing at all.[11] The Muslim tradition says much the same: force may be used only under the leadership of a suitably qualified *imam*, or leader.[12]

Aquinas does not elaborate directly on this generally accepted principle, although elsewhere he clearly supports Augustine's opposition to private killing, permitting it only as an unintended consequence of a legitimate act of self-defence. His focus is rather upon defining, in the context of feudal society, who has the responsibility as a 'lawful authority' for initiating war. Classical Islam takes a somewhat similar view, but from a rather different angle. Under the Abbasid Caliphate (749–1258), it was certainly not for the individual Muslim to initiate war: only the head of the Muslim 'state' could ensure that the correct Qur'anic procedures would be followed (for example inviting the opponent to accept Islam, or to pay the tax which was its substitute) or assess the likelihood of the Muslim forces winning. In effect, the principle of lawful authority in Islamic warfare, as in the Christian tradition, was to limit the means and use of military force to those who, in theory, could be trusted to use it responsibly.[13] In effect, then, both traditions nowadays subscribe to the view that, subject to the UN Security Council's role as defined in Articles 42 and 51 of the UN Charter, only sovereign states possess the authority to undertake international war justly.

Reasonable prospect of success
War undertaken recklessly, without due calculation of the chances of winning, is clearly irresponsible and condemned in both traditions because of the unnecessary suffering and destruction it causes. As has been pointed out, one of the tasks of the Abbasid Caliphate was that the Caliph should assess the likelihood of winning before initiating warfare.[14]

Last resort
This condition is a difficult one to apply in practice. Both traditions seem to accept it in some form. But it can hardly entail a requirement for the parties to have tried every possible alternative to the use of force whatever the consequences of doing so would be. For one thing, surrendering rather than fighting is always possible for one or other party (although Muslims are not permitted to surrender to oppression and must always strive against it in whatever way is compatible with

Islamic teaching (Qur'an 4: 75). For another, attempts at all costs to use diplomatic or other non-violent methods of resolving the conflict before resorting to force may well jeopardize the successful application of other criteria, notably that of reasonable chance of success. In the classical Islamic tradition, the nearest approximation to the last resort criterion is perhaps the requirement that, given the immediate prospect of hostilities, the adversary be invited either to accept Islam or to pay the necessary tax before being forced to fight.[15] But this is certainly not the same thing as requiring every alternative to be used first. In the case of humanitarian intervention the last resort criterion becomes especially problematic; in the case of Bosnia, for example, a limited but forceful intervention early on might have averted the need for a much more destructive operation later.

Proportionality
War may be undertaken only in so far as the harm done by it is proportionate to the good achieved. So far, the two traditions agree. The criterion of proportionality, in the Christian tradition, is both an *ad bellum* and an *in bello* matter. In deciding whether or not to go to war, the authorities have to decide whether the harm likely to be caused by the war as a whole will be outweighed by the benefits of winning it or by the unfortunate consequences of not going to war at all. While this may look like common sense, it is hard in practice to calculate the right answer, and every state is likely to favour its own point of view.[16] Furthermore, in the conduct of war, every operation and every strategic or tactical decision has to be governed by the same consideration, for not every means of winning is legitimate. The Qur'an tells believers 'whoever attacks you, attack him just as he has attacked you' (2: 194), an injunction reminiscent of the Jewish law of 'an eye for an eye and a tooth for a tooth' (5: 45, Exodus 21: 24). This gives rise to the general principle in Islamic law that harm should not be removed by a greater harm. However, the Qur'an also recommends mercy and forgiveness as an alternative to strict proportionality (5: 45) and urges Muslims to repel evil with what is better.

In bello conditions for a just war

Proportionality
In bello proportionality is of special significance in the case of modern weapons of mass destruction. Given the likelihood of massive

collateral damage and unintended innocent deaths, can the use of such weapons ever be justified as duly 'proportionate' in the pursuit of a just cause? We have no room here for a full discussion of the huge literature produced in the West on the ethics of nuclear weapons. But it is worth noting one particular Muslim observation at this point. The Iranian submission to the International Court of Justice, on nuclear weapons, insisted that 'the right to self-defence as provided in Article 51 of the Charter, cannot be invoked to justify the use of nuclear weapons. The right to self-defence is limited by the general principles of necessity *and proportionality* as well as those of international humanitarian law'.[17]

The question of proportionality in the case of *threats* to use nuclear weapons raises somewhat different considerations. Muslims are not allowed to frighten neighbours, although they can deter potential enemies by a show of strength (Q. 8: 59). Nevertheless, it can be pointed out that according to the International Court of Justice the notions of 'threat' and of 'use' of force stand together in the sense that if use is illegal, so too is the threat of use.[18]

Discrimination
This principle concerns attacks on civilians and non-combatants in war. Both traditions have much to say on this subject. Following Vitoria's condemnation of all killing of the innocent in war, Catholic tradition insists that it is never licit intentionally to kill the innocent in warfare, and that such killing may be allowed, if at all, only through the principle of 'double effect', that is as the unintended consequence of legitimate military actions. But some Christians disagree, holding that, for the greater good, a consent to some voluntary killing of the innocent is licit.[19] The Muslim tradition has some parallels. The Qur'anic verse 'Fight in the way of God those who fight against you, but do not transgress. God does not love the transgressor' (2: 190) permits fighting against actual fighters, but civilians are protected. Thus wars and weapons of destruction that destroy civilians and their towns are excluded by the Qur'an and the word and deed of the Prophet, these being the only binding authority in Islamic law. The word 'transgression' (according to Baydawi, commenting on 2: 190) means 'initiation of fighting, fighting those with whom a treaty has been concluded, surprising the enemy without first inviting them to make peace, destroying crops or *killing those who should be protected*'. (Compare Aquinas's teaching that an *impugnatio* is permissible only when a provocative move has already been made by the opponent[20]).

Vitoria seemed to cast doubt on his own principle of the inviolability of the innocent in his treatment of the innocent in conditions of siege.[21] So does Ibn Rushd: 'Most scholars agree that fortresses may be assailed with mangonels, no matter whether there are women and children within them or not. This is based on the fact that the Prophet used mangonels against the population of Ta'if...'.[22] If there were women and children behind such fortifications, some scholars called for stopping using the catapult, while others merely 'disapproved' in accordance with the *ayah*: 'If they had been apart, we should certainly have punished the unbelievers among them with a grievous punishment' (Q. 48: 25). The use of catapults indiscriminately is here either forbidden (*haram*) or 'disapproved' (*makruh*) which is the lowest category of the permissible. A parallel inconsistency remains concerning nuclear weapons today, in both traditions. There is an extensive literature on the Christian teaching about discrimination in the context of nuclear weapons. Christians such as John Finnis and colleagues insist that consenting to kill innocents intentionally is absolutely forbidden, and that this makes nuclear deterrence a wholly illicit policy. Others, such as Arthur Hockaday and David Fisher, think that the prohibition is not absolute, and that the benefits of deterrence can outweigh the ban on some limited consent to killing of the innocent.[23]

Similarly, uncertainties about discrimination can be detected in Islamic circles, although there is relatively little written from a specifically Islamic standpoint on the ethics of the use or threat of use of weapons of mass destruction, or on other modern weapons systems. This is a point at which we can note a divergence between the two traditions. In saying to the believers 'whoever attacks you, attack him just as he had attacked you' (2: 194) the Qur'an is *limiting* the fighting to combatants (that is those who have attacked you) and excluding others. As we have already pointed out,[24] the Prophet and his successors gave their soldiers clear instructions not to attack civilians – women, old people, religious people engaged in their worship – or to destroy crops or animals because discrimination and proportionality were to be strictly observed. Yet some Muslim writers say that the deaths of the innocent, even if brought about by the deliberate use of naturally indiscriminate weapons, are to be classed merely as 'mistakes'.[25] On the other hand, although deterrence by accumulation of weapons is permitted in the Qur'an (8: 59–60), nuclear weapons would be against Islamic law on a number of counts:

- that they use fire to burn the enemy – forbidden by the Prophet.[26]
- that they cause 'destruction on the earth' – forbidden in the Qur'an (2: 60)
- that they cause the deaths of many innocent non-combatants – forbidden by the Prophet and the Qur'an (2: 19)[27]
- that the results of using them could be suicidal – forbidden in the Qur'an (2: 19)

There has hitherto been little serious discussion, in the Muslim literature, of the application of the discrimination principle to modern weapons of mass destruction. Doubtless because few predominantly Muslim states are known to have aspired to nuclear status (Pakistan is the major exception), there was little motivation among Muslims during the cold war to engage in profound ethical debate on the issue. Today, however, with several Muslim states suspected of nuclear (not to mention chemical and biological) ambitions (Iraq, Iran, Libya) and following the Nuclear Non-Proliferation Treaty review conference of 1995, the International Court's judgement on the legality or otherwise of nuclear use and threats of use, the findings of the Canberra Commission on the global elimination of nuclear weapons and the 'Abolition 2000' campaign organized by several hundred non-governmental organisations (NGOs), such a debate is perhaps beginning in the Muslim world. Certainly Iran's submission to the International Court included a section on 'Discrimination Between Combatants and Non-Combatants' which insisted that the modern humanitarian laws of war prohibit nuclear attacks, or threats of attack, because of their necessarily indiscriminate nature.[28]

We turn now to a number of other, related themes.

THE TREATMENT OF PRISONERS OF WAR

In the case of prisoners of war, while the Muslim contributors to this book hold that there is nothing in the Qur'an or Hadith which would authorize Muslims to do anything other than follow the present international humanitarian conventions, some early Muslim scholars tended to hold that it was one allowable option for the *imam* to kill able-bodied male prisoners of war (the other options were to enslave them, ransom them or set them free). The *Siyar* of Shaybani (second Islamic century) allowed the killing of male captives if there was no other way the *imam* could dispose of all the prisoners because there were insufficient means available to transport them back to a place of safety. This view is not based on the Qur'an or Sunnah, but is simply '*ra'y*' (personal opinion), based on utilitarian reasoning as commonly seen in the West. The Qur'anic verses about prisoners of war quoted in Chapter 3 above ('Prisoners of war') were arguably misinterpreted by some classical scholars, who ignored the spirit of the verses, and tried to contradict them with other verses and some instances of practice by the Prophet Muhammad, in order to make killing allowed.[29] Yet others, however, even in those times, using their 'literal' interpretation of the Qur'anic verses, held that captives may not be slain, and earlier still, the Prophet's Companions were unanimous that captives should not be slain. In fact the Prophet's treatment of captives was usually extremely kind, and his good example has been followed by many later Muslims, for example Salah al-Din (see page 9).[30]

THE TREATMENT OF THE ENVIRONMENT

Islam preceded Christianity in limiting warfare which involved the destruction of crops, or of what we would nowadays call 'the environment'. Muslim insistence that human beings are not sovereigns over the earth but are its vicegerents, was strong from the beginning, as the frequency of Qur'anic verses on this subject reminds us (for example 2: 20, 2: 30, 3: 10, 7: 56, 30: 26, 30: 41). The same point about the environment is nowadays made by Christians,[31] but it would be hard to find it being made, or made as strongly by Christians of ancient times as it was by Muslims in the earliest days of Islam. On the other hand, there are clear parallels between the Qur'anic concern for the protection of crops and the duties laid down in the book of Deuteronomy: 'When you besiege a city for a long time, making war against it in order to take it, you shall not destroy its trees by wielding an axe against them; for you may eat of them, but you shall not cut them down. Are the trees in the field men that they should be besieged by you? Only the trees which you know are not trees for food you may destroy' (Deut. 20: 19–20). Indeed the parallels between the laws of warfare laid down in Deuteronomy 20 and those of early Islam are striking, suggesting perhaps a common culture of conflict-regulation in the ancient Middle East shared between Jews, Christians and Muslims.[32]

THE CRUSADING SPIRIT

Despite the agreed limits which the authentic traditions of each side clearly lay down, both have notoriously failed in the past – and present – to keep to them in practice. As our historical survey in Chapter 1 shows, military leaders with large imperialistic ambitions and insoluble political dilemmas have led both traditions to betray, often egregiously, their best intentions and insights. In particular, both traditions have displayed in the past a 'crusading spirit' against the other, in which the pursuit of holy war against the infidels has distorted the true meaning of the scriptural texts and their interpretation in both traditions.[33]

It is perhaps an open question just how far these ancient failures of understanding have been overcome today. In the Iran–Iraq war of the 1980s both sides invoked God, in a crusading spirit, against the other.[34] The wars in Bosnia, Sudan and East Timor have all too easily resurrected the ancient enmities between Christians and Muslims, leading to 'holy war' fanaticisms by people on both sides. Much intra-state conflict today is also infected with the virus of a crusading spirit. On the international plane, that spirit was not wholly absent from the rhetoric of either side during the Kuwait conflict of 1990–1. Yet in modern times we have come to understand more clearly the evils of racism and xenophobia – fundamental ingredients of the crusading spirit. Despite this, neither tradition has managed to expunge these tendencies. Perhaps it is necessary for each to learn more from the mistakes of the other, in order for each to appreciate how far the crusading spirit is from the true meaning of its own teaching. For it is quite clear that such a spirit is illegitimate in both traditions. The question is how to give effect to this theoretical illegitimacy in practice, and to expose it when it is used by powerful politicians for their own ends.

FUNDAMENTALISM

A 'crusading spirit' is especially evident among so-called 'fundamentalist' movements with significant political ambitions, which exist in both traditions, but globally speaking only in patches. The term 'fundamentalist' is hard to avoid here, given its prevalence in much contemporary discussion and propaganda. Indeed the starting point of this book was a recognition by those responsible for it that in many parts of the developed world so-called Islamic 'fundamentalism' has come to be regarded as the most dangerous threat to international peace and security to have emerged since the end of the cold war.[35] Yet the term 'fundamentalism' is deeply ambiguous. Every religion must constantly be probing its authentic roots, or 'fundamentals', if it is to remain true to its essential insights. On the other hand, there is always a danger, for any religion, of becoming fixated on the past, or on certain allegedly unchanging certainties, to the exclusion of 'development' in doctrine. This too is a sort of (aberrant) fundamentalism.

While latching on to some genuine element of the faith, 'fundamentalism' is usually based, in both traditions, on over-simplified and often unscholarly interpretations of the scriptural texts and of the tradition which has emerged from them. 'Fundamentalists' tend to focus on a narrow range of issues, which are then taken to be *the* key issues for today. They align themselves with particular political tendencies, claiming not only to be the authentic voice of Islam or of Christianity, but to hold the key to the political and social problems of the modern world. They often do so fanatically, claiming for themselves the right to foist their views onto the rest of the population, whether by manipulation of the liberal democratic process or by bullying and even violence where that process does not effectively exist.

In this book, 'fundamentalism' is an issue in so far as so-called fundamentalist movements are commonly wedded to a certain view of the relation of means to ends. As 'extremist' or 'fanatical', these movements disregard, or believe themselves to be exempt from, the strict limits on the use of force which are – in the opinion of those responsible for the present book – *fundamental* to genuine faith. In the absence of such limits, extremist movements tend almost inevitably to move towards the use of terrorism as a legitimate, even a preferred, means of getting their message across. Such methods are, in our opinion, ethically illicit and forbidden by the tenets of both faiths. Genuine Islam condemns terrorism as clearly as the bishops in Ireland condemn the IRA. Both insist that the end does not justify the means, and that innocent non-combatants may never be made targets of reckless attack.

Yet it is also true that the motivation of extremist movements is often the defence of the oppressed, or rebellion against unjust and undemocratic regimes. This is as true of Islamic fundamentalists as it is of those motivated by Liberation Theology. In this study, we have presented some material concerning Islamic fundamentalism as promoted by two of its best known founders: Mawdudi of Pakistan and Qutb of Egypt. Many Muslims, including those represented in this study, regard both men as unscholarly and one-sided in their interpretations of the Qur'an, and of the essentials of the message of Islam. Yet they have helped to create large followings, not merely in their own countries and the Middle East generally, but elsewhere too (for example in the Maghrib, Sudan, Bosnia, Turkey, Afghanistan, the Central Asian republics and even among the black population of the United States). It is a major object of this study to draw attention not only to the shaky legal and theological foundations of such fundamentalism – which may nevertheless be a serious danger simply because of the numbers of people liable to accept it – but to the unacceptable means often used to promote what might otherwise be a legitimate cause.

But it would be a mistake to focus solely on a 'threat' from the Islamic quarter. For Christian fundamentalism, though it preoccupies European thinkers and politicians much less than the neighbouring Islamic variety, is nevertheless a force to be reckoned with, especially in the United States. The Christian 'right' has gone a long way to capturing the inner citadels of the Republican Party in that country. Its influence outside the United States has so far been felt most keenly on the Western side of the Atlantic, its principal activities consisting of proselytizing activities in Latin America and elsewhere, especially among the ill-educated urban poor of the cities. While Christian fundamentalism in the United States has its deepest roots within Protestantism, especially in the Bible belt of the southern states, it has captured many in the Catholic community who were former adherents of a simplistic anti-communism and have been looking for a new crusade to join since the end of the Cold War.

Christian fundamentalism of this kind is deeply political in its aims and influence, despite its claims to be a purely 'religious' movement concentrating on saving people's souls rather than liberating them from political or economic oppression. Such an 'anti-political' stance is itself a political position, although Christian fundamentalists are less obviously concerned with issues of social justice than some of their Muslim counterparts.[36]

It might be thought that here is a clear divergence between Christian and Muslim fundamentalism. For while the latter is frequently violent, often terroristic in its methods, the former largely confines itself to evangelism and non-violent persuasion (albeit some right-wing fundamentalist Christians in the USA called for Iran to be 'nuked' during the siege of the US embassy in Teheran). However, few fundamentalist Christians have been conspicuous for *opposing* military activity by their governments, however dubious the methods used. Fundamentalist evangelists in Latin America in the 1980s were seldom regarded as a threat by the military authorities, because they did not take a political stance against them. Fundamentalist South African Christians in the apartheid era were prepared to go along with the violence perpetrated by the authorities. And some fundamentalist Christians, often but not exclusively of Catholic persuasion, have adopted methods in the cause of opposing abortion in America which are tantamount to terrorism, and may even include murder.

IRREGULAR WARFARE

This lies at the heart of our concern, since most of the current and most likely future conflicts are not international but intranational in character. Both traditions have a good deal to say, and share, on this topic. For in both, the impetus to engage in irregular war comes from a demand for social change in the name of justice, restoration of land and a better deal for the underdog. Here Liberation Theology in Latin America and elsewhere shares much, both good and bad, with Islamic militancy in the Middle East, the Maghrib and elsewhere.

Both traditions have tended to be highly suspicious of the use of force, or violence, in rebellions. In terms of state practice, they still are. The use of force, without lawful authority in the shape of the state's consent, has been generally regarded as likely to bring in its train more harm than good. Even a bad ruler, or a tyrant, may be better than no ruler at all. In the classical tradition of Islam rebellion, or irregular war, was thought likely to have tragic consequences for everybody, because of the chaos and disorder that it brought. It ought therefore to be avoided at almost all costs. Yet the right of just rebellion has long been recognized in theory in both traditions. From the Christian side, Aquinas justifies rebellion against an unjust tyrant on the ground that it is the tyrant who is responsible for the injustice against which the rebellion is taking place, as well as for the harm done in the course of the conflict.[37] Rebellion is therefore just provided that it is kept within the bounds of proportionality, that is, provided that the harm caused to the people by the rebellion is not worse than the harm done by the unjust ruler. In the Reformed (Calvinist) tradition just rebellion against a tyrant is a matter for the 'lesser magistrates'. That is to say, if the head of a state becomes a tyrant, then it is up to those lower down in the governing hierarchy to depose him.

This point was also much discussed by early Islamic scholars, and there are some *hadiths* on the subject of when and whether to rebel against an unjust ruler:

> The Prophet (peace-be-upon-him) said: The best fighting (*jihad*) in the path of Allah is (to speak) a word of justice to an unjust oppressive ruler.   (*Abu Dawud*)

> The Messenger of Allah (peace-be-upon-him) said: The best of your rulers are those whom you love and who love you, who invoke God's blessings upon you and you invoke His blessings upon them. And the worst of your rulers are those whom you hate and who hate you, and whom you curse and who curse you. It was asked (by those present): Shouldn't we overthrow them with the help of the sword? He said: No, as long as they establish prayer among you. If you then find anything detestable in them, you should hate their administration but do not withdraw yourselves from their obedience.   (*Muslim*)

> The Prophet (peace-be-upon-him) said: 'A Muslim has to listen and obey (the orders of his ruler) whether he likes it or not, as long as his orders do not involve him in disobedience (to Allah); but if an act of disobedience (to Allah) is imposed, he should not listen to it or obey it.'   (*Bukhari*)

Despite the hesitancies of scholars and politicians in both traditions, Francis Lieber, writing about the American Civil War, argued that rebellion could be justified.[38] In contemplating (without approving) the case for the southern confederacy, Lieber came to the conclusion that what mattered was not so much whether the rebels had lawful authority for taking up arms (for this was a genuinely open question), as whether their conduct of the war remained within the limits set out in the just war tradition and in the humanitarian laws of war in so far as they existed in his time. Rebels were not necessarily criminals, but might have just cause on their side against an unjust government.[39] His case against rebellion, then, is that rebels who fight outside the ordinary framework of law are peculiarly liable to engage in acts of barbarism, contrary to all humanitarian limits: for example assassination, hostage-taking, terrorism and atrocities against the innocent, in order to achieve political objectives.

There is an Islamic justification of rebellion in terms similar to those which Lieber proposed. Modern Islamists sometimes characterize irregular war as a 'people's struggle' (equivalent to some forms of 'Liberation Theology') designed to regain what has been stolen: territory, property, rights – for example in the case of the Palestinian struggle against Israel.[40] This view has a long ancestry. Classical Muslim scholars like al-Shaybani, reflecting on the early conflicts in Islam in the time of Ali, recalled that the rebels were still Muslims, and had to be treated differently from mere criminals or apostates. They had rights simply because they belonged to the family of Islam, despite having criticized and even made war upon the established Muslim ruler (Qur'an 49: 9–10) Some modern Muslim proponents of irregular war, for example the authors of *The Neglected Duty* (the 'testament' of Islamic Jihad[41]) go further, claiming that no blame can be attached to the irregular fighter who kills a soldier who is in service with the army of an allegedly apostate government (such as the government of modern Egypt) even if the latter is personally a devout Muslim. For it is impossible for the irregular fighter to tell whether such a person has willingly allied himself to apostasy or has simply been coerced into military service and cannot extricate himself.[42] It is up to God finally to judge of the rights and wrongs of the issue: in the end all will be well for all of them in the hereafter. Meanwhile, in the here and now, killing the Muslim soldier may be both necessary and morally licit in order to attain a true victory for Islam. Such is the reasoning of those who have come to the conclusion that the rulers of states like Egypt are, in effect, apostates and that it is therefore necessary to fight them.

What is missing from modern Islamic organizations engaged in irregular war is any deep discussion of the *in bello* limits to be placed on the means to be used. Neither the Charter of Hamas, nor *The Neglected Duty*, which represents the thinking of Islamic Jihad, has much to say on the subject, though they give much attention to *ad bellum* considerations. Perhaps this is only to be expected of all such organizations wherever they are. After all, their leaders and ideologues are not normally scholars of theology or ethics, although they often deploy religious texts to very persuasive effect.[43] Yet surely such discussion of the means used is crucial, given the publicity given in the media and elsewhere to the atrocities allegedly perpetrated by such organizations, especially against innocent non-combatants. Here is a point, within the modern debate, at which Muslims and Christians (especially those sympathetic to Liberation Theology) need to come together to agree, at least in principle (whatever the actual practice) on the limits that their traditions ought to set to the kinds of tactics they employ.

PACIFISM

A major point at which the two traditions seem to diverge, at the level of practical action and attitude, concerns pacifism, or the principled refusal to take part in warfare of any sort.

At its root, *absolute* pacifism is a refusal to co-operate with the military organs of state power.[44] This is why the absolute pacifist refuses not only to kill, but even to be conscripted into any kind of wartime state service, including non-combatant service. It was undoubtedly Protestants, especially those belonging to churches which were not established or co-opted by the state, who led the way in pacifist protest, with the Quakers at their head. In so far as pacifism is itself a form of principled protest, it is hardly surprising that Protestantism should have sponsored most of the pacifism that has been in evidence in this century, for in so far as Protestantism rests ultimately upon a belief in the validity of 'private judgement', or the primacy of conscience, it is not surprising that a form of protest which is so clearly a matter of conscience and private judgement, often against the pressures exerted by the surrounding society, should have taken root in Protestant rather than Catholic circles.

Until very recently the authorities of the Roman Catholic Church were solidly opposed to pacifism. Nevertheless absolute Catholic pacifists existed, in small relatively isolated groups, in a number of democratic states.[45] But in many Catholic countries the Church had, as it were, sold itself in advance to the state, and therefore found it impossible to permit its believers to take up such a stance. Even a modified pacifism, that is, a refusal to bear arms or kill anyone combined with a readiness to be conscripted to do something else instead, was long condemned by the Catholic Church in Europe as a dereliction of the duty to defend fellow citizens. It was not until the post-World War II revelations of state-sponsored atrocities on a huge scale became undeniable, and major powers took to threatening massive indiscriminate killing as a means of deterring their enemies, that pacifism became an option approved by the Catholic Church, provided that the objector was prepared to do some alternative service in place of bearing arms.[46]

Killing human beings is condemned in the Qur'an in general (5: 32), and killing Muslims in particular (4: 92). The Muslim is *actually forbidden* to obey any call from the state which is contrary to God's will for, as the Prophet said, 'No obedience for evil deeds, obedience is required only in what is good' (Hadith: *Bukhari*). During the first civil war between Muslims one group of people (the Qa'ada) refused to fight on either side on the grounds that the war was wrong.[47]

The Qur'an exhorts *all* Muslims to 'stand up for justice as witnesses to God' in a way which avoids prejudice and passion, even against their own interest and that of those closest to them (4: 13). This is done preferably by peaceful means: 'the best fighting (*jihad*) in the path of Allah is to speak a word of justice to an oppressive ruler' (Hadith: *Muslim*). If it is possible to avoid persecution by moving away, this is advocated (16: 14). Talking in a good way to believers in other faiths (29: 46, 16: 12), and consultation between people generally, are also advocated to avoid conflict (42: 38).

If conflicts arise between two parties of Muslims, the other Muslims are commanded to try to make peace between them (49: 9) even if this involves restraining the oppressive one by force. The Prophet was a practised arbitrator and peacemaker from an early age, when he arbitrated between rival Makkan clans, and it is a matter for rejoicing that Allah can bring people's hearts together when human efforts cannot (8: 63).

However, where parties will not listen to good words, and begin hostilities, persecution or oppression, it is justifiable to use force to stop them, and defend those people who wish to live in peace. In this context refusal (without a good excuse) to fight in the way of God is condemned (4: 75), but no punishment is specified, and there is no 'conscription' in Islam.

CONCLUSION

Both Christianity and Islam claim to preach truths universally valid for all human beings, irrespective of race, nationality, gender or social status. Yet these claims are, in certain respects, incompatible with each other. This is particularly clear concerning belief about divine revelation. Islam rejects the Christian teaching that Jesus is both God and man. Christianity rejects the Muslim teaching that the Qur'an is God's definitive message about His will for human beings, superseding every other prophetic 'word'.

There is no way of evading this incompatibility and what it necessarily entails in terms of ethical obligations laid upon individual human beings. True, in each tradition there are divergencies of belief about what exactly is entailed, at the level of personal practice, by faith in the revealed 'word'. Nevertheless it is common ground, for example, that

Christians do not recognize any obligation laid by God upon humankind to fast during Ramadan or to undertake the pilgrimage to Makkah. Conversely, Muslims do not admit any obligation laid by God upon humankind to be baptised or to partake in the eucharist. At this level, those responsible for the present book recognize a degree of incompatibility not only concerning the theology of divine revelation but also concerning the obligations laid upon people as the result of it.

However, we are not here concerned with the implications of this dichotomy for domestic societies, the rights of citizens or the internal governance of states, important though these are. Our concern in this book is with the ethical obligations laid upon nation-states, and other actors on the global stage, as a result of commitment to a divine revelation. At this level, we believe that there is already a great deal of common ground between the two traditions – far more than is commonly recognized, even by the political élites on both sides.

First of all, whenever conflict occurs between states or between intra-state groups, there is a primary obligation to pursue non-violent solutions. The use of force of any sort must always be a last resort: for both religions are founded on a divine imperative of peace and reconciliation among humankind. This point is of special importance today, in a world riven by violent conflict, but also equipped with weapons of unprecedented destructiveness. Even if a heavy price has to be paid, especially by the relatively rich, in terms of social or economic hardship, in pursuit of 'justice, peace and the integrity of creation', such consequences have to be squarely faced by governments and those with the power to influence global events. For we are deeply concerned about the difficulties in exercising the use of force justly.

Nevertheless we recognize that resort will probably be had to force, including military force, in numerous situations. Whenever this happens, it must be confined, by all the parties, to the very narrow limits set by the criteria of justice in warfare (most of which are accepted by both traditions) and by international law, humanitarian law and the laws of war. No infringement of these laws, observance of which is obligatory upon all states and actors, is permissible. In particular the use of force or coercion to persuade individuals or groups to accept belief in either Islam or Christianity is completely unacceptable.

Today both traditions endorse the objects enshrined in Article 1 (1) of the UN Charter:

> To maintain international peace and security, and to that end: to
> take effective collective measures for the prevention and removal of

threats to the peace, and for the suppression of acts of aggression or other breaches of the peace, and to bring about by peaceful means, and in conformity with the principles of justice and international law, adjustment or settlement of international disputes or situations which might lead to a breach of the peace.

But neither has fully lived up to its own beliefs in this respect. It is an obligation, under both traditions, for every state to support and further the work of the UN and its various agencies, including the judgements of the International Court of Justice. This obligation includes a recognition that, as the Court has said, 'there exists an obligation to pursue in good faith, and bring to a conclusion, negotiations leading to nuclear disarmament in all its aspects under strict and effective international control'. Whatever may be the legal arrangements within a state, we are unanimous that both religions are committed today to the rule of international law in all its aspects, and that every state must abide strictly by its international legal obligations, including of course any obligations it may incur as international law develops in the future.

NOTES

1. See Rabbi David Goldberg, *The Jewish Approach to the Just War*, address to Council on Christian Approaches to Defence and Disarmament (CCADD) (London, 10 November 1993, available from CCADD) and Chapter 2 above, pp. 25–7.
2. See Chapter 3 above, pp. 60–1.
3. In Shia Islam the *imams*, as descendants of the Prophet himself through his daughter Fatima, have always had special authority in interpreting the Qur'an and Hadith. Nevertheless their powers were limited by the demands of fidelity to the letter and spirit of the Arabic text of the Qur'an and to the collections of Hadith.
4. See Chapter 3 above, pp. 61–41.
5. Compare Chapter 2 above, pp. 44–61 on Grotius, with Chapter 3 above, on prisoners of war, p. 72. See also Chapter 5, pp. 135, 139 for discussion of the modern law on prisoners of war.
6. See Chapter 2 above, p. 34; see also Robert Markus, 'Augustine on the Just War', in *The Church and War* (Oxford: Blackwell, 1983), p. 4.
7. See Chapter 2 above, pp. 42–3.
8. See Chapter 3 above, p. 66 and note 8. The reference to pre-empting attack is comparable to Aquinas's implication that a belligerent may be permitted to get his retaliation in first against a provocative move by the opponent (see Chapter 2 above, p. 39).

9. See Chapter 2 above, on right intention, p. 39, and Chapter 6, editorial comment, pp. 143–4
10. See Chapter 3 above, pp. 66–7.
11. Augustine, Ep. 57.5, referred to in Markus, *Augustine on the Just War*, p. 4.
12. See Chapter 3 above, 'Who can call for a jihad?', p.68, and note 10 of that chapter.
13. See John Kelsay, *Islam and War* (Louisville: John Knox Press, 1993), Chapter 2, 'The Islamic View of Peace', pp. 32–4.
14. Kelsay, *Islam and War*, Chapter 2, p. 36.
15. Kelsay, *Islam and War*, p. 36.
16. See Brian Wicker, 'A just defence of just prices', *New Blackfriars*, 77 (904) (May 1996), pp. 231–3.
17. Submission by HE Mr Javad Zarif, representative of Iran, to the International Court of Justice on *Legality of the Threat or Use of Nuclear Weapons*, given at a public sitting on Monday, 6 November 1995 in the Hague, Part II, No. 28, p. 25 (our italics).
18. *Legality of the Threat or Use of Nuclear Weapons*, International Court of Justice, The Hague, 8 July 1996, No. 47. See also UN Charter, Article 2, No. 4; R. Green, *Implications of Advisory Opinion by the International Court of Justice*, World Court Project (Twyford, Berkshire, 1996), p. 16; Javad Zarif's Iranian submission to the International Court of Justice, No. 32.
19. See Chapter 2 above, note 13; and see note 23 below.
20. See Chapter 2 above, p. 39.
21. See Chapter 2 above, pp. 43–4.
22. Ibn Rushd, *Bidayat al-Mujtahid*, The Book of Jihad, 1: 3.
23. John Finnis, Joseph M. Boyle and Germain Grisez, *Nuclear Deterrence, Morality and Realism* (Oxford: Clarendon Press, 1987), p. 78: 'The norm excluding intentional killing of the innocent is the core of one of the Ten Commandments: "Do no murder" (Exodus 20: 2–17 at v. 13; Deut. 5: 6–22 at v. 17). In the Jewish and Christian scriptures, and the common morality of our civilisation, this ban on murder did not mean "Do not kill unless killing is necessary to secure some great(er) good." Rather it meant that the killing of human beings is excluded save where divinely authorised ... while the precept also condemns some forms of reckless homicide, its core is the more specific norm: It is always wrong deliberately to kill the innocent.' David Fisher, *Morality and the Bomb*, p. 45: 'War ... causes immense human suffering. The value of the principle of non-combatant immunity is that it provides a reasonably clear-cut and justifiable way of restricting that suffering ... None the less, if, after taking all these and other imperfections of human reasoning into account, it remains true that military action causing non-combatant casualties is the only way to prevent a very great harm and where the good achieved will clearly and decisively outweigh the harm, such action – however morally repugnant – may be licit.' Arthur Hockaday, 'In Defence of Deterrence', in Geoffrey Goodwin (ed.), *Ethics and Nuclear Deterrence* (London: Croom Helm, 1982), p. 84: 'What I am arguing is that, although the conditional intention (sc. of nuclear deterrence) may contain an ele-

ment of moral evil, a strategy of deterrence involving the conditional intention may be the most effective way of securing the twin objectives of preventing war and checking political aggression and may therefore be a morally acceptable price to pay to achieve these objectives.'

24. See Chapter 3 above, pp. 68–9.

25. See M. Hamidullah, *Muslim Conduct of State* (Lahore: Sh. Muhammad Ashraf, 1945), pp. 219–20, quoted in J. Busuttil, 'Slay them wherever you find them: Humanitarian law in Islam', in *Revue de Droit Militaire et de Droit de la Guerre* (1991), pp. 113–40 at p. 122 and note 103.

26. The Prophet was reported to have said: 'Do not punish anybody with Allah's punishment (fire)' (Al-Bukhari). See also Ibn Rushd, Bidayat 1: 3: 'the prophet said to a certain man: "If ye should seize him, then slay him, yet do not burn him. No one is free to punish by means of fire, save the Lord of the (Hell) fire (i.e. God)" '.

27. See Malik, Al-Muwatta, 21: 3: 9: 'The Messenger of Allah, may Allah bless him and grant him peace, saw the corpse of a woman who had been slain in one of the raids, and he disapproved of it and forbade the killing of women and children.'

28. International Court of Justice, *Legality of the Threat or Use of Nuclear Weapons*, Nos 48–56. The accusation that Iran is developing nuclear weapons of its own is unproven, although there appear to be some in the Iranian leadership who would like to go down the nuclear road, for a variety of not very coherent reasons (see Sharam Chubin, in *Survival* (London: International Institute for Strategic Studies), **38** (1) (1995), pp. 86–104; and Fawaz Gerges, in *Survival*, **38** (4), pp. 5–15). But internal wrangling, if any, in no way invalidates the arguments the Iranian regime put to the international court, for they relied simply on established international law as their starting point. Following the publication of the court's opinion, a resolution promoting the elimination of nuclear weapons (Res. A/C 1/51 L.37) has been sponsored by a largely Muslim state (Malaysia) and on 11 December 1996 it received 115 votes, with 22 against and 32 abstentions. This resolution insists 'that the continuing existence of nuclear weapons poses a threat to all humanity and that their use would have catastrophic consequences for all life on earth'.

29. For example, Ibn Rushd, *Bidayat al-Mujtahid*, 'Damage allowed to be inflicted on the enemy'.

30. Ibn Rushd, in *Bidayat al-Mujtahid*, Book of *Jihad* 1: 3, reminds his readers that Al-Hassan Ibn Muhammad al-Tamimi related that the Companions of the Prophet unanimously agreed that a captive should not be killed, and went on to say that the *ayah* (47: 4) when taken literally suggests that the *imam* has either to give amnesty to the captive or ask for ransom. See also Busuttil, 'Slay them wherever you find them', p. 123 and notes.

31. For example by the RC bishops of England and Wales in their document *The Common Good* (London: Catholic Bishops' Conference of England and Wales, 1996), No. 106.

32. For a detailed discussion of Jewish and Christian scriptural beliefs about the sacred character of the 'environment' in the ancient world,

see Robert Murray SJ, *The Cosmic Covenant* (London: Sheed and Ward, 1992). Murray argues convincingly that Biblical beliefs about the sacred character of the environment were long overlaid in mainstream Christianity, but that this concern is being revived in modern times.

33. See Chapter 1 above. In the Great War of 1914–18 slogans like 'Gott mit uns' and 'God save the King' were commonly used by each side against the other.
34. Kelsay, *Islam and War*, Chapter 3.
35. This thesis has become widely accepted since the appearance of Samuel Huntington's essay 'The clash of civilisations', *Foreign Affairs*, 72 (3) (August 1993), pp. 22–49. This essay has been expanded into *The Clash of Civilisations and the Remaking of World Order* (New York: Simon and Schuster, 1996).
36. Islamic revivalism in Egypt, for example, 'is expressed not only in formal religious practices but also in the social services offered by psychiatric and drug rehabilitation centres, dental clinics, day-care centres, legal aid societies as well as organizations that provide subsidised housing and food distribution or run banks and investment houses' – (John Esposito, *Islam: The Straight Path* (Oxford University Press, 2nd ed., 1991) p. 171.
37. Aquinas, *Summa Theologiae*, IIa IIae, Q. 42.
38. Kelsay, *Islam and War*, Chapter 5, pp. 78–81; Chapter 2 above, 'Modern applications', pp. 52–3
39. See Kelsay, *Islam and War*, Chapter 5 for equivalent Islamic injunctions.
40. For a full discussion see Kelsay, *Islam and War*, Chapter 5.
41. Kelsay, *Islam and War*, pp. 100–5.
42. There is no conscription in Islam, as we note above, pp. 79,127. To this extent a government which compels a soldier into the army has *ipso facto* breached a tenet of Islamic faith.
43. See Kelsay, *Islam and War*, Chapter 5.
44. See Chapter 2 above, pp. 48–9
45. For example Dorothy Day's 'Catholic Worker' group in the United States, and the 'PAX' society in the UK.
46. See the Second Vatican Council's 'Pastoral Constitution' on 'The Church in the Modern World', *Gaudium et Spes* (1965), para. 79.
47. *Encyclopaedia of Islam*, entry under 'Ali'.

5 The Modern International Laws of War: Christian and Muslim Approaches

Coming to terms with the evolution of the institutions and practices of what has been called the 'international society of states'[1] has been a slow process in which Christians have had to accommodate themselves to secularization and to the prevailing erastian tradition of church/ state separation in which international politics have been firmly alloc- ated to the latter, while Muslims have been subjected to the more brutal experience of colonial domination and belated incorporation into what is widely seen as a largely European and Western interna- tional order. Central to most definitions of international society is the evolving corpus of conventions, customs, principles and decisions known as international law, together with its recognized and accepted processes of authoritative decision-making.[2] Both Christian and Mus- lim states have been part of this development, and have formally accepted the rules and processes of modern international law.

THE *AD BELLUM* PROVISIONS OF INTERNATIONAL LAW

Article 2 (4) of the United Nations Charter outlaws interstate war under the guise of the 'threat or use of force':

> All members shall refrain in their international relations from the threat or use of force against the territorial integrity or political independence of any state, or in any manner inconsistent with the purposes of the United Nations.

The idea behind this provision is simple: if all states were members of the UN and obeyed this injunction, there would be no interstate war, thus fulfilling the first stated purpose of the new organization: 'to save succeeding generations from the scourge of war, which twice in our lifetime has brought untold sorrow to mankind'.

Restrictionists adopt a broad interpretation of Article 2 (4) in order to rule out all cross-border acts of force including what some have seen as interventions which do not threaten territorial integrity or political independence, and they combine this with a narrow interpretation of allowable exceptions. In fact, on strict readings, only two legal exceptions to the ban on 'the threat or use of force' are seen to survive, namely action in response to a threat to peace, and self-defence.

The UN authorizes collective action with respect to threats to the peace, breaches of the peace and acts of aggression (Art. 39) and if necessary 'such action by air, sea or land forces as may be necessary to maintain or restore international peace and security' (Art. 42). The original intention was for decisions about the use of force under Article 42 to be as binding on members as are decisions under Article 41, which concerns actions not involving the use of armed force. To this end, Articles 43–7 set out mechanisms whereby members would contribute to a Security Council operation run by a UN military staff committee. So far this has not happened, however; so the Security Council has done no more than 'authorize' members to act voluntarily under Article 42, and, more controversially, has even delegated responsibility almost entirely, as in the 1990–1 Gulf War.[3] Article 42 decisions are, therefore, not binding on members, although they remain binding for the target state, which is thereby barred from invoking self-defence under Article 51.

Article 51 states:

Nothing in the present Charter shall impair the inherent right of individual or *collective* self-defence if an armed attack occurs against a member of the United Nations, until the Security Council has taken measures necessary to maintain international peace and security.

Article 51 comes after Article 42, thereby emphasizing that in the original conception even self-defence was considered an interim recourse until collective mechanisms could be activated. Those invoking self-defence still had to report immediately to the Security Council.[4]

Many of the *ad bellum* provisions common to Islamic and Christian tradition can be recognized here, including provisions concerning legitimate authority, restriction to 'necessary' measures, and the stipulation that a collective use of force should only be used as a last resort after Article 41 measures have been deemed inadequate. Perhaps the key principle at issue, however, is 'just cause', now confined in the eyes of restrictionists to self-defence and collective action to maintain or restore international peace and security, as against the somewhat broader Muslim and Christian tradition.[5] From a Muslim/Christian perspective possibly the most difficult question is whether restrictionists are right to rule out 'defence of the innocent', which both traditions have long recognized as a legitimate *casus belli*, from the canon of the modern *ad bellum* provisions allowed in international law. We will return to this in Chapter 7.

THE *IN BELLO* INTERNATIONAL LAWS OF WAR

International law concerning the conduct of war once begun deals with the attempts that have been made, especially since the middle of the last century, to humanize military conflict between states. Muslims and Christians have both come to accept that the international 'humanitarian laws of war' represent obligations which all states, of whatever religious provenance or none, are bound to accept.

The international humanitarian law of armed conflict consists of two legal systems which theoretically are quite separate. The Law of the Hague concerns the rights and duties of belligerents. The Law of Geneva is designed to secure protection and humane treatment of those taking no direct part in the fighting (or who can do so no longer).

The core of the Law of the Hague is embodied in the Hague Convention of 1907. The regulations forbid the killing or wounding of a surrendered enemy; destruction of enemy property unless 'imperatively demanded by the necessity of war'; and killing or wounding 'treacherously'.[6] It is forbidden to attack undefended towns or dwellings. All possible steps must be taken to protect churches, art galleries, charitable foundations, historic monuments and hospitals. An occupying power must preserve public order and respect the law of the land. It must protect family honour and rights, the lives of persons, private property and religious convictions and practice. And it may not inflict general penalties on account of actions by individuals.[7]

The Law of Geneva consists of the Geneva Convention of 1949 and two Protocols added in 1977. It deals with sick and wounded combatants, victims of shipwreck, prisoners of war (POW), and civilians in the hands of a foreign power. It is based on the principle that persons who are placed *hors de combat* and those taking no part in the war shall have their lives spared and be treated humanely. The taking of

, arbitrary executions, torture, cruel or degrading treatment ials are prohibited. The wounded, the sick and all medical resources are to be respected under the sign of the Red Cross or Red Crescent: likewise chaplains are to be protected. Prisoners of war must receive the food and medical care they need, be allowed to write home, and have their names given to the International Committee of the Red Cross who are then entitled to visit them. Civilians are to be allowed to live normal lives so far as circumstances permit: deportations, pillage and indiscriminate destruction of property are all ruled out. The additional Protocols of 1977 set out the basic rule that acts of war are specifically disallowed which cause 'superfluous injury... unnecessary suffering or widespread, long-term and severe damage to the environment'. Everything possible is to be done to avoid harming civilians and to ensure that incidental damage is not excessive in relation to the 'concrete and direct military advantage'. The Protocols extend the Convention to cover wars of liberation and internal conflicts against dissident armed forces or other organized armed groups.[8]

CHRISTIAN AND MUSLIM IDEAS OF INTERNATIONAL LAW

The modern international humanitarian laws of war may be properly regarded as outgrowths of ethical principles subscribed to by both Christians and Muslims. Its aim has been to codify these principles, so far as the effects of armed conflict are concerned, in ways acceptable to the membership of all nations regarding themselves as civilized. For Christians, Jesus's parable of the sheep and goats sets out the main targets of this activity with precision:

> Then the king will say to those at his right hand...I was hungry and you gave me food, I was thirsty and you gave me drink, I was a stranger and you welcomed me, I was naked and you clothed me, I was sick and you visited me, I was in prison and you came to me. (Matthew 25: 34–6. A Muslim *hadith* says something very similar[9].)

The Geneva Convention has accordingly reflected a widening concern, first with the sick (and wounded), then the prisoner (POW), then the stranger (those under foreign occupation) and finally the hungry and thirsty (which can stand for whole populations of countries in conflict). The Law of the Hague goes somewhat further in extending protection to public and private property, setting out some rules of fair play in combat and finally attempting through arms control to outlaw weapons of peculiar horror.

The point need not be laboured that this whole undertaking is derivable from Christian ethical concerns. It would be wholly cynical to argue that the behaviour of nations in combat has not, in some measure at least, been rendered more humane as a result. It will be useful to pick out certain key ideas.

A good starting point is protection of the innocent. In the words of a seventeenth-century Puritan divine, William Ames: 'Charity and aequity doth require that the Warre be so managed that the innocent may bee as little damnified as possible.'[10] It is an obvious consequence of just war doctrine that combatants are the main force of resistance and the legitimate target of military operations and that the innocent may neither participate in nor be subject to hostilities. The question arises, who are the innocent? Derived from 'doing no hurt', 'innocent' in the earliest English uses means 'unoffending', 'not deserving of the suffering inflicted'. We take it here in this sense: the innocent are simply those whose life and work in no way contribute to prosecution of the war. Everyone would agree that this applies to old people, the sick in body or mind, children and nursing mothers. It is an obvious extension to include clergy and members of religious orders, medical and nursing personnel.[11] It was the intention of those who negotiated the 1977 Protocols to include civilians engaged even in 'non-peaceful' activities such as scientists, and those working in industries closely associated with the war.

There is an obvious gap of logic here. In terms of moral guilt (if any) as well as in simple fact, a war effort depends crucially upon a vast unseen cohort of helpers which includes not only workers in armaments but in logistics generally (telecommunications, supply, transport, repair) and even more crucially upon those who direct affairs – civil servants and their political masters. It seems quite unfair to regard these people as 'innocent' in the sense of not contributing to the active prosecution of the war. Two things, however, are clear. First, that it would be quite impossible for commanders on active operations to winnow out those who are in this practical sense implicated directly in the war effort from those who are strictly 'innocent'. Second, the law distinguishes only between civilians and combatants. The Additional Protocol I to the Geneva Convention accordingly defines as civilian, and as such not to be the object of attack, anyone who is not a member of organized armed forces, militias, volunteer corps, resistance movements or who does not spontaneously take up arms against an invader. This will remain the case, like it or not.

It is but a short step from the concept of innocent immunity to the concept of persons being *hors de combat*.[12] Clearly the laying down of arms may be due to surrender or to capture on the battle-field; *a fortiori* it may result from being incapacitated due to sickness (historically by far the largest category) or wounding. All these cir-cumstances can cause a person to revert to 'the condition of men pure and simple', and thus to enjoy the full protection of the law.

But it also follows that to inflict damage on men and women, even if combatant, beyond what is needed to render them *hors de combat* is unnecessary and therefore wrong. Thus the idea of *unnecessary suffer-ing* emerges as a further step. In the words of the St Petersburg declaration: 'the necessities of war ought to yield to the demands of humanity'. Hence the first principle of qualitative arms control as set out in that declaration: that states should abstain from 'the employ-ment of arms which uselessly aggravate the suffering of disabled men or render their death inevitable'.

So this idea leads in turn to the concept of a war crime such as murder, ill treatment, deportation, genocide, plunder or wanton destruction *not* justified by military necessity. In elaborating this idea the International Law Commission laid particular emphasis on personal responsibility and moral choice, thus reverting to a cardinal principle common to Christians and Muslims, namely the respons-ibility of the individual conscience before God.

And this opens the way for a final move away from any formal code via natural law to the bracing air of the Martens Clause: placing all mankind under the safeguards and government resulting from 'cus-toms established between civilized nations, the laws of humanity and the demands of public conscience'. This is a high plateau indeed, and the question is whether any can breathe at so great an altitude.

Muslims have no quarrel with any of this, for they are urged to co-operate with others in doing good, so there is nothing to debar them from co-operating in international treaties and organizations like the United Nations, as indeed they have, bringing the ethics and experi-ence of their Islamic background to bear on issues which concern every nation.

Muhammad Hamidullah, in his book *Muslim Conduct of State*[13] points out that every nation has perforce to develop some form of law in dealing with other nations. Much of European law is based on Roman law, which also influenced the interpretations of Islamic law.

However, there was a gap of a thousand years between the Roman Empire and the emergence of modern European international law, in which European writers like Oppenheim state that 'there was no international law in Europe... [and] and there was no need of such at that time'.[14] It was during this time that the Muslims were developing their own international laws on the basis of the Qur'an and Hadith, intermingled with influences from other cultures.

In this field, the *siyar* of al-Shaybani is acknowledged to be the earliest Islamic work to deal with relations between the Muslims and those at war with them, with intricate problems of property rights and the rights of conquered persons. This became the basis of the division of the world in Islamic law into the *Dar al-Islam* and the *Dar al-Harb*.[15] The word *harb* (destructive war-mongering) is distinct from *jihad*, which is striving 'in the way of Allah' to bring order and justice in place of savagery. *Dar al-Harb* did not include 'those lands further afield who have not yet heard the call of Islam', as is stated quite clearly by al-Mawardi.[16]

Whereas Roman law allowed no right for the belligerent, and nothing but discretion regarding the non-Roman enemy, Islam allocated many rights to the non-Muslim enemy,[17] whether as a non-combatant, a prisoner of war, a slave (to be treated like a member of the family and freed as soon as possible), or a non-Muslim resident in conquered territory. The prophet Muhammad is reported to have said, 'Hate your enemy mildly for he may one day become your friend.' This concept of rights for the barbarian was an important restraint on war.

The crucial question, in accepting parties to (or 'subjects' of) a body of international law, appears to be their willingness to implement it. Islamic law requires of its participants a common ground of belief (or at least recognition for such belief) in God and accountability in the next world, which should ensure that they will comply even against their own material interests. The common ground of UN legislation appears to be something akin to 'peer pressure' or 'collective will', but is still hotly debated,[18] since few members actually adhere to the laws to which they have agreed, and some are allowed more power than others so that they can afford to impose, obey, or ignore the rules as it suits them.[19] All kinds of treachery, breaking treaties or agreements are outlawed in Islam, however powerful the Muslims are, unless the enemy breaks them first, and then only after due warning is given.[20]

Modern international law recognizes and has force mainly over sovereign states.[21] Islamic law, like all ancient law, 'was inherently

personal rather than territorial, for if Islam were intended for all
mankind, the territorial basis of law would be irrelevant'.[22] It re-
sembles human rights law in its concern for the individual, and
recognizes the sovereignty of different 'peoples' only in so far as
they have made treaty agreements with the Muslims, either as a
community or as individuals. Governments, as legal personalities, do
not even make an appearance. Even the ruler of the Muslims is there
to uphold Islam within and outside the Muslim community, and can
legally be removed if he fails in this task. Racism, nationalism, tribal-
ism and class discrimination are forbidden as 'no one is superior to
another except in awareness of God' (Qur'an 49:13).

Muslims anywhere are like parts of a single body, so that the pain
of one part affects the others (Hadith: *Bukhari*). It is a duty to
intervene when called upon and to help others 'except against a people
with whom there is a treaty'. Military force is sanctioned in this cause.
The United Nations is still ambivalent on the degree and circumstances in which force may be used to protect the weak against
oppression, and the international definition of such oppression is
still not clear. In Islam the definition is clearer: it is where people
are being forced from their homes, tortured – Ibn Rushd says that
'enemies must not be tortured, nor must their bodies be mutilated'[23] –
and killed for their beliefs. Even so, Muslims living outside the *Dar al-
Islam* still have to obey the laws there that do not conflict with Islam,
and migration to a better place is encouraged as a way for the weak to
escape from oppression (Q. 16: 41).[24]

NOTES

1. Hedley Bull and Adam Watson describe a transition from an anarchical
   international 'system' of states constituted as such by the bare fact that
   'the behaviour of each is a necessary factor in the calculations of others'
   to an international 'society' in which states have 'established by dialogue
   and consent common rules and institutions for the conduct of their
   relations, and recognise their common interest in maintaining those
   arrangements'; Hedley Bull and Adam Watson, *The Expansion of International Society* (Oxford: Clarendon Press, 1984), p. 1.
2. Rosalyn Higgins sees international law as a process of authoritative
   decision-making 'directed towards the attainment of certain declared
   values' rather than a 'system of neutral rules'; Rosalyn Higgins,

Problems and Process: International Law and How We Use It (Oxford: Clarendon Press, 1994), p. 2 and back cover.

3. But see Ramsey Clark, *The Fire This Time* (New York: Thunder's Mouth Press, 1994), p. 155.

4. Article 51 concludes: 'measures taken by members in the exercise of this right of self-defence shall be immediately reported to the Security Council and shall not in any way affect the authority and responsibility of the Security Council under the present Charter to take at any time such action as it deems necessary in order to maintain or restore international peace and security'.

5. A number of other possible justifications for the legitimate use of force remain contentious, such as belligerent reprisal against cross-border attacks (for example, Israeli punitive expeditions in South Lebanon, or US air raids on Libya); pre-emption against what is known to be an imminent assault (for example Israeli initiation of the 1967 six-days war); enforcement of treaty obligations (for example allied action in 1956 in response to Egyptian nationalization of the Suez canal); response to an invitation to intervene by a foreign government (for example the Soviet invasion of Afghanistan in 1979); cross-border action to rescue nationals (for example the raid on Entebbe in 1977). There are also questions of definition, such as how long a time has to elapse after an act of aggression before 'self-defence' ceases to be a legitimate justification for counteraction.

6. Ruses of war and measures 'necessary for obtaining information' are acceptable.

7. More than 50 states have acceded to this body of regulations. They were held by the Nuremberg Tribunal to have been recognized by all civilized nations and thus become declaratory of the laws and customs of war.

8. There are over 170 parties to the Geneva Convention and more than 110 to the Protocols.

9. Compare the following Hadith (*Sahih Muslim*): 'Allah's Apostle (peace be upon him) said, Verily, Allah, the Exalted and Glorious, will say on the Day of Resurrection: O son of Adam, I was sick but you did not visit Me. He will say: O my Lord, how could I visit Thee when Thou art the Lord of the worlds? Thereupon he will say: Didn't you know that a certain servant of Mine was sick but you did not visit him, and were you not aware that a certain servant of Mine asked you for food but you did not feed him, and were you not aware that if you had fed him you would have found Me by his side? (The Lord will again say): O son of Adam I asked for something to drink but you did not provide Me with any. He will say: My Lord, how could I provide you with something to drink when Thou art Lord of the worlds? Thereupon He will say: A certain servant of mine asked you for a drink but you did not provide him with one, and had you provided him with a drink you would have found Me near him.'

10. See Chapter 3 above, 'Who should be fought?', pp. 68–70. For further Christian views on 'discrimination' and protection of the innocent see Chapter 2 above, pp. 40–1, and note 24; Chapter 4, note 23.

11.   Grotius included a further category: those whose manner of life is 'opposed to war', such as writers, farmers, merchants, artisans and other workers.

12.   See Rousseau: 'The object of the war being the destruction of the enemy state, a commander has a perfect right to kill its defenders so long as their arms are in their hands; but once they have laid them down and submitted they cease to be enemies... and revert to the condition of men pure and simple, over whose lives one can no longer exercise a rightful claim' (*Social Contract*, Book I, iv).

13.   Muhammad Hamidullah, *Muslim Conduct of State* (Lahore: Sh. Muhammad Ashraf, 1et ed., 1935).

14.   L.F.L. Oppenheim, *International Law* (4th ed., 1928), I, A. 62, quoted in M. Hamidullah, *Muslim Conduct of State* (Lahore: Sh. Muhammad Ashraf, 1945).

15.   See Chapter 3 above, p. 71.

16.   Abu'l Hasan al-Mawardi, *The Laws of Islamic Governance*, trans. A. Yate (London: Ta Ha Publishers, 1996), p. 60.

17.   Hamidullah, *The Muslim Conduct of State*, p. 62.

18.   M.T. Ghunaimi, *The Muslim Conception of International Law and the Western Approach*, (The Hague: Martinus Nijhof, 1968), p. 164.

19.   See Clark, *The Fire This Time*, Chapter 8: 'The Trashing of the UN Charter and the US Constitution'.

20.   For discussion of this point in connection with the Iraqi invasion of Kuwait, see Chapter 6 below, pp. 162–3.

21.   Hence the confusion over whether Bosnia and Croatia were sovereign states or parts of Yugoslavia.

22.   Majid Khadduri (trans.), *Shaybani: The Islamic Law of Nations* (Johns Hopkins Press, 1966), Introduction pp. 7–8.

23.   Ibn Rushd, *Bidayat al-Mujtahid*, Book of the *Jihad*, 1: 3, in R. Peters, *Jihad in Classical and Modern Islam* (Princeton: Markus Wiener Publishers, 1996), p. 35.

24.   Around 80 per cent of the world's present refugees are Muslims.

6 Christian and Muslim Approaches to the Gulf War, 1990–1

Editors' note

This chapter is a case study in which the principles presented earlier are put to the test of a concrete example: the Gulf War of 1990–1. In 'Desert Justice?' David Fisher asks how far Christian just war criteria were applied in practice, and how far they stood up to the test of that application. His answer (in which he expresses his own views, not necessarily to be taken as reflecting official policy or thinking) is that they performed well, and that the war itself can be judged to have been a just one for that reason. The next section, 'The Gulf War: Another Christian view', for which Roger Williamson and Brian Wicker are responsible, then inserts a note of Christian scepticism about that conclusion, and suggests that it rests on the omission of some essential analytical elements. The chapter continues with two Muslim responses: first an analysis by Judge Al-Hajri of Qatar of the legality of the invasion of Kuwait under Islamic international law; and second an overview of Muslim reactions to the war as a whole, largely contributed by Abdel and Harfiyah Haleem, but with the concurrence of Zaki Badawi and Haifa Jawaad.

The editors wish to emphasize that the divergent views contained in this chapter do not separate along a 'Christian' versus 'Muslim' fault-line. Differences of ethical assessment emerge within each tradition. A particular divergence emerges over the true aim ('right intention' to use just war terminology) of the coalition powers. This is an issue of fact rather than principle. Were they primarily aiming to remove Saddam's forces from Kuwait, thus putting right the wrong of international aggression? Or were the Americans really using the Kuwait crisis to further their own interests by establishing a degree of hegemony over the whole oil-rich region? And if the latter, was this a 'right intention' or not? We do not attempt here to reconcile the diverging views about this question within the group, but to let them stand as products of a sharp but disciplined debate on the application of ethical principles to concrete cases, which has occurred among the contributors to this book.

DESERT JUSTICE? A CHRISTIAN ETHICAL APPRAISAL OF THE GULF WAR

Earlier chapters have traced the development of the Christian just war tradition and explored the common themes shared between it and the Islamic doctrine of *jihad*. This chapter seeks to answer the key question whether the just war theory is of mere antiquarian value, of interest only to scholars and theologians; or whether it has practical utility in guiding how states should behave, particularly in the crucial choice between peace and war. The test case to be examined is that of the Gulf crisis that commenced with the Iraqi invasion of Kuwait on 2 August 1990 and finished with the declaration of a ceasefire at midnight on 27 February 1991. Our aim will be to assess whether the allies' actions during that period and, in particular, their resort to war and their conduct of the war, were justified according to the criteria of the just war. The allies' actions after the war are beyond the purview of this section.

The lively debate over the ethics of nuclear deterrence in the West in the 1970s and 1980s had revived interest in the just war tradition.[1] As a result, the theory had been brought up to date and was ready and available for use from the moment the first major conventional war of the post-Cold War period loomed in prospect. Much of the debate over the morality of the Gulf War in both the United States and United Kingdom was thus conducted in the terms of the just war tradition. Echoes of the tradition could even be heard in some of the political rhetoric of the coalition leaders. Perhaps not since Vitoria's development of the theory in the sixteenth-century to criticize the wars being waged by his Spanish contemporaries in the New World has there been such an immediate application of the theory to events, as they unfolded.

Use of the just war tradition does not of itself establish its utility. For what matters is whether it helped those applying it to reach determinate ethical judgements. This is far from a foregone conclusion. There were and are many shades of opinion amongst Christians as to the justice of the Gulf War. There were also differences of view between Christians in the West and those in the Middle East – those closest to the conflagration – with the latter, on the whole, being opposed to the use of force by the West. The Pope, while not entirely excluding a military response, was concerned over the tragic consequences of a war in the region and underlined to President Bush his 'firm belief that war is not likely to bring an adequate solution to international problems'.[2]

The just war theory was appealed to on both sides of this debate, by opponents and supporters of the 'military option'. Indeed, the inconclusiveness of the US Catholic theological debate led Father Francis Winters SJ to conclude that the Gulf War 'has been a fair test of just-war theory' but that 'on balance the theory failed the test of providing wise judgement'.[3]

In the UK there were also divided counsels. A lively debate took place amongst Christians prior to the start of coalition operations, with, for example, Philip Crowe[4] and Roger Williamson[5] urging caution because of doubts as to whether the just war criteria would be met, while Richard Harries and Arthur Hockaday argued that a coalition operation to free Kuwait, provided it was suitably conducted, could meet the criteria.[6] The Anglican hierarchy finally concluded on the eve of the allies' offensive:

> We have been extremely reluctant for a long time to acknowledge the necessity of war, but we see that there does come a point when this is the only option left. In our statement, we have recognised that this time may have come...[7]

Meanwhile, in Iraq Saddam Hussein viewed matters in a rather different light. Shortly before the allies' attack commenced, he claimed:

> We are taking the right path for peace and jihad, not only for all Muslims but for all nations.[8]

Saddam's right thus to speak 'for all Muslims' was debatable given that: it was a Muslim country he had invaded and was busy despoiling; many of the leading coalition members were Muslim; and all were operating from and with the support of Muslim Saudi Arabia. Equally questionable was his appeal to the Islamic concept of *jihad* since, as argued in an earlier chapter, this rules out, as does the just war theory, any war undertaken for aggressive purposes, such as Saddam had undertaken against Kuwait.

In order to try to assess the practical utility of the just war tradition, let us consider its detailed application to the Gulf crisis. This should help in determining whether the different conclusions reached at the time by Christians arguing within the just war tradition reflected a fundamental weakness of the theory or arose from different reasons.

The just war tradition starts from a moral presumption against war: war stands in need of justification. The tradition thus seeks to define circumstances in which a state may legitimately resort to war – the *jus ad bellum* – and the way in which the war should be conducted – the *jus in bello.*[9]

The *jus ad bellum* prescribes that war is permissible if and only if: war is declared by a competent authority; all available peaceful means of settling the dispute have been tried and failed so that war is a last resort; the war is undertaken for the sake of a just cause; and the harm judged likely to result from the war is not disproportionate to the likely good to be achieved, taking into account the probability of success.

The *jus in bello* adds two further conditions governing the conduct of war: the harm likely to result from a particular military operation should not be disproportionate to the good it might achieve; and non-combatant casualties should be minimized.

How, in retrospect, did the allies' actions in the Gulf crisis measure up against each of these conditions?

The first requirement – of competent authority – is usually interpreted within the tradition to mean that war can only be declared by governments, not individuals. Some modern interpreters have suggested that the only competent authority in the latter half of the twentieth century should be the United Nations. While the importance of UN sanction cannot be gainsaid, this may be unduly restrictive: for example, the Tanzanian intervention to prevent genocide in Uganda was not authorized by the UN and yet would still appear justified. But even if UN sanction is not always necessary, it is certainly sufficient proof of competent authority.

On this basis the coalition operations fully met the requirement of competent authority since they were authorized by the UN both implicitly under the provisions of Article 51, allowing for the inherent right of self-defence, and explicitly under Resolution 678. The latter provided that, in the event of Iraqi failure to comply by 15 January with the relevant UN resolutions requiring their withdrawal from Kuwait, member states, co-operating with the Government of Kuwait, were authorized 'to use all necessary means to uphold and implement' these resolutions and to 'restore international peace and security in the area'.

The next requirement – of last resort – occasioned much dispute at the time. Many opponents of the war argued that the coalition military operations had been embarked on prematurely and that more time ('one year') should have been given for sanctions to work.[10] There was also criticism that the timing of the military operation had been dictated by its own logic and, in particular, the need to attack when the troops were at peak readiness and before either Ramadan or the very hot season might interfere with military operations.

These criticisms appear, however, to be misplaced. The just war tradition does not argue that every other means should be applied before war, but rather that all available peaceful means of resolving the dispute should be used. War causes harm and it is only sensible to try other available means first, if there be such. Equally, if war is the only way of resolving the dispute, it may be justified. It does not, therefore, follow that other options should always be preferred to the military or that the military option should always be applied temporally last: indeed, an early limited application of force may be more effective than a late one, by which time the problem may have become more intractable.

In the present dispute it can hardly be claimed that the military option was resorted to with undue haste given the lengthy pause between the Iraqi invasion of Kuwait on 2 August 1990 and the start of coalition operations on 16 January 1991. Diplomatic efforts to resolve the dispute continued right up to the last moment, with the Baker–Aziz talks in Geneva on 9 January and Perez de Cuellar's trip to Baghdad on 11–14 January, which culminated in his memorable quip: 'You need two to tango. I wanted to dance but I did not find any nice lady for dancing with.'[11]

As regards the argument that economic sanctions should have been given more time, this would have been true if sanctions had had some prospect of success. Economic sanctions are a weapon of indiscriminate harm. Indeed, their object is to harm innocent civilians as a means of bringing pressure to bear on wayward governments. According to the just war tradition such an indiscriminate weapon should only be used if there are very strong grounds for supposing that more good than harm will result. Such reasons are hard to find. Despite the readiness of the international community to resort to general economic sanctions, their success rate has been very limited.

In the present case it was suggested that they might fare better given the extent of the international coalition ranged against Saddam (thereby reducing the risk of leakage) and his dependence on oil (a prime target of the sanctions) as a source of revenue. What was never made clear, however, was how the sanctions were supposed to work, even after ample time. For even if they led to extremes of suffering and deprivation amongst ordinary Iraqis, it was never explained how the people were supposed to bring effective pressure to bear on a ruthless dictator who held all the reins of power. The logic of this process was as mysterious and unconvincing as was that whereby area bombing in World War II was supposed to bring about the overthrow of Hitler. Saddam's survival long after the war, despite continuing sanctions, attests only too clearly to the ineffectiveness of this particular mechanism.

The third requirement of the just war tradition is that there should be a just cause for the war and that the war should be undertaken for the sake of this cause. In the words of Vitoria, 'there is one and only one just cause for waging war viz. an injury received'.[12] The war should be embarked on in order to remedy that injury and hence with an appropriate 'right intention'.[13] Right intention is often treated in the tradition as a separate condition. The merit of thus treating it as a necessary adjunct to just cause is that this restricts the intention with which war is waged to remedying the wrong that occasioned it. This thus inhibits the expansion of war aims that has been a depressing feature of modern conflicts: pre-eminently during World War I, where as carnage grew, so the war aims were expanded retrospectively to try to justify the suffering. Moreover, the broader the war aims, the more difficult it is to conduct the moral calculus to determine whether more good is achieved than harm and the greater the consequent risk of licensing excessive harm. Given the moral presumption against war from which it starts, the just war tradition seeks to limit the suffering caused by war, while at the same time not precluding action that may be morally required by setting unachievably ambitious aims: the fallacy of supposing that unless we can redress every wrong we should not attempt to address some. In international law, at least until recently, the requirement for a just cause has been interpreted narrowly to refer to rectifying a specific act of aggression against the territory of a sovereign state. Iraq's aggression against Kuwait would thus appear a paradigmatic just cause. Nonetheless, the justice of the allies' cause was one of the conditions most argued over at the time.

There were few, if any, who accepted Saddam's claim to have right on his side, given the brazen nature of his aggression. But some opponents of the war claimed that remedying aggression was not the allies' real motive – for if it were, why had the West not intervened against other aggressions, including those of Israel against the Palestinians? It was also argued that the West bore some responsibility for the present crisis as a result of its past tacit support for Saddam's regime, not least through the supply of arms. The West's real motive, it was suggested, was the need to protect its supply of oil. The unprecedented response to Saddam's aggression was, according to Naom Chomsky, only 'because he stepped on the wrong toes'.[14]

Many factors undoubtedly played a part in the allies' motivation. Oil was certainly a factor in the crisis. Indeed, without Kuwait's oil wealth, Saddam would never have been tempted to invade, nor would the US have moved so rapidly to protect Saudi Arabia. Moreover, the protection of the world's oil supplies, from which the poorer nations benefit at least as much as the wealthier, is not an ignoble motive. Nonetheless, the conclusions of the historians of the war are that:

> There seems little doubt that Bush was influenced most of all by the need to uphold the principle of non-aggression and the analogy with the failure of appeasement in the 1930s.... When he spoke to Congressmen the day he took his decision on doubling forces, he reported that he had been reading Martin Gilbert's lengthy history of the Second World War.[15]

Such motivation would also appear to have been paramount with Mrs Thatcher who as early as 5 August 1990 told a US audience:

> Iraq's invasion of Kuwait defies every principle for which the UN stands. If we let it succeed, no small country can ever feel safe again. The law of the jungle would take over from the rule of law.[16]

Such sentiments echoed the shock and revulsion very widely felt against Saddam's behaviour – one UN member invading and seeking to annihilate another – just when, with the demise of the cold war, prospects for the UN and world peace had appeared brighter than ever before. Consonant with such betrayed optimism, Bush's political rhetoric at times soared even higher:

> What is at stake is more than one small country: it is a big idea: a new world order – where diverse nations are drawn together in common cause, to achieve the universal aspirations of mankind: peace and security, freedom and the rule of law.[17]

Even if such poetic flights of rhetoric are to an extent discounted, the more prosaic motivation enunciated by Mrs Thatcher would still constitute a paradigmatic just cause. Nor does the fact that such noble motives were allied with self-interest (protection of oil supplies) invalidate them. For human endeavours are typically undertaken from a variety of motives, without this necessarily undermining the more altruistic reasons for action. Indeed, it is a fallacy of post-Kantian Protestantism to suppose that the categorical imperatives of morality must be entirely distinct from the hypothetical imperatives of other actions; and that duty and self-interest must, therefore, necessarily be divorced from each other as motives.[18] This was not how the Greeks viewed ethics, for whom happiness (*eudaimonia*) was the natural end of virtue, just as heavenly bliss was the culmination of earthly goodness in mediaeval Christendom.

It is also unclear why the allies' alleged past misdemeanours, in failing to respond to earlier aggressions or in supplying arms to Iraq, should necessarily detract from the rightness of their action in the Gulf crisis. To suggest this is, indeed, alien to Christian thought, whose Founder constantly taught, most memorably in the Parable of the Prodigal Son, the intrinsic value of the present right act, whatever past failures there may have been. Nor is it valid to argue that all wrongs need to be righted before any one can be – for that way leads to moral impotence in the face of a suffering world. In any case, the allies could point to good reasons for at least some of their past caution in responding to aggression, in view of the risks of nuclear escalation endemic in the cold war period. Indeed, it was only with the ending of the cold war that the diverse utility of military force had once more been rediscovered.

The final *jus ad bellum* requirement is the application of the principle of proportion to the war as a whole: to assess whether it is likely to produce more good than harm, taking into account the probability of success. The just war tradition counsels caution in applying this test. For the suffering caused by war is likely to be direct and immediate; the good may be speculative and uncertain. War can thus only be justified if there are very good reasons for believing that the good will, indeed, outweigh the harm; we must also ensure that no more harm is brought about than is necessary to achieve the good result.

The application of this principle occasioned much dispute. Few doubted that the allies would achieve military success given the weight and sophistication of the firepower they had assembled. What was doubted, however, was whether the war could be kept limited or whether it would escalate out of control, particularly if Israel became involved. There was widespread concern that the casualties, among both the allies and Iraqis, would be out of all proportion to any objectives achieved, thus rendering any military victory hollow. Roger Williamson, for example, presented military planners with an unpalatable moral dilemma of either risking through wrong decisions enormous military casualties in a 'Vietnam in the desert', or else seeking to evade these by massive air strikes leading to high civilian casualties. Either way it was doubtful whether the principle of proportion could be met.[19] There were also fears that ecological catastrophe would ensue if Saddam fulfilled his threat to fire the oil wells.

In order to weigh up the balance sheet of gains and losses, it is necessary first to assess how many of the allies' objectives were achieved. These objectives were outlined in discussing the just cause requirement. First and foremost was the objective to free Kuwait by ejecting the aggressor, thereby upholding the rule of international law and, in particular, the prohibition on external aggression. President Bush claimed this would help inaugurate a 'new world order'. There was also some suggestion that 'to restore international peace and security' (as required by Resolution 678) might necessitate the removal of Saddam Hussein, although this never became an explicit war objective, nor would it have been likely to have commanded the assent of all coalition members.

Of these objectives, the first – ending the aggression – was fully achieved. The coalition operation also upheld the principle of non-aggression and so served to strengthen the authority of the UN. Indeed, if the allies had not so acted, the authority of the UN, which in 1990–1 was only just being reasserted after the prolonged paralysis of the Cold War, would have been very seriously and perhaps fatally weakened.

The war did not lead to Bush's 'new world order', although arguably it may have contributed indirectly to the 1993–4 rapprochement between Israel and the Palestinians. The war certainly did not bring about the overthrow of Saddam, as his subsequent oppression of his people, particularly the Kurds in the north and Shi'ites in the south, has borne grim testimony.

It is thus pertinent to ask whether the allies should have prolonged the war until Saddam was overthrown and his regime replaced with a more internationally acceptable alternative. With the benefit of hindsight and the knowledge of the appalling suffering he has wreaked upon his people, it is tempting to answer in the affirmative. At the time, the extent of his subsequent oppression of his people was not known, while the difficulties and uncertainties involved in ousting him from power (to be replaced by whom?) were all too evident. Given the caution admonished by the just war tradition, the allies were thus perhaps prudent not to have expanded their war aims to include Saddam's overthrow.

Turning to the costs of the war, it is clear, in retrospect, that these were massively overstated by the opponents of the war (and, indeed, some of its supporters). The war remained limited; it did not escalate out of control; and despite all Saddam's provocations through the Scud missile offensive, Israel kept well out of the war. Ecological catastrophe did not happen, even though Saddam fulfilled his threat to fire the oil wells. The overall casualties were relatively modest. The allies lost 240 dead (many killed through friendly fire and accidents). Iraqi casualties in the war are more speculative. They were, however, assessed by Freedman and Karsh (on the basis of Iraq's own claims) to be 30 000 dead, of which 2000 to 3000 were civilians. The Iraqi figure for civilian deaths was the very precise 2278.[20]

Not all of the allies' wider objectives (in particular, Bush's new world order) were achieved. Nonetheless, the key objective, which constituted the paradigmatic just cause, of reversing Iraqi aggression and thereby upholding international law, was fulfilled, at an overall cost that, however regrettable, was relatively modest. The principle of proportion was thus satisfied.

Reaching such a judgement is very much easier with hindsight than it was at the time. While there were, in David Fisher's view, good reasons for supposing even then that the allies' objective of expelling the Iraqi aggressor could be achieved without disproportionate cost, the contrary concerns felt by many Christians were very genuine. What this analysis, however, makes clear is that the nature of the dispute between opponents and supporters of the war over the application of the principle of proportion was primarily a factual one, mainly about how many casualties would arise from military operations. In turn, this suggests that the dispute reflects less a radical indeterminacy in the just war criteria than the ineluctable fact of our moral lives that we have to reach difficult ethical judgements in conditions of uncertainty. In trying to decide what is the right thing to do, we all too often have no choice but to weigh up the incommensurable and uncertain outcomes of our actions.

We turn now to the *jus in bello* conditions that have to be satisfied in the conduct of war. The first of these is a second application of the principle of proportion, this time to assess whether the cost of individual military operations is proportionate to the value of the objectives achieved, with the good outweighing the harm and no more harm being caused than is needed to achieve the good. The allies' conduct will be assessed in relation to two such operations: the overall air campaign and the killing in the final days of the war on the road to Basra.

The objective of the allies' air campaign was to contribute to winning the war: either on its own, if that were possible (as advocates of the strategic use of air power hoped); or, at the least, by substantially reducing Iraqi opposition, to prepare the way for a ground offensive. To achieve this overall objective, a number of different targets were attacked. These included nuclear and chemical weapon facilities, Scud missile sites, air defence installations, command and control facilities, civilian infrastructure used in support of military operations, and Iraqi ground forces, particularly those occupying Kuwait. The next section will assess the justice of allied attacks on civilian infrastructure. In this section, I shall consider whether the extent and duration of the campaign as a whole was excessive in relation to its objectives.

The air campaign was outstandingly successful. The question at issue is whether it was perhaps too successful and that the objectives could have been achieved at less cost. In particular, it may be suggested that the intensity of the air campaign was primarily motivated by a desire to minimize allied casualties – to keep down the 'body bag count' about which the US, in particular, was very sensitive following its Vietnam experience. Indeed, in responding to criticism of the scale and intensity of the air campaign, the British Gulf War commander, Sir Peter de la Billiere, appeared to concede this: 'My answer is that if we stop early we pay in British lives, and this is not a deal I wish to do.'[21]

It would be impossible on ethical grounds to justify a trade in military casualties based on a calculus that equated, say, three Iraqi soldiers' lives with those of one British soldier. For from a moral viewpoint one life counts the same as another. But this does not mean that ethics would have to preclude the sensible military strategy of inflicting enemy casualties, while minimizing one's own. For what the principle of proportion requires to be weighed in the balance is not one side's military casualties against another's but rather the much more complex and difficult judgement of whether the good to be achieved by an operation would outweigh all the harm achieved. In the present case, this involves assessing whether the contribution of the air campaign to winning the war (and hence to the objective of ending Iraqi aggression) was such as to outweigh the disbenefit of the casualties (military and civilian) on both sides. Military casualties are thus weighed on the same scale with each other, not against each other on different scales.

In retrospect, it may appear that the air campaign was excessive when we know how little resistance was encountered once the ground campaign commenced. This was, however, hardly known at the time and, indeed, the allies began ground operations before their objective had been secured of a 50 per cent attrition of key equipments (tanks, armoured vehicles, artillery). It is also salutary to recall that at the time the allies faced critics arguing in favour of a greater air campaign to avoid the need for any ground offensive. On balance, therefore, it can be concluded that the overall air campaign was justified.

A particular incident in the campaign that provoked much criticism was the air attacks against the Iraqi soldiers and others fleeing on the road to Basra. On 25 February coalition F15E aircraft had bombed the front and rear of the convoy of some 1000 vehicles, so that the fleeing Iraqis were trapped. The next day waves of aircraft, and subsequently artillery, attacked the remnants of the convoy in what became known as the 'turkey shoot'.

It was argued in favour of these attacks that they were destroying military assets (men and equipment) that might otherwise be used to prolong the war. Against this, however, the Iraqi occupation of Kuwait was by then at a virtual end and the Iraqis on the verge of accepting cease-fire terms. Once the convoy had been stopped, those being attacked had no chance of escape: it was, as one pilot remarked with evident distaste, like 'clubbing baby seals'.[22] The carnage caused would thus appear disproportionate to the objective. Indeed, the widespread revulsion aroused by this incident encouraged President Bush promptly to call a halt to allied military operations.

The final *in bello* condition to be satisfied is the principle of discrimination or non-combatant immunity. This principle has at times within the tradition, and particularly in recent years, been treated as an absolute condition, admitting of no exception. Within the historic development of the tradition, the principle has not always been so regarded; and with good reason, given the complexity of our moral life. For we may be faced, like Agamemnon at Aulis, with circumstances in which 'there are no ways that do not lead to ill',[23] and hence where the right choice may be of a lesser evil. To avert a very much greater harm it may, therefore, be justifiable to take action, even if civilian lives are thereby put at risk. The principle of discrimination is thus perhaps well encapsulated by the seventeenth-century Puritan divine, William Ames:

> Charity and Aequity doth require that Warre be so managed as the innocent bee as little damnified as possible.[24]

Nonetheless, even if not absolute, the principle of discrimination does impose an important constraint additional to that of proportion, requiring that civilian casualties be minimized. Allied policy was designed, according to its spokesmen, to achieve just that. As General Schwarzkopf put it:

> We are doing everything we possibly can to avoid injuring or killing or destroying innocent people. We have said all along this is not a war against the Iraqi people.[25]

Moreover, uniquely in recent history, technology had furnished the means of using modern weaponry to attack military targets with minimum collateral damage. The Gulf War marked the major debut on the world stage of precision guided munitions. The allies thus had an avowed policy of discrimination and the means to fulfil it. Concern was, nonetheless, voiced among Christians that in a modern war and, in particular, with the employment of aerial bombardment the principle of non-combatant immunity would inevitably be breached.[26] Were there, therefore, lapses?

The difficulty of justifying the allies' imposition of general economic sanctions because of the indiscriminate harm caused has already been addressed. In the conduct of the war itself, the strategic air campaign, while directed primarily against military targets, did include targeting of civilian infrastructure used to support the war effort, such as fuel, electricity and telecommunications. These attacks were designed to weaken the Iraqi war effort, for example by disrupting Saddam's command and control of his forces. (Towards the end of the war it took Saddam 24 hours to communicate with his front line.) Unfortunately, in the heavily militarized Iraqi society these same utilities also served the civilian population (for example, electric power for sewage works or water purification). The attacks thus caused massive disruption to civilian life, with particularly harmful effects in the longer term. For example, post-war assessments suggested it could take up to nine years fully to restore the electrical power system.

It could perhaps be argued that since the primary objective of these attacks was military, any civilian casualties were merely incidental side-effects – foreseen but not intended – for which the allies could hardly be held responsible. But such an argument from 'double-effect' takes too short a route. For the conceptual distinction between consequences intended and foreseen does not appear sufficiently clear-cut to bear the weight of the moral distinction placed upon it. If the consequences of an action, while not intended, are still both within the agent's control (they would not have happened if he had not acted thus), and consented to by him, at least in the minimal sense that having foreseen their occurrence he, nonetheless, persisted in the action, the agent cannot surely be acquitted of all responsibility. For such control over and consent to events appears precisely what underpins our attribution of moral responsibility for them.

In the present case, it can perhaps be argued that not all the civilian casualties were within the agent's control. Damage immediately caused (for example, to water purification plants) was within the allies' control. But the worst effects on civilian life came about as a result of the prolonged breakdown of the infrastructure, even after the war. The causal linkage of such later effects to the allies' bombing is leaky. For it would always have been open to Saddam (or any successor) to seek a massive injection of international humanitarian aid to restore the infrastructure once hostilities had ceased. Such considerations seem to have underlain General Kelly's remark at the time that, 'If there is an additional effect on the civilian population, it is one that Saddam chooses, not one that we did'.[27]

General Kelly's claim is, however, only partly true. For the allies were responsible for the foreseeable damage brought about by their actions, even if they cannot be blamed for the extent to which these effects were prolonged after the war and worsened as a result of Saddam's obduracy. Such arguments cannot, therefore, be used to evade all responsibility for civilian damage, some of which was the direct result of allied actions. Given that the main aim and effect of these attacks were military, they can, on the whole, be held consistent with the principle of discrimination. In retrospect, however, the intensity of some of the attacks on infrastructure does appear questionable. Indeed, after the war the Air Force conceded that the strikes against electricity generators might have been more effective than intended.[28]

Moreover, even if the campaign, as a whole, was thus justified, one particular incident provoked considerable criticism. This was the attack on the command bunker/air raid shelter on 13 February at Amiriyah in the suburbs of Baghdad, which killed 314 civilians. In this case there was no dispute that the deaths were within the allies' control: they would not have have happened if the Air Force had not directed two laser-guided bombs at the bunker. What the allies claimed in their defence was that they had not known that civilians were sheltering in the bunker, which they had evidence was being used as a back-up command and control facility. Without such knowledge they could not be held to have consented to the deaths. One of the two conditions for attributing responsibility – consent – was thus missing.

It is perhaps arguable that the allies should have made more effort to verify the absence of civilians, although such criticism is easier made with the benefit of hindsight than at the time when quick decisions were required. What does, however, seem clear is that the Amiriyah incident did not portend – as some feared at the time that it might – a switch to a deliberate policy of targeting civilians. On the contrary, the target list was immediately revised to ensure that such an accident did not recur and nine similar bunkers were removed from the list.

It is thus concluded that, while there were some lapses, overall, the coalition operations to liberate Kuwait, in both their origin and conduct, satisfied the criteria of the just war. On balance, the Gulf War can thus be held to have been a just war. Moreover, whether or not this is accepted, this analysis has helped demonstrate that the just war tradition does provide a useful framework for assessing such questions. The lively debate and conflicting views among Christians as to the application of the tradition to the Gulf War reflect less an inherent weakness of the theory than the hard choices we face in making ethical judgements in conditions of uncertainty. We cannot escape this ineluctable feature of the human condition simply by changing our moral theories.

THE GULF WAR: ANOTHER CHRISTIAN VIEW

The previous section ('Desert Justice?') argues that the war over Kuwait was 'just' according to criteria long established in the Christian tradition. Hardly anyone doubted that the invasion of Kuwait by Iraq was a case of blatant aggression. Saddam had committed just the kind of offence which Christian teaching on the 'just cause' for war describes, and which the UN Charter was established to deal with. One UN member had swallowed up another, and justice cried out to have this aggression reversed.

But in the months leading up to the start of military operations in January 1991, little else was as morally clear-cut as this. There was worldwide doubt whether the other conditions that needed to be fulfilled before a resort to arms could be licit (lawful authority, last resort, right intention) would be met. In a paper titled *Just War in the Gulf?*[29] Roger Williamson quoted numerous statements from Church of England sources, together with statements from Christian American denominational leaders and the National Council of the Churches of Christ,[30] as well as from Christians in the Middle East,[31] which supported sanctions against Iraq, but urged continuing UN-sponsored negotiations as the best way forward. Many, especially in America, were deeply suspicious of any US Government military action in response to the crisis. A NCCC statement of 15 November 1990 was typical: 'the US administration increasingly prepares for war, a war that could lead to the loss of tens of thousands of lives and the devastation of the region...In the face of such reckless rhetoric and imprudent behaviour, as representatives of churches in the United States we feel that we have a moral responsibility publicly and unequivocally to oppose actions that could have such dire consequences'. On 15 January 1991 (the UN's deadline date for Iraq's withdrawal) the NCCC wrote to President Bush: 'Once begun, it is unlikely that this battle can be contained in either scope, intensity or time. And this we know out of bitter experience: in the paths of these armies will be ground to death aggressors and victims alike; the Kuwaiti lives, national dignity and property which you deployed troops to rescue are likely to be destroyed; and very many of our own beloved countrymen and women will die. This sacrifice is out of all proportion to any conceivable gain which might be achieved through military action.' True, as things progressed, the question of lawful authority was answered to most non-pacifist Christians' satisfaction by the passing of UN Resolution 678, authorizing 'all necessary means' to eject Saddam from Kuwait. And once the coalition forces were assembled, there seemed a reasonable chance that they would be successful in removing Saddam's forces.

But all the really problematic questions remained. For one thing, precisely because of the enormous assemblage of overwhelming force which the coalition led by the US had provided, might not the war be a grossly *disproportionate* response to the offence that had been committed? And what of the fate of the Iraqi civilian population, whom international law forbade the coalition intentionally to attack? Would they remain as inviolable as international law demanded? What about the destruction of the very means of sustenance (water, electricity) on which they depended? 'Was this not likely to happen as the coalition closed in on Baghdad for the kill? And for how long should economic sanctions be allowed to take their course before it could be said that war had become truly the *last resort*? Only six months were given: perhaps another six months would have done the trick. All of these questions were being asked, with increasing urgency as time went on.

It is easy with hindsight to argue that some worries were (as it happened) misplaced, largely because the Iraqi army proved no match for the coalition forces, and because Saddam conducted a militarily inept campaign, as well as because of the intensity of the air assault before land operations began. But it was not at all easy, at the time when decisions had to be made, to believe that these worries would be satisfactorily responded to. There was a massive, well-argued Christian hesitation, based on just war reasoning, from all quarters of the globe, about endorsing the war option. Indeed, Saddam was counting on this to avert the fate that he otherwise saw coming.[32] Furthermore, it was widely estimated that the number of casualties on both sides, but particularly among Iraqi civilians, would be huge, leading to difficult, not to say callous, calculations of how many would be too many.[33] And would the enormous firepower of the coalition forces be used with strict discrimination against military targets only? It seemed unlikely. There was widespread and justifiable scepticism about the concept of 'surgical strikes'.

It is an axiom of just war thought that intellectually a war can be distinguished, as a discrete action, from much of its surrounding context, including events that happen before it begins and events that continue as a result of it afterwards. But we cannot wholly disentangle a war from the rest of what has happened, is happening and will happen in the world. It was partly because of unclarity about the limits of what needs to be brought into the calculation that many Christians were especially exercised about the disproportion between the offence committed and the punishment likely to be meted out.

This unclarity was present in several ways. The first concerned the purpose of the war. If the goal of the war was simply to punish aggression, by ejecting Iraq from Kuwaiti soil, then (it was continually pointed out) why did the West not do the same when Israel grabbed the West Bank, or Indonesia grabbed East Timor? Of course it has been argued that the West's failure to do anything about those cases does not entail that it would not do better in the Kuwait case.[34] Yet a degree of consistency is relevant to our judgement of the probity of the motives of those claiming to act with a 'right intention' in the here and now. Given the clamour of claims and counter-claims going on all around, doubts about the assertion that the goal of the war was simply to reverse Saddam's aggression were certainly legitimate at the time, given the West's poor past record in reversing other cases of aggression, and given the manifest interest that it had in Kuwait's oil. And anyhow, President Bush was making loud noises about the 'new world order' he was expecting to create out of the conflict in Kuwait.[35] His publicly stated goal was much more than simply ejecting Saddam from his ill-gotten territorial gain: it was 'to achieve the universal aspirations of mankind: peace and security, freedom and the rule of law'.[36]

But a deeper unease comes out when we examine some of the most significant doubts expressed by Christian leaders before the military operations to eject Iraq began. One of the most important of these, summing up much of the Christian protest during the previous months, was the message sent by Pope John Paul II to President Bush on the very day the UN deadline expired (15 January 1991):

> In recent days, voicing the thoughts and concerns of millions of people, I have stressed the tragic consequences which a war in that area could have. I wish now to restate my firm belief that war is not likely to bring an adequate solution to international problems and that, even though an unjust situation might be momentarily met, the consequences that would possibly derive from war would be devastating and tragic. We cannot pretend that the use of arms, and especially of today's highly sophisticated weaponry, would not give rise, in addition to suffering and destruction, to new and perhaps worse injustices.

The Pope sent a similar message to Saddam on the same day:

> No international problem can be adequately and worthily solved by recourse to arms, and experience teaches all humanity that war, besides causing many victims, creates situations of grave injustice which in their turn constitute a powerful temptation to further recourse to violence.[37]

The Pope's conviction that war would not solve the problem of Iraq's aggression is in no way incompatible with the claim made in 'Desert Justice?' above that, in strict just war terms, the war that took place was licit. It is simply that it is possible to view things through a wider-angle lens than that commonly used by military strategists or even some just war philosophers. There is no contradiction in saying that, although the war was fought for a just cause, it quite failed to solve the underlying problem, and therefore should not have been fought. One could put the point by saying that the criterion of 'right intention' was inadequately formulated by the Western coalition. Certainly the goal of ejecting Saddam was licit: but doing this was not the same thing at all as making the world safer for long-term peace.

Much of the Christian protest against the coalition's case implied that, however just a war to eject Saddam from Kuwait might be, waging it would not serve the long-term interests of peace. Now, it might be argued that this large ambition was too remote and cloudy to be the subject of an intention in the modern sense of that word.[38] But the meaning of 'intention' in the just war criterion of 'right intention' as formulated by, say, Aquinas is not quite what it usually means today.[39] It seems to refer less to the righteousness of what is going on in the mind of the actor and more to the rightfulness of what he is attempting to do. Anyhow, in today's 'global village' the effects of a war are felt everywhere. And of course this was just the point of Bush's rhetoric about seeking, through the war, to establish a 'new world order'. While this rhetoric may have been hyperbolic, it was understandable, for it answered to the felt needs of a post-cold war generation yearning for a more peaceful environment, in which human beings could flourish better than they had been able to for the past forty years.

The point is not that the *cause* for which the war was fought was not just, if by this term we refer simply to the project of ejecting Saddam. And of course, getting him out of Kuwait may well have been a necessary preliminary to creating the larger peace. But, as many Christians saw it, the problem was that doing so by means of military force employed on a huge scale, was not compatible with that larger aim, or 'right intention': namely, peace, or a 'new world order'. The motives of the actors were too mixed, the rhetoric too confused, the politics too dubious, the violence too blatant. And who is to say that they were wrong? Saddam was certainly ejected from Kuwait, but he is still in power in Iraq, and his people continue to suffer from the damage the coalition did to them. That they are still subject to indiscriminate sanctions may not be strictly a direct, let alone an intended, consequence of the military operations: but it is a consequence all the same, for which the coalition must take some blame. And of course, Bush's rash outsider's call to the Iraqi people to rise up and themselves overthrow Saddam has only made things far worse for them.

It is hard to find any fault in the Pope's caution that the war would give rise 'to new and perhaps worse injustices' and that it quite failed to solve the real problems of the region, let alone create a new world order of peace and security.

WAS THE INVASION OF KUWAIT BY IRAQ PERMISSIBLE UNDER ISLAMIC INTERNATIONAL LAW?

This question has been studied in a recent unpublished doctoral dissertation by Ali Bin Ghanim Ali Al-Shahwani Al-Hajri, of Qatar.[40] He summarizes his findings as follows:

The Iraqi invasion of Kuwait constituted an unprecedented event in the history of modern Islamic states. A Muslim state invaded another without any prior warning or without any regard for the sanctity of Islamic international law. Islamic international law is perceived by all Muslims as binding on every member and state and no deviation is permitted at all.[41] This law differs in both form and procedures from modern international law, but echoes it in its condemnation of war,[42] its declaration that treaties are sacred[43] and its insistence that human rights must be upheld.

According to Islamic international law the world in theory is divided into *Dar al-Islam* and *Dar al-Harb*, where in the former the rule of peace is prominent and in the latter the rule of war prevails. In practice, however, relations between the two worlds are regulated through certain modes and forms of agreement.

The Iraqi invasion was a clear violation of the rules of *Dar al-Islam* where war should not be resorted to unless in exceptional cases, such as self-defence. Under the principle of self-defence Islamic international law permits force to be used to repel aggression[44] or in response to treaty violation[45] in order to protect the religion of Islam. Iraq failed to prove that its invasion was undertaken in self-defence, for Kuwait did not instigate an actual armed attack[46] which would have necessitated the action of self-defence on Iraq's part. It was Kuwait which was invaded and not Iraq, and yet Iraq claims that it was acting in self-defence.

Islamic international law has clearly banned what is called anticipatory self-defence. Moreover, Islamic international law stipulates that, whenever war is contemplated, a state cannot initiate it without prior warning.[47] The practices of Muslim states in the past have proved that if a war is fought without any declaration, the attacking state must annul its action and pay adequate compensation to the afflicted party. Again Iraq initiated its war without any regard for this principle. For it is documented that Iraq, while negotiating with Kuwait, was busy preparing plans for invasion.

In addition, Iraq, by its aggressive action, violated its peace treaties with Kuwait. These treaties, though signed within the framework of modern international law, are valid by Islamic international law.[48] Violation of a treaty in Islamic law is not permitted at all unless the treaty has expired or has been breached by another party to it.[49] Even where the treaty has been breached, war cannot be conducted instantly: a Muslim state is obliged to communicate its intention to the (potential) violator in order that negotiations might prevent it occurring.[50]

As to Iraq's challenge to the legality of the alliance of the Western powers with Kuwait, Iraq interpreted Islamic law as forbidding such an alliance with non-Muslims against a Muslim state. In fact Islamic international law appears to recognize such alliances.[51] The issue of alliance with non-Muslim states occupies an important chapter in the literature of Islamic international law. Views on the subject were and continue to be diverse, but a common stand is possible. Jurists have been divided into two: pro-alliance and anti-alliance.[52] Both of the camps, however, agree that an alliance with non-believers is permissible when Muslims are weak and cannot combat aggression with their own resources.[53]

The pro-alliance jurists justified force against a Muslim state by invoking the Holy Book which affirms that if two groups of believers fight each other, then peaceful settlement must be the rule.[54] As Iraq rejected the peaceful settlement, and in view of the Muslim states' weakness, an alliance with Western powers became permissible. The argument of those jurists who rejected the alliance was not based on the illegality of war against Iraq as such, but on the alliance itself. They called for war against Iraq, but not with Muslim and Western forces. However, due to the weakness of Muslim states, an alliance with Western powers became a necessity, otherwise Kuwait and possibly other Gulf states afterwards would have succumbed to Iraqi rule.

In conclusion, the Iraqi invasion of Kuwait was contrary to Islamic international law, and the alliance of Kuwaiti–Western powers was legal. Such an alliance was based on the principle of necessity (*masla-hah*) which is recognized by a majority of jurists.

A MUSLIM VIEW OF RECENT EVIDENCE ON THE KUWAIT WAR

All views of the Gulf War are only as good as the evidence on which they are based, and to find the truth, it is necessary to do thorough research into the facts. David Fisher's account draws mainly from *The Gulf Conflict 1990–91* by Freedman and Karsh. Ramsey Clark's book *The Fire This Time*[55] is based on research undertaken internationally by a team of dedicated researchers (with perhaps political aims), his own eye witness, and reports from journalists mainly working for US and UK newspapers and journals. Official figures and reports and speeches made by US leaders are also quoted. In addition, a review by the late Khurram Murad in *The Muslim World Book Review*[56] covers eight other books on the war written from various points of view since 1992. What he finds in some of them substantially agrees with Ramsey Clark's conclusions. Evidence from both these sources is the basis for the following argumentation, together with additional information given in an interview by Dr Zaki Badawi.

Alliance with non-Muslims

The discussion about the legality of non-Muslims helping Muslims against another Muslim is the crucial one for Muslims, since it gave an opening for the non-Muslims to establish a permanent military presence[57] on the ground in the Middle East and thus to enforce their control of the area, which arguably was the reason for the whole exercise.[58] Hence continuing attempts by Muslim militants to highlight the presence of the US forces still in the Holy Land of Arabia. This land has a special status in that it should be dedicated completely to Islam, according to traditional Islamic law, based on the words of the Prophet, 'Two religions cannot be professed together in the peninsula of Arabia' (*al-Hidayah* – a Hanafi legal textbook). The permanent US military presence is therefore seen by some as a sacrilegious occupation and a danger to the integrity of the whole of the Islamic Middle East.

Right intention?

If the real intention behind the war was to extend US hegemony over its oil interests in the Middle East,[59] that would, to some extent, supersede the arguments from just war and *jihad* theory that it was a war to right a wrong, since that wrong (the invasion of Kuwait) was part of the plan in the first place, and intentionally provoked.[60] It was not *that* wrong the US sought to redress, but a wrong against US 'national interests': the emergence of a hostile rival power which might 'dominate a region whose resources could...generate global power'. Zaki Badawi said that among Muslims, in the build-up to the war, 'there was apprehension that Israel, with US connivance, harboured a secret project to encourage Iraq to disintegrate into its three natural parts, that is into three small states which would be in competition with each other: a Kurdish North, a Shi'ite South and a Sunni centre. So here was a powerful Arab country being subjected to the over- whelming might of the West with the ultimate objective of being destroyed by it.'

In both just war and *jihad* traditions, the pursuit of power and national economic interest are invalid intentions. However, this would apply to the US intentions, not those of the Muslims involved, who made some attempt to prevent the war, and limit it to the just aims of reversing Iraq's aggression on Kuwait. The Saudis, appar- ently, were only persuaded to allow the Americans in by deceptive use of aerial photographs to make them think that Iraq was poised to invade their country.[61]

Proportionality and discrimination?

According to the reports gleaned by Ramsey Clark and his associates, the conduct of the Kuwait war, behind the propaganda facade, was far from the restrained and focused attack on military targets it purported to be. On the contrary, what he describes was an all-out attack on the civilians and civilian infrastructure from the beginning which broke both international and US laws of war, constituting war crimes on 19 counts.

Liberation of oppressed people?

Far from liberating the Iraqi people from oppression by a 'new Hitler' (according to some reports they were considerably less oppressed before the war than many other Muslim countries in the Middle East),[62] the war left Saddam Hussein still in place, angry and vengeful against his perceived enemies who were encouraged by the US to try and overthrow him, and so caused more oppression than there was before. The Kurds, supposedly under US protection, are still being oppressed by Turkey, and in the south the Shi'i marsh-dwellers, supposedly protected by the allies from air attack, are reportedly being deprived of their habitat by Saddam's drainage of the marshes.[63] In addition, the continuation of sanctions has made life for Iraqi civilians harder than ever before and caused many needless deaths. Iraq and its people are broken and weak and unable to challenge either US hegemony or Saddam Hussein.

The state of Kuwait was liberated from Iraq and its sovereignty restored, but nothing else has changed there. It was said during the war that women would have voting rights, but they still do not, and the US is not interested in this. As a result of the war, the Palestinians had to leave Kuwait, which had been one of their few remaining refuges in the Middle East. The Kuwaitis, too, are still campaigning for the release of 700 Kuwaiti hostages held in Iraq, presumably as bargaining chips.

Some maintain that popular political opposition has been encouraged, by the war and the American effort for 'democratization', to grow in the area, particularly in Saudi Arabia and Iraq. The Saudis have reactivated a nominated *shura* (consultative council); and the dissident Committee for the Defence of Legitimate Rights has emerged, currently based in Britain. There have also been at least two failed coup attempts against Saddam Hussein encouraged by the CIA in Iraq.[64]

Whatever the intention behind them, so far these opposition attempts have merely had the effect of destabilizing and putting pressure on the regimes, like earlier US efforts to destabilize Iraq using the Kurds, and US support for Iraq's aggression against Iran after the revolution, rather than constituting serious attempts by widespread popular movements to provide an alternative government.[65] Such irritations can only make governments *more* repressive.

Making mischief on the earth

In achieving Arab and UN backing for the war, the US apparently bribed, deceived, and threatened Middle Eastern states, who are now retreating from further involvement. These actions constitute corruption and oppression and are all illegal under Islamic law. Fomenting dissent and instability can also be seen as making mischief in the land.

Environmental damage caused by the war, mainly by US action, spread far beyond Iraq and Kuwait, for example black snow in the

Himalayas, oil slicks in the Gulf, increased carbon emissions.[66] A full assessment still has not been made of radiation leakage from nuclear plants destroyed by bombs and other pollution from crudely destroyed chemical weapons and biological weapons (attacks on which are illegal under a Protocol to the Geneva Convention).[67] Nor have the effects of Gulf War Syndrome on allied troops been taken into account in the balance of harm caused.

Do the good effects outweigh the harm?

The Kuwaiti and other Gulf governments obviously derived some good from the war in that they retained their sovereignty. However, they remain in fear of another Iraqi threat, and so more dependent than ever on the Americans for protection.

Another possible benefit from the war was to deter Saddam from expansionist aggression. However, it has not been proved that he had any such intention,[68] and the power of his military machine was greatly exaggerated in the build-up to the war, judging by the almost total lack of resistance faced by the US and allied forces from the Iraqis.[69] Indeed some suspected, and Saddam Hussein said, that the whole thing was an elaborate charade organized by the US in order to demonstrate the effectiveness of their arms – with television coverage as advertising – to promote sales in the Middle East and elsewhere and frighten governments into buying weapons.[70] This can hardly be seen as a good effect from a Muslim point of view. More arms purchases mean less money spent on welfare of citizens, danger to dissidents, danger of government debt to the arms producers and consequent weakness in the face of financial pressure.[71]

In fact the war was seen by some as a defeat for Islam, since the war propaganda effectively cast Saddam as one force potentially strong enough to stand up for Islamic causes – for the Palestinians, for a rise in the price of oil, and the consequent increase in the wealth of Muslim countries. Saddam said at the time, using rhetoric borrowed from his erstwhile enemies in Islamic revolutionary Iran, that he was fighting for all these causes and thus gained support from not a few Muslims (mostly young) who believed him, or at least shared these aims.

The elimination of such an 'Islamic' challenge to the status quo may have been seen by those in power as a 'good' outcome, deterring any future attempts to wage open military *jihad* in the cause of Islamic 'fundamentalism'. Murad says that:

the US and the West are convinced that their interests will not be secured merely by making Israel strong, or by propping up despotic but friendly regimes in Muslim countries, by keeping them divided and destroying their armed strength. The real threat lies in the resurgence of Islam, which must be combated, controlled and eliminated by whatever means possible.[72]

In any case, the repression of Islamic forces keeps the Middle East regimes busy, divided and too weak to resist US/Israeli domination:

On the one hand the US stands at the top of the world, all the Middle East regimes have become subservient to the American dictates and interests, they are weak and divided as never before, they are busy suppressing the popular Islamic forces within. On the other, Israel's military might stands supreme in the region, and the Arabs' potential to deter Israel has been reduced to almost nil.[73]

Human rights consequences of increased Western hegemony in the Middle East

Muslim peoples have a long historical experience of Western hypocrisy and double-dealing, violence, oppression, and exploitation, all under the guise of 'civilizing' non-Christian nations.[74] Following assassinations of earlier rulers aided by the CIA,[75] Saddam Hussein has enjoyed much Western military and other support, especially in his war against Iran, a war far more heinous than the invasion of Kuwait, when this support was channelled through the Gulf states. It was the debts incurred by Saddam during this war which made him turn to Kuwait for help, and Kuwait's refusal which sparked the invasion.

Muslims, in some of their own countries, are being prevented, by other Western-sponsored rulers, from practising the simplest aspects of their own religion:

- In Turkey, the army is trying to stop women in government jobs choosing to wear the *hijab* (headscarf), and prevent a more general introduction of Shari'ah law, in spite of the attempts of the democratically elected government to allow these.
- In Egypt, free speech in the mosques is a thing of the past, since all such speeches must now have a government licence, and ordinary Muslims are not allowed to do *i'tikaf* (staying in the mosque) in the

last 10 days of Ramadan; even charitable collections have to be licensed.[76]

- In Algeria, following a long tradition of electoral rigging and military oppression by the French, the people have not been allowed to elect the government they want and are now embroiled in brutal repression and military resistance.
- In Tunisia, some women are reported to have been arrested for wearing the *hijab*.
- Across the Muslim world, Western laws have supplanted some of the most vital Islamic ones, especially in the field of business economics, like those forbidding usury, resulting in what, according to Islamic teachings, are regarded as perversions of justice.
- Military courts are reported to pronounce death sentences on Muslim activists who have been tortured in jails, and the FBI is reported to be setting up a network of intelligence bureaux across North Africa to share information about 'terrorists'.[77]

The US Government is being revealed increasingly as interested only in oil and money, and caring nothing for the human rights of Muslims. They are seen as allied with, or even subject to, the power of Israel and the Zionist lobby and, because of this, actively hostile to Islam and Muslims, as witnessed by their recent veto of an otherwise unanimous UN motion condemning Israel's annexation of the Abu Ghoneim/Har Homa site in Jerusalem, and their alleged funding of an illegal invasion of southern Sudan by soldiers from neighbouring countries in support of rebels attempting to unseat the Islamic government in the North.[78]

Long-term consequences for the regulation of wars

Ultimately, if the US Government can get away with breaking most of the rules of international law, as Ramsey Clark alleges it did, and as it apparently continues to do in Sudan, there is no safeguard for human beings who try to stand up for any kind of justice. It was somewhat encouraging to hear the Western powers for once invoking God and justice and talking of limiting their action over Kuwait, but the facts on the ground appear to have been as bad as could be expected from the most hardened unbelievers, even worse than the previous World Wars, at least as calculated according to the quantities of ordnance said by some sources to have been launched at Iraq.[79] The US showed scant regard for the humanity of Iraqi people,[80] in spite of all the claims to the contrary, or for the welfare of the planet as a whole.

Lawful authority?

Since the US is not Muslim it is not subject to Islamic law. It is, however, or ought to be, subject to modern international law, and it is up to the international community, including the Muslims, to decide how to deal with this problem. The Muslims, for their part, are increasingly distrustful of the UN as a source of lawful authority in the regulation of wars. Especially since the demise of the USSR's balancing influence, the UN is seen to be a tool of the US, which uses its veto and manipulates the members of the Security Council at will to achieve its own ends in a way that is unjust and biased towards the agenda of Israel in the Middle East.[81]

The constitution of the UN as set up after the last war is widely seen, not just by Muslims, to be anachronistic and unjust, giving far too much power to the five veto states, and excluding the vast majority of other states. It is not based on any objective concept of justice, or belief in accountability to God, and is therefore fundamentally flawed. Muslims therefore warmly support moves to reform the UN's constitution, particularly the removal of the five power veto (especially that of the US which has not even paid its dues). However, this enterprise does bring to mind the story of the mice arguing about who should put the bell on the cat!

In the absence of effective international law, or where it conspicuously fails to do justice, then the Muslims are bound by Islamic law to combat the transgressors, in whatever way is possible, until they submit to the rule of justice. For Muslims now, it is necessary first of all to determine, on the basis of all the evidence, whether they can continue to treat the US as friends and military allies, or should attempt to make a stand in whatever ways they can, at least by collectively withdrawing their co-operation in matters proved to be damaging to Muslim interests and principles, as they appear to be doing over the Israel/Palestine 'peace process'.

It would not be surprising if more people despaired of struggling for justice by non-violent means and resorted to clandestine militarism to combat their oppressors. One man who has taken this path is Usama bin Ladin, interviewed in the *Independent* (22 March 1997) by Robert Fisk, who quotes him as saying that the US was in Saudi Arabia because of its oil but – more importantly – because it feared ('along with the Zionists') that 'they and their local agents would drown in the Islamic uprising'. On being told that the US regarded him as the foremost 'terrorist' in the world, he said, 'If liberating my land is called terrorism, this is a great honour for me.'

Other Muslims, remembering how the peoples of the all-conquering Byzantine, Persian, and later Mongol superpowers eventually accepted Islam, and that the true victory in Islam is the opening up of hearts and minds to God's truth and the turning of enemies into friends, will continue in the time-honoured tradition of *jihad* of the tongue and pen, of peaceful preaching and teaching, following the Qur'anic verse:

There is no compulsion in religion: truth stands out clear from falsehood.... God is the Protector of those who have faith: from the depths of darkness He will lead them forth into light ... (2: 256–7)

NOTES

1. See David Fisher, *Morality and the Bomb* (London: Croom Helm, 1985; New York: St Martin's Press, 1985). This book was the outcome of a debate held in Oxford in Hilary Term 1984 between Fisher and the then Master of Balliol, Anthony Kenny, both sides of which were published. See also Anthony Kenny, *The Logic of Deterrence* (London: Firethorn Press, 1985).
2. Pope John Paul II, letter of 15 January 1991 to President George Bush, printed in the English language edition of *Osservatore Romano*, 21 January 1991. See below, p. x and Note 37.
3. Francis X. Winters SJ, 'Freedom to resist coercion: Augustine, Aquinas, Vitoria', *Commonweal*, **118** (1991). The US debate is well summarized in John Langan, 'The just war theory after the Gulf War', *Theological Studies*, **53** (1992), pp. 1–18.
4. Philip Crowe, 'The doctrine of a just war', in *CWN Series*, 26 October 1990, pp. 8–9.
5. Roger Williamson, *Just War in the Gulf?* (Uppsala, Sweden: Life and Peace Institute, 1991).
6. Richard Harries, 'The path to a just war', *Independent*, 30 October 1990; and Arthur Hockaday, 'War and justice', *The Tablet*, 27 October 1990.
7. John Habgood, then Archbishop of York, reported in *The Times*, 16 January 1991, summarizing the statement of the Church of England bishops, 15 January.
8. Saddam Hussein, quoted in the *Guardian*, 12 January 1991, p. 1.
9. Fisher, *Morality and the Bomb*, Chapters 2–3.

10. Williamson, *Just War in the Gulf?*, p. 62.
11. Perez de Cuellar, quoted in the *Daily Telegraph*, 15 January 1991.
12. Franciscus de Vitoria, *De Indis Recenter Inventis et de Jure Belli Hispanorum in Barbaros*, ed. Walter Schatzel (Tubingen: J. C. B. Mohr (Paul Siebech), 1952), No. 13.
13. See Chapter 2 above, pp. 39–40 and below, note 39.
14. Naom Chomsky, 'The use (and abuse) of the United Nations', in Micah L. Sifry and Christopher Cerf (eds), *The Gulf War Reader: History, Documents, Opinions* (New York: Random House, 1991).
15. Lawrence Freedman and Efraim Karsh, *The Gulf Conflict 1990–1991* (London: Faber and Faber, 1993), p. 212.
16. Rt Hon Margaret Thatcher, speech to the Aspen Institute, 5 August 1990.
17. President George Bush, State of the Union speech, 29 January 1991.
18. Alasdair MacIntyre, *Against the Self-Images of Ages* (London: Duckworth, 1971), Chapters 15 and 16. See also Alasdair MacIntyre, *After Virtue: A Study in Moral Theory* (London: Duckworth, 1981), pp. 44–5.
19. Williamson, *Just War in the Gulf?*, p. 19.
20. Freedman and Karsh, *The Gulf Conflict*, pp. 408–9 and 329.
21. Sir Peter de la Billiere, *Storm Command, A Personal Account of the Gulf War* (London: HarperCollins, 1992) p. 279.
22. Freedman and Karsh, *The Gulf Conflict*, p. 403.
23. Aeschylus, *Agamennon*, v. 211, quoted in Kenneth Dover, *The Greeks* (BBC Publications, 1980), p. 86.
24. William Ames, 'Conscience, with the power and cases thereof', quoted in James Turner Johnson, *Ideology, Reason and the Limitation of War* (Princeton University Presss, 1975), p. 199. But see also above, pp. 117–18 and p. 130, and note 23.
25. General Norman Schwarzkopf, CENTCOM briefing, Riyadh, 18 January 1991.
26. Williamson, *Just War in the Gulf?*, pp. 19–23.
27. Lieut-General Thomas Kelly, US Department of Defense News Briefing, Washington DC, 11 February 1991.
28. Freedman and Karsh, *The Gulf Conflict*, p. 322.
29. Roger Williamson, *Just War in the Gulf?* (Stockholm: Life and Peace Institute, 2nd ed., 5 September 1991).
30. *Ibid.*, pp. 24–32.
31. *Ibid.*, pp. 56–8.
32. See Freedman and Karsh, *The Gulf Conflict*, p. 434: 'Until quite a late stage in the conflict the Iraqi leader remained confident that through a combination of bluster and inducements he might strengthen the peace camp in the West to such an extent that war would be averted.'
33. See Roger Williamson, in Brien Hallett (ed.), *Engulfed in War* (University of Hawaii, 1991), p. 57. Williamson points out that Bush's intention to avoid another Vietnam in the desert implied that the US was preparing a crushing air-onslaught with a probability of high Iraqi casualty figures: 'No price was too heavy to pay' to achieve Iraqi withdrawal, Bush had said.
34. David Fisher, see above, p. 150.

35. See above, p. 149.
36. State of the Union message, 29 January 1991.
37. *L'Osservatore Romano*, English weekly edition, 21 January 1991. The Pope did not desist from his view that war was not a solution to any international problem, as *Centisimus Annus* (1 May 1991) No. 52 makes clear. An even more categorical rejection of war as a solution to any modern problem was to be found in an editorial in the Rome-based journal *Civilta Cattolica* Vol. 142, pp. 3–16, dated 6 July 1991.
38. See Barrie Paskins on intentions in nuclear deterrence, in 'Deep cuts are morally imperative', in Geoffrey Goodwin (ed.), *Ethics and Nuclear Deterrence* (London: Croom Helm, 1982), p. 99: avoiding war 'is indeed the motivation of our deterrent activity, but intention and motive are different things. What I *intend* to do is what I judge, correctly or incorrectly, to lie within my power to do...What I hope thereby to achieve is a further good, beyond my unaided powers'.
39. See Aquinas, IIa *Summa Theologiae*, IIae, Q. 40, Art. 1 ad 3 for a clear statement that a 'right intention' (*recta intentio*) in war must be the pursuit of peace. In this context it is important to note that for Aquinas *intentio* can signify exertion, effort or purpose. Just war must be waged with a right purpose and not for any less worthy reason.
40. Judge Al-Hajri, dissertation on *The Iraqi Invasion of Kuwait and the Legality of Its Claims in International Law and Islamic International Law*, presented to the Department of Public International Law at the University of Kent at Canterbury, February 1997. The following end-notes are based on material contained in earlier parts of this dissertation, especially Chapter 5.
41. The primary source of Islamic international law is Allah himself, as evidenced in the Qur'an, the Sunnah and those actions of the 'Rightly Guided Khalifas' which were considered binding on all Muslims. Al-Hajri, *The Iraqi Invasion*, Chapter 5, p. 9 quotes the Hadith which reads: 'follow my tradition and the tradition of the Rightful Khalifas who succeeded me and never deviate from it'.
42. 'According to Al-Mawdudi...Islam avoided the reference to war for one reason. Its expansion through conquest was considered morally legitimate for it was perceived to represent the means to achieve happiness and prosperity for all people...Jihad is undertaken to propagate and defend Islam, not to wage war arbitrarily'. (Al-Hajri, *The Iraqi Invasion*, Chapter 5, p. 14)
43. On the sanctity of treaty promises see Qur'an 9: 13, 16: 91.
44. See Qur'an 2: 194: 'If then anyone transgresses the prohibition against you, transgress ye likewise against him.' Jurists regarded this verse as a clear illustration of the justice of Islamic law as it permits fighting only to repel injustice and aggression and in accordance with the principle of proportionality.
45. See Qur'an 9: 13, 16: 91.
46. 'Defensive war must be initiated in response not to an anticipated attack but to an actual one, and must be proportional...the practice of the Prophet reveals that self-defence was exercised only when Mus-

lims were exposed to a real attack'. (Al-Hajri, *The Iraqi Invasion*, Chapter 5, pp. 26–7)

47. Under Islamic international law, any armed attack must be preceded by a declaration of war. The Prophet stipulated that a war cannot be undertaken unless a warning is given to the other party informing them of such an attack, thus allowing them the opportunity to avoid it. It was narrated that the Prophet, whenever he dispatched a military mission, would order the commander to present the enemy with a choice of two alternatives to war: either to pay the *jizya* (poll tax) in return for their protection or convert to Islam...According to the Shafi'ite school of law if Muslims launched an attack without prior warning then they were obliged to pay compensation (Al-Hajri, *The Iraqi Invasion*, Chapter 5, p. 36).

48. Iraq had signed the UN Charter, The Charter of the Arab League and the Charter of Organization of the Islamic Conference (all of which include pledges of peaceful negotiation of disputes and of the inadmissibility of force) and Islamic international law requires strict observance of (secular) pledges made by any Muslim party. Iraq was also party to the treaty of Joint Defence and Economic Co-operation among states of the Arab League, which included a similar pledge to settle disputes by peaceful means.

49. If an agreement is breached by another party, then Islamic law stipulates that Muslims must inform the enemy that the agreement is no longer valid and as such a state of war exists. Thus it is regarded as a serious breach of Islamic law to unilaterally annul a treaty without valid reason (Al-Hajri, *The Iraqi Invasion*, Chapter 5, p. 42).

50. It was argued by several leading jurists, especially Muhammad Ibn al-Hassan al-Shaybani, that it is obligatory on the ruler of a Muslim state to inform his enemy that, upon a conflict instigated by the latter, the treaty between them becomes invalid. Whenever it is breached by the latter then the treaty between them becomes invalid. A war in short cannot be initiated unless the enemy is informed thus. By such action Muslims would not be able to take the enemy by surprise (Al-Hajri, *The Iraqi Invasion*, Chapter 5, p. 42).

51. The Prophet made several alliances not solely between Muslims but also between Muslims and non-Muslims. In Medina he made a pact of fraternity between the Muslims and Jewish community. However, the Prophet extended the concept of alliance to include non-believers. In the first year of emigration (Hijra) the Prophet made an alliance with the chief of the Mutam Ibn Aumair tribe. The purpose of this pact with a non-believer tribe was mutual self-defence where each party pledged to help and defend the other if one of them was subjected to an attack (Al- Hajri, *The Iraqi Invasion*, Chapter 5, p. 50).

52. Al-Hajri, *The Iraqi Invasion*, Chapter 5, pp. 53–4 identifies the Abu Hanifa school of law as being 'pro- alliance' and the Hanbali school as being 'anti-alliance'. The Shafi'ite school does not permit such alliances except where there is extreme necessity. In general, disagreement among Jurists was common as their opinions were motivated by the circumstances of each case. There is no doubt that all of them built their

decisions on the Qur'an and Hadith but they gave different interpretations.

53. See Al-Hajri, *The Iraqi Invasion*, Chapter 5, pp. 55–7.

54. Qur'an 49: 9.

55. Ramsey Clark, *The Fire This Time* (New York: Thunder's Mouth Press, 1992).

56. Khurram Murad, 'Book Review', *The Muslim World Book Review* 17(3) Spring 1997, The Islamic Foundation, Leicester, pp. 3–11.

57. Murad, *ibid.*, p. 4, quotes William Perry, the US Defense Secretary in his 3 May 1995 report to the Congress on the *US Security Strategy for the Middle East*, as saying that the 'US capabilities to defend its vital interests in the Middle East are at an all-time high, in stark contrast to the situation two decades ago: ... Now we have 20 military bases, and 20,000 troops are permanently stationed there. Equipment for a further two divisions lies in place. Except Iraq, Iran, Lebanon, Syria and Yemen, we have strong military co-operation agreements with all the countries; they all allow us the free and unconditional use of their ports and air bases, and conduct with us more than 20 joint exercises every year. But above all, we are Americanizing the Arab forces, making them exclusively dependent upon American weapons, methods and training. The forces we took three months to mobilize in 1990, we could now do in three days.'

58. Clark, *The Fire This Time*, p. 62.

59. Murad, *op. cit.*, pp. 3–4, quotes a Pentagon document of February 1992 which clearly sets out the aims of the Gulf War: it describes the war as 'a defining event in US global leadership', and its after-world as a 'new international environment'. In this new environment, the Pentagon confidently envisages, America could easily remain the 'one and only unrivalled superpower', and 'retain the pre-eminent responsibility ... for addressing those wrongs' which 'threaten her interests', or 'seriously unsettle international relations'. She should therefore prevent 'the re-emergence of a new rival' and 'any hostile power from dominating a region whose resources could ... generate global power'. She must also establish a new order which would convince 'potential competitors [like Germany and Japan] that they need not aspire to a greater role or pursue a more aggressive posture to protect their legitimate interests'; and must 'account sufficiently for the interests of the advanced industrial nations to discourage them from challenging our leadership' (*New York Times*, 8 March 1992). Eliot Cohen, Professor of Strategic Studies at the Paul H. Nitze School of Advanced International Studies, Johns Hopkins University (*Foreign Affairs*, March–April 1996, p. 52) boasts, 'America has the prospect of military power beyond that of any other country on the planet, now and well into the next century. But, it may drive the revolution in military affairs only if it has a clear conception of what it wants military power for.' Joseph Nye Jr., Dean of the John F. Kennedy School of Government at Harvard University, and former Chairman of the National Intelligence Council, and William Owens, former Vice-Chairman of the Joint Chiefs of Staff, say that the emerging capabilities of the US must be linked to its foreign policy, for

military force is still the final arbiter of disagreements. America is better positioned to enhance not only the effectiveness of its raw military power through its information edge, but also its soft power – power 'to set the agenda in ways that shape the preferences of others' and persuade 'them to agree to norms and institutions that produce the desired behaviour'. Thus, as they say, 'the new political and technological landscape is ready-made for the US to capitalize on its formidable soft power to project the appeal of its ideals, ideology, culture, economic model, and social and political institutions' (p. 24).

60.   Clark, *The Fire This Time*, p. 15; Murad also agrees that 'It is now more than evident that Saddam Hussain was almost invited by the US into Kuwait, and soon after, within three days, by 5 August, America got itself invited, too, into Saudi Arabia to wage war against Iraq.' (Murad, *op. cit*)

61.   The story was 'uncovered by Bob Woodward of Watergate fame in his *The Commanders*' (*ibid.*, pp. 5–6).

62.   Clark, *The Fire This Time*, pp. 60 ff.

63.   *Independent*, 24 April 1997.

64.   *Independent*, 11 April 1997. This was published on the same day that the US was trying to make Europe withdraw its ambassadors from Iran because of a political assassination in Germany (five years earlier) in retaliation for earlier destabilization by American-backed rebel *mujahidin*!

65.   This continues with support for the rebels in Sudan, and recent calls (by Newt Gingrich) for the US to attack Iran.

66.   Clark, *The Fire This Time*, Chapter 5.

67.   *Ibid.*, p. 286.

68.   *Ibid.*, p. 28, and see note 61 above. The cause of the invasion of Kuwait was a local dispute over money when Iraq emerged from its war with Iran heavily in debt and Kuwait not only refused to help, but actually made things worse by over-producing on its oil quota using oil from a disputed oilfield on its (also long disputed) border with Iraq.

69.   *Ibid.*, p. 29; see also p. 31 for the discrediting of US propaganda on Iraqi atrocities in Kuwait.

70.   *Ibid.*, p. 218 gives details of increased arms sales in the year following the war, when the 'US made two thirds of all arms sales in the region'.

71.   Murad queries Faisal al-Mazidi's assessment (*The Future of the Gulf*, London: I. B. Tauris, 1993) of the need for 'massive external support' from the US 'to deter or defeat any aggression', asking 'Then why such massive expenditure on arms purchases and defence forces?' Murad, *op. cit.*

72.   *Ibid.*, p. 11; Murad refers to two articles by Ali Mazrui and Richard Falk in T. Y. Ismael and J. Ismael, *The Gulf War and the New World Order: The International Relations of the Middle East* (Gainesville: Florida Press, 1994).

73.   Murad, *op. cit.*, p. 10.

74.   *Ibid.*, p. 9: 'American leaders from the beginning have always been convinced that they had been chosen by God and history, were under a covenant, it was their manifest destiny to use its power to generate

and civilize mankind, and to be the guardian at the gate against barbarians. Hence they had a right to dominate, even push back and exterminate, people who stood in their way, the savages as they called them then, (or terrorists and extremists now)...'.

75. Clark, *The Fire This Time*, pp. 5–6
76. The *Independent*, week beginning 17 March 1997, interview with the editor of the Egyptian opposition newspaper *Al-Sha'ab*.
77. Clark, *The Fire This Time*, pp. 5–6.
78. Jimmy Carter's visit *may* have injected a note of sanity into the situation there.
79. Clark, *The Fire This Time*, p. 58 (88 500 tons of explosives).
80. *Ibid.*, p. 42: 'When asked his assessment of the number of Iraqi soldiers and civilians killed, General Colin Powell answered, "It's really not a number I'm terribly interested in." '
81. See *ibid.*, pp. 153–6: 'The Corruption of the UN'.

7 Humanitarian Intervention and the Bosnian Conflict

Do governments have a right, if not a duty, to intervene forcibly to protect indigenous populations in other countries whose own governments are either incapable of defending them or are themselves responsible for the suffering? Both Muslims and Christians are often implicated as aggressors and suffer as victims in these situations. In some cases Christians persecute Muslims (Bosnia); in other Muslims persecute Christians (Sudan); in others again Christians persecute Christians (Croatia) and Muslims persecute Muslims (Iraq).[1] Neither faith community is free from blame – and the challenge of what, if anything, to do about it confronts both alike. In this chapter we first consider the question of forcible humanitarian intervention in general, then apply our conclusions to the question of humanitarian intervention in Bosnia.

The question of humanitarian intervention is not a new one, but it has assumed new dimensions since the end of the cold war. In terms of international law there has been a shift of concern from UN Charter Article 2 (4) (the legitimacy of cross-border military action by states) to UN Charter Article 2 (7) (the legitimacy of intervention by the UN in the internal affairs of states).[2] This revives older conceptual categories and raises deep questions about conflicting values of order and justice enshrined in the Charter, about the desirability or possibility of reform of the UN and about the whole nature of the international collectivity. At its heart lies the dilemma well expressed by Tesón:

> The first horn of the dilemma [intervention] opens the door for unpredictable and serious undermining of world order. The second horn of the dilemma [non-intervention] entails the seemingly morally intolerable proposition that the international community, in the name of the non-intervention rule, is impotent to combat massacres, acts of genocide, mass murder and widespread torture.[3]

These issues are of urgent concern to Muslims and Christians alike. Passionate calls for intervention have come from both Muslims and

Christians, outraged by the large-scale suffering of whole populations in other countries, whether by gross deprivation in chaotic war conditions and state collapse, or as direct victims of vicious assault. Agonized debate has gone on within Muslim and Christian countries about what measures can and should be taken, when, where, how and by whom. Certainly, there can be no prospect of collective response – or even, we would argue, of genuine humanitarian response – unless this represents a cross-cultural international consensus which must include both global faith communities, represented as they are in every major region of the world.

One of the main arguments against humanitarian intervention has been the relativist claim that human rights norms are 'Western' values not shared in other cultures. We cannot enter this debate in detail here. Three points can be made, however.

First, 'Western' is not the same as 'Christian'. As Harries points out, the historic relationship between Christianity and secularist formulations of human rights concepts has not been easy, in so far as some Christians have maintained that: (a) creatures have no inherent rights in relation to the Creator; (b) a Christian ethic is one of duty, not rights; and (c) in the spirit of the Sermon on the Mount, Christians should be concerned to waive rights, not assert them.[4] The relationship between Islam and human rights has also been problematic and much discussed.[5] Although some Muslim commentators have found incompatibilities between certain post-1945 formulations of human rights and Islam, others agree with A. Brohi that 'the Universal Declaration of Human Rights of 1948 can be seen as a basic corollary or extension of the programme laid down in the Qur'an'.

Second, although particular items included in detailed 'lists' of human rights have caused problems for Muslims (perhaps explaining the abstention of Saudi Arabia in the original 1948 vote on the Universal Declaration of Human Rights), this is hardly the case with the gross violations of basic human rights at issue when humanitarian intervention is contemplated.[6] Predominantly Muslim countries have endorsed all the post-1945 international human rights treaties, including the 1948 Genocide Convention. Some governments in these states have been slow to ratify in some cases – but so have the governments of predominantly Christian countries. The United States only ratified the Genocide Convention in 1989, lodged careful reservations – and even then refused to call the 1994 massacres in Rwanda genocide for fear of incurring unwanted obligations.[7] Although the 1993 World Conference on Human Rights, attended by 171 countries, found unanimity difficult to achieve on a number of issues, each of the prior regional meetings as well as the final Declaration and Programme of Action of 25 June affirmed the universality of the concept of human rights.[8]

Third, as noted above, in the post-cold war world it is in any case not only human rights that are at issue, but the entire range of humanitarian concern. This is traditionally seen to include the international humanitarian law (of armed conflict) and the cluster of activities known as 'international humanitarian assistance' (refugee, hunger and relief work). We have already seen that the former is underpinned both by Muslim and by Christian tradition. The latter is also central to the universalist ethic professed within both Islam and Christendom. All three fields of humanitarian concern are integral to the question of humanitarian intervention after the cold war. From this perspective, Isaac is surely right to say that 'all peoples respect and appreciate humanitarian activities that form part of a common human vocabulary'.[9] This is expressed in the 1965 'fundamental principles' of the Red Cross, subscribed to by all members of League of Red Cross and Red Crescent Societies, and generally accepted within the wider humanitarian community: principles of humanity, impartiality, neutrality and universality.[10]

But do these rights and duties of governments to act across borders in defence of humanitarian values without the consent of host governments extend to the use of military force? We consider, first Christian, then Muslim responses.

CHRISTIANITY AND FORCIBLE HUMANITARIAN INTERVENTION

With the slow emergence of the concept of the secular sovereign state, heralded by Jean Bodin and Alberico Gentili in the sixteenth century and adumbrated in the *cuius regio eius religio* clauses of the Peace of Westphalia, the earlier unity of Latin Christendom was progressively replaced by the 'international anarchy' in which states no longer recognized superior universal jurisdiction.[11] In that case, did states have the right to wage war, not only in defence of their own interests, but also in order to protect the citizens of other states from abuse by their own governments? Early commentators such as Gentili thought that they did. Grotius endorsed Gentili's position (as in much else, Grotius did not acknowledge his debt):

The fact must also be recognised that kings, and those who possess rights equal to those of kings, have the right of demanding punishments not only on account of injuries committed against themselves or their subjects, but also on account of injuries which do not directly affect them but excessively violate the law of nature or of nations in regard to any persons whatsoever.... Truly it is more honourable to avenge the wrongs of others rather than one's own...[12]

Here was an adaptation of earlier traditions in which 'defence of the innocent' was allowed as a 'just cause' for war. Gentili and Grotius did not have a modern conception of intervention because they still envisaged a 'solidarist' international community of humankind in which natural law applied to individuals as well as states.[13] It was in the eighteenth century, in the writings of Christian Wolff and Emerich de Vattel, that the principle of non-intervention received its first explicit manifestation, although not its technical definition.[14] From then on, what came to be called 'international law' was seen by most jurists to apply solely to states, not individuals, and, as Vattel put it: 'the natural society of states cannot continue unless the rights which belong to each by nature are respected'.[15] At this point the new statist non-intervention prohibition, championed as the foundation of *international order* by some, came into direct conflict with the older solidarist tradition which recognized governments' duties and rights to defend humanitarian values wherever they were threatened in the name of *international justice*. This discrepancy was never satisfactorily overcome, reappearing in nineteenth- and early twentieth-century discussion about the rights and duties of 'Christian' European powers to intervene to protect threatened populations elsewhere, particularly in the Ottoman Empire,[16] and in the UN Charter in 1945 in the form of an underlying tension between what Lori Fisler Damrosch has called the two 'clusters of values' that lie at its core: 'state system values', protected by the non-intervention norm enshrined in articles 2 (4) and 2 (7), and 'human rights values' enshrined in articles 1 (3), 55 and 56.[17]

All of these inner contradictions and disputes can be found reflected in contemporary Christian thinking, with Christian realists in the tradition of Reinhold Niebuhr and Christian pacifists as unlikely bedfellows in opposing the concept of forcible humanitarian intervention, albeit on very different grounds, and many Christians in what might be called the broad 'just war' tradition prepared to countenance it under certain circumstances. It is difficult to find a consensus, or even a central tradition here. In the transformed post-cold war situation, however, where egregious human suffering is associated with protracted internal conflict and incipient state collapse, where the question of 'consent' is ambiguous, and where the possibility of concerted action through regional organizations and the UN is possible, interviews conducted for this chapter strongly suggest that there is a majority acceptance that Christian doctrine teaches: (a) that governments are not only responsible for their own citizens, but also have a duty of concern for people in other countries, (b) that the non-intervention rule in international law should not be a shield behind which atrocities can be perpetrated with impunity, (c) that, where basic subsistence and security needs or rights are threatened, international action to sustain and protect below the level of the use of military force should be pursued vigorously and with as much material provison as is required, and (d) that, *in extremis*, and given certain necessary circumstantial conditions, military force can and should be used by governments to protect the innocent in other countries.

The theoretical basis for this doctrine is quite widely seen to be provided by natural law, as a manifestation of the divine law, which clearly imposes a duty of concern across borders and cultures. Whether or not in particular cases such use of force is justified is seen to depend upon circumstances, and here various criteria might be invoked as in just war theory. For example, the greater possibility of collective measures by the United Nations since the end of the Cold War would count as new circumstances which might widen the scope for legitimate action. Some, however, doubted whether circumstances were ever likely to be right, given the international system as it is today (along the lines of those who accept just war theory in principle, but do not think that any war has yet satisfied the criteria). Others, while endorsing vigorous cross-border humanitarian concern, rule out the use of force for Christians on pacifist grounds. Here, even an apparently benign use of military force was seen to presuppose the whole machinery of militarism, itself an evil which Christians should not condone. Resort to force was seen to represent a tragic failure by the international community to act better.[18]

There is, therefore, no general approach common to these various Christian perspectives, but within them we may note the persistence of what Alan Donagan calls the 'common morality' of the original natural law tradition, which, implying 'positive concern for the welfare of people outside one's own community', is seen by many

Christians to provide the normative ground for a justified humanitarian use of force across international borders.[19] This is also reflected in the papal insistence that:

> The conscience of humankind, sustained henceforth by its liability to international human rights, asks that humanitarian interference be rendered mandatory in situations which gravely compromise the survival of entire peoples and ethnic groups: this is an obligation for both individual nations and the international community as a whole.[20]

ISLAM AND FORCIBLE HUMANITARIAN INTERVENTION

What of Muslim responses? We will briefly consider the political, legal and ethical dimensions of this question.

At the political level, since the 1950s there has been as much inconsistency within the Islamic as within the Christian world on the issue of humanitarian intervention. On the one hand, many governments of predominantly Muslim countries have been consistently opposed to anything that might revive colonial domination by the powerful, and thus antipathetic to the very idea of humanitarian intervention. For example, the principle of non-intervention has been regularly cited as foundational for regional organizations with a strong Muslim membership, such as the OAU and ASEAN. In the case of ASEAN, since its formation in 1967 members have explicitly adhered to the 'Asian way' in which governments support each other – for example against communist insurgents – but on no account do they meddle in each other's domestic affairs, observing the 'rule of silence' when disagreement threatens.[21] Western attempts to link aid to human rights or to orchestrate protest against Indonesia for the Dili massacre in East Timor are branded 'cultural imperialism' and seen as part of a global campaign 'to make us permanent developing countries' (Prime Minister of Malaysia).[22] On the other hand, in different circumstances, the governments of predominantly Muslim countries have been prominent in not only allowing, but demanding intervention to uphold international human rights. For example, with reference to South Africa, it was the Tunisian representative at the United Nations who in 1961 declared that protection of human rights and fundamental freedoms was the essential purpose of the United Nations, and that the organization would dig its own grave if it tolerated abuses and failed to intervene. It was the South African representative who appealed to 'the principle and attributes of sovereignty' as foundational and declared that South Africa would never have joined the UN had Charter Article 2 (7) not been included.[23] The interventionist case has been argued with equal vehemence in response to the political victimization associated with recent 'complex emergencies'.

Turning to the legal dimension, we have seen in Chapter 3 how the concept of the *umma wahida* or single community of Muslims (potentially a community of all humankind) long predates the modern secular state, and is widely seen to overrule it. All other divisions, including ethnic, racial or national differences, are secondary: Allah made humankind into 'nations and tribes' for self-understanding and interaction 'so that you may get to know one another' (49: 13), but for no deeper purpose. Exclusive nationality and state sovereignty are not foundational concepts in Islamic law.

Most of the fifty-odd states which are members of the Organization of the Islamic Conference (OIC) are recent creations, often within what are seen as artificial ex-colonial borders. As members of the United Nations, their governments have signed up to the international instruments which define statehood in contemporary international law. But, it seems fair to say, there is still a great deal of work to do to relate traditional Islamic law to this relatively recent set of circumstances in a way which satisfies Islamic legal principles. The OIC itself, for example, which voted in 1980 to set up an 'International Islamic Law Commission' to 'devise ways and means to secure representation in order to put forward the Islamic point of view before the International Court of Justice and other such institutions of the United Nations when a question requiring the projection of Islamic views arises therein', has in the event as yet failed to do so.[24] The import of all this for our question is that Muslim jurisprudence overwhelmingly tends to recognize the Qur'anic *umma*, not the state, as the foundational element in international law, so that the question of overriding a statist non-intervention norm in the case of protecting the vulnerable technically does not arise. The onus is all the other way: 'the burden of proof lies with those who would challenge the right of intervention on grounds of sovereignty rather than on those who assert it'.[25]

How can the political espousal of statist non-intervention principles by a number of governments of Muslim countries and the absence of clear teaching on the status of the modern state in Islamic law be reconciled? We turn, finally, to the ethical dimension, taking as our main guide Sohail Hashmi's fine paper on the Islamic ethic of humanitarian intervention – recognizing that the political, the legal and the ethical are inexorably intertwined in Islamic doctrine. A moral obligation is laid upon Muslims 'to order that which is right and to forbid that which is wrong' (3: 104), which includes the defence of the vulnerable against injustice and oppression. This is the authentic voice of humanitarianism, in which principles of humanity, impartiality and universality are now firmly grounded in the duty of obedience all Muslims owe to divine command.

What, then, when these injunctions are violated, and vulnerable populations are threatened by or actually suffer injustice and oppression on a massive scale, either in Muslim or in non-Muslim countries? Hashmi identifies three strands of modern Islamic thought on the relationship between Islamic tradition and the nation-state. The first is a diffuse secular school in which the traditional concept of the Muslim community (*umma*) is 'stripped of substantive political content', and in some cases rejected in favour of rapid modernization and state-building. Despite its historical significance in relation to modernizers like Kemal Ataturk in Turkey and Reza Shah in Iran, this group is seen to be marginal today. The second group tries to reconcile Islamic tradition and the modern state system – for example by arguing along the lines of Muhammad Iqbal (influential ideologue of the new Pakistani state) that nation-states represent a temporary phase of human development, useful in this era, but to be condemned strongly when 'regarded as the ultimate expression of the life of mankind'. As Hashmi puts it, 'even modernist Muslim intellectuals cannot escape the conclusion that even the nation-state with liberal institutions cannot be embraced as the *summum bonum* of Islamic political life'.[26] Finally, as we saw in Chapter 3, there are those such as Hasan al-Banna and Sayyid Qutb of the Muslim Brotherhood in Egypt, Abu'l-A'la Mawdudi in the Indian subcontinent, and Ayatollah Ruhollah Khomeini in Iran, who reject the nation-state as an unIslamic relic of European colonialism. From this latter perspective the significant distinction is not between states, but between the *Dar al-Harb* (home of war) and the *Dar al-Islam* (home of Islam).

These debates are as yet unresolved. But, within what is broadly the second approach, which we tentatively take as indicative of mainstream academic Muslim opinion, there is still a clear bias in favour of humanitarian intervention. As Zaki Badawi puts it:

The notion of the state is not very clear in the Muslim perspective; but we have now recognized and accepted it, so a Muslim country may not intervene in the internal affairs of another state, provided – and this is a very important proviso – that the internal war is not a war against a Muslim community or a weak community. If it is a power struggle between two generals, say, you would not intervene. But if a minority is singled out for oppression, then it is incumbent on Muslims, or for that matter the international community, to intervene.[27]

To this extent, Islamic teaching coincides with the Christian natural law tradition in recognizing a theoretical basis for humanitarian intervention, and forcible humanitarian intervention takes its place within the broad tradition of *jihad*. The command to act justly and enforce justice clearly includes a duty to wage war for the protection of the weak, the vulnerable and the helpless, as laid down in the Qur'an:

> How should ye not fight for the cause of Allah and of the feeble among men and of the women and children who are crying: Our Lord! Bring us forth from out this town of which the people are oppressors! Oh, give us from Thy presence some protecting friend. Oh, give us from Thy presence some defender! (4: 75)

Further questions include the following. Should Muslims intervene on behalf of Muslims oppressed by non-Muslims as in Palestine, or in Afghanistan during Soviet occupation, or in Bosnia? Here the Qur'an enjoins that oppressed Muslims (*mustad'afun*) should either remove themselves physically from the land of their oppressors (4: 97), or there should be a collective response from the Muslim community in defence of the oppressed (4: 75).[28] Should Muslims intervene when Muslims are oppressing other Muslims as in Southern Iraq? In Sunni Islam this was treated as a special case of civil discord (*fitna*) between Muslims, in Shi'a tradition as part of *jihad*. Here the Qur'an teaches:

> If two parties of the believers fall into a quarrel, make peace between them; but if one of them transgresses beyond bounds against the other, then fight all of you together against the one that transgresses until it complies with the command of God. But if it complies, then make peace between them with justice, and be fair: For God loves those who are fair. (49: 9)[29]

Finally, should Muslims intervene when Muslims are oppressing non-Muslims as in Nigeria or Sudan? In particular, 'Can Muslim states ally themselves with non-Muslim powers to fight another Muslim state that may be committing massive human rights violations against its own people?' On this contentious issue, Hashmi concludes: 'The answer on a superficial level is self-evident: of course Muslim states should be foremost in undertaking humanitarian intervention and conflict resolution within the Muslim world. This is unambiguously demanded by Qur'anic ethical principles[30]. Badawi agrees: the international community, supported by Muslim governments, should 'without question' intervene, even if the oppressing government is Muslim. 'The Prophet said "your brother right or wrong", a dictum from ancient Arabia, is a good dictum, but it should be interpreted so that if your brother is in the right you support him, but if he is in the wrong you prevent him from doing the wrong, because to prevent what is morally wrong is to support the right.'[31] This receives ringing endorsement in the Qur'an: 'Oh, you who believe! Stand out firmly as witnesses to Allah, even as against yourselves, or your parents, or your kin, and whether it be against rich or poor' (4: 135). As to alliance with non-Muslims, this is forbidden if the non-Muslims are hostile to Islam, but, according to Hashmi, not if they are sympathetic. For the Iranian scholar Ayatollah Murtaza Mutahhari 'no one should have any doubts that the most sacred form of *jihad* and war is that which is fought in defence of humanity and of human rights', and, if non-Muslims join this *jihad*, their action is also sacred.[32]

In short, summing up Christian and Muslim responses to the question of forcible humanitarian intervention, it appears that, despite considerable internal controversy, there is substantial support in principle in extreme conditions, subject to two as yet unresolved clusters of problems: (a) the lack of clear agreement about how to decide which humanitarian crises merit such action, and (b) the absence of legitimate and effective institutional machinery for implementation. We will return to these two issues at the end of the chapter.

HUMANITARIAN INTERVENTION IN BOSNIA

The war in former Yugoslavia erupted with devastating force in Bosnia in April 1992. Although in theory the international community had three broad military options, in effect it was already committed to one of them.

The first option was *enforcement* – whether at the outset in response to President Izetbegovic's initial appeal for military help to restore order, or later to impose the Vance–Owen agreement, coupled in the eyes of many commentators by a lifting of the arms embargo to allow the new Bosnian government to arm itself. From the perspective of the Bosnian government, in terms of international law the whole situation had changed at the beginning of 1992 with the recognition of Bosnia-Herzegovina. From now on the war was interpreted as one of aggression waged primarily by Serbia-Montenegro against the integrity of the pluralistic Bosnian state. Arguments in favour included: (a) the moral humanitarian case, (b) the fact that the international community had recognized Bosnia and should therefore defend it, (c) the dangerous precedent of allowing ethnic cleansing to succeed, (d) the danger of rising Muslim resentment worldwide, and (e) the danger that the war might spread.

The second option was *abstention* or *withdrawal*. For the Serbs, for example, the situation was structurally different to that envisaged by the Bosnian government. As in Croatia, they now, as Bosnian Serbs, found themselves against their will transformed into a threatened minority. They had not voted in the Bosnian referendum. The internal borders of Yugoslavia were not sacrosanct, having been deliberately drawn to include Serbs in other republics. Izetbegovic was seen as a dangerous Islamic fundamentalist intent on establishing an Islamic state. The breakup of Yugoslavia was seen as a German-inspired plot. From this perspective, the other two options were interpreted as politically biased against Serbs. Arguments against forcible intervention included: (a) that there was no agreed or sustainable political settlement to enforce, (b) that the military force required and likely losses would be prohibitive (some, invoking Nazi difficulty in subduing the region, spoke of the need for 500 000 troops), (c) that outsiders would be sucked into a Balkan morass, (d) that there was insufficient international solidarity and domestic support, and (e) that it would jeopardize existing deployments and risk escalation.

In contrast to the first two options was the third, *non-forcible peacekeeping*, the option that the international community drifted into during the first six months of the war by simply extending UNPROFOR's existing mandate (originally for Croatia). Behind the policy stance lay a third interpretation of the conflict, incompatible with those of the Bosnian government and the Bosnian Serbs, and highly offensive to the other two: namely that this was a civil war within Bosnia in which various 'factions' labelled 'Serb', 'Croat' and 'Muslim' were scrapping with each other, and that the best that could be done was to offer some protection to civilian populations, and perhaps some encouragement towards a political settlement.

The depth of the political impasse can be gauged when it is seen that there was no neutral description of the situation free from prior assumptions already integrally contested within it. For Croats, UNPROFOR was protecting Serb gains in Croatia; for Serbs, UNPROFOR was serving hostile outside interests; for Muslims, UNPROFOR was condoning 'ethnic cleansing' and conspiring to prevent the legitimatè Bosnian government from defending itself.

There can be little doubt as to the remarkable international effort by UN humanitarian agencies led by UNHCR, hundreds of NGOs and UNPROFOR troops in sustaining more than 4 million people throughout the former Yugoslavia (as calculated, for example, during the period of the eighth UN Consolidated Appeal, 1 July to 31 December 1994). The conclusion of an official UN report in May 1994 was that in former Yugoslavia 'the United Nations humanitarian assistance operations have succeeded in alleviating suffering and in saving hundreds of thousands of lives'.[33] Does this, therefore, represent the best that the international community could have done in the circumstances, a remarkable demonstration of concerted action which would have been impossible during the cold war, as the main troop-providing governments, as well as many UN officials, argued?

Muslim responses

The answer to this question from the Muslim world seems to have been almost unanimously 'no':

> On the basis of these two factors alone – Serbian aggression and Bosnia's militarily weak position – the people of Bosnia-Herzegovina would have deserved help from a strictly Islamic perspective. But what strengthened Bosnia's case was the actual oppression and suppression of the people. 200,000 Bosnians were killed in the 43 month long war; 50,000 women and girls were raped; 2 million were rendered refugees. The degree and extent of oppression suffered by the oppressed would have justified intervention in the eyes of Islam. Besides, most of the oppressed were Muslims – an added reason, as it were, for intervention.[34]

Vigorous early response, it is argued, would very likely have prevented this.[35] As it was, the gap between forcible rhetoric and non-forcible deployment of UNPROFOR, accentuated by unplanned accretion of mandates and 'mission creep', created an equally wide gap between public expectations and operational realities. Safe areas were besieged, bombarded, and eventually, as in the case of Srebrenica and Zepa in July 1995, overrun, their inhabitants seized under the noses of helpless UNPROFOR troops, thousands never to be seen again.[36] What was regarded as culpable inaction by those governments with the military capacity to protect the suffering populations was roundly condemned, and interpreted as deliberate hostility to the idea of a Muslim state in Europe:

> The EC's and US-controlled UN's refusal to use military force to stop the holocaust in Bosnia is absolutely disgusting and hypocritical. Their enmity against Islam and the Muslims has now been fully exposed.[37]

Treating the crisis as 'humanitarian', rather than as an assault on the independence and integrity of a predominantly Muslim but pluralistic state, was regarded as deliberate avoidance of international responsibilities. UNPROFOR was seen to be intent upon protecting its own troops, not the civilian population, and to be using the fact of its vulnerability as a deliberate excuse for not using force. This constituted *de facto* support for Serb (and, between May 1993 and March 1994, Croat) aggression and atrocities, and was seen to contrast distastefully with earlier Western alacrity in using force against Iraq in defence of oil interests: 'Western policies do amount to intervention – on the side of the aggressor.'[38]

Nor were the governments of Muslim states exonerated. The record of the OIC states in responding to international humanitarian crises is described as 'dismal' by Hashmi. Failing to respond to Pakistani atrocities in what is now Bangladesh in 1971–2, to condemn Iraq for the 1981 attack on Iran, or to take a lead in the 1990–1 Gulf crisis, the OIC is seen to have been similarly supine during the Bosnian debacle. Hints of collective Muslim intervention, either unilaterally or through the UN, since the time of the 17–18 June 1992 meeting of foreign ministers in Istanbul, were in the event seen to amount to little more than rhetoric (including the unanimous demand that the international community should 'take armed action by land, sea and air' to end the atrocities in Bosnia). Other than limited arms shipments by individual OIC states, some humanitarian aid, support for UNPROFOR, and perhaps covert encouragement of a small number of ex-mujahedin irregular volunteers,[39] OIC member states undertook no concerted intervention during the critical years of the conflict.[40] Hashmi concludes:

The crisis in Bosnia, as well as the many other humanitarian crises in other parts of the Muslim world, have created a popular climate that not only permits but demands consideration of principles of intervention. Indeed, in all crises to date, the OIC member-states have been moved to whatever belated action they have taken by strong internal pressures.[41]

Zaki Badawi, arguing for an immediate military response at the outset against the aggressor in June 1991 at the time of the Slovene and beginning of the Croat war, claims that the case for forcible intervention in this instance 'would be accepted by almost all Muslims'. Non-forcible attempts to reconcile peoples might work in some cases, but people like Milosevic, Karadzic and Mladic wanted power at any cost and could only be restrained by force.[42] In his view, this would not have entailed the deployment of ground forces, but air strikes and the threat of escalation, together with the provision of the legitimate means of defence for the Bosnians.

On 23 April 1994 a large number of prominent British Muslims signed a letter to UN Secretary-General Boutros Ghali demanding action or his resignation:

The international community must be ashamed of its double-standards: bombing Iraq to enforce safe havens while allowing Gorazde, another safe haven, to be butchered. When Muslims took exception to the insults and profanities in *The Satanic Verses*, the so-called liberal world was hysterical with anger. Muslims had become the new barbarians. Civilization, progress, culture were all threatened by them. Now where are the voices of the so-called civilization, progress and culture?

Similar sentiments were voiced by Muslim leaders from Turkey[43] to Malaysia.[44] Speaking on behalf of the Arab group at the United Nations on 30 June 1993, Jordan's permanent delegate, Abu Odeh, accused the Security Council of denying the people of Bosnia-Herzegovina their right to self-defence:

Numerous as they are, the public arguments boil down to the fact that influential and powerful countries, as is well known to everybody, have seen fit to deal with the tragedy in Bosnia-Herzegovina within a framework of their financial calculations and perceived interests, completely ignoring ethical, moral and legal responsibilities.[45]

The demand was for the lifting of the 1991 arms embargo, because 'it was understood right from the beginning that the adoption of the arms embargo Resolution 713 by the Security Council implied that the United Nations itself would undertake on behalf of the victim the task of repelling the aggressor'. At the time of the fall of Srebrenica in July 1995, demands for action reached a crescendo: King Hussain told President Chirac of France that Jordan would pull its troops out of UNPROFOR 'if no military action was taken to stop Serb attacks against Muslim enclaves in Bosnia'.[46] After the Dayton agreement, foreign and defence ministers of Islamic contact group countries and countries with troops in Bosnia, meeting in Kuala Lumpur in March 1996, repeated earlier calls for 'assistance to maintain and create a military balance' in Bosnia.

Let us leave the last word with the Reis-ul-Ulema (leader of the Muslim Religious Council) in Bosnia-Herzegovina, Mustafa Ceric, sending out a tragic appeal 'to whom it may concern' from Sarajevo in July 1993:

A fascist invasion has taken over 200,000 lives, raped tens of thousands of Muslim women, destroyed over eight hundred Muslim holy places, and driven more than a million Muslims from their homes.... Therefore we address ourselves to all Muslim imams throughout the world in the name of Islamic compassion; to all Christian dignatories – of the Catholic, Orthodox and Protestant churches – in the name of Christian love; to all Jewish rabbis in the name of Talmudic justice; to all Buddhist priests in the name of the Buddha's enlightenment; and all those who nurture in their hearts a spark of humanity: we call upon them, through the force of their faith and love, to open up a path to Sarajevo, and thus save hope and belief in the dignity of man and universal divine and human values.... But we Bosnian Muslims, in this Sarajevo, and throughout Bosnia, with you or without you, shall continue amid all our sufferings and torments to defend the authentic Bosnian spirit of living together. Alive or dead we remain loyal to God's words and loyal to our Bosnia. It is up to you to decide whether you will help us live or watch us die.

Christian responses

Turning to Christian responses to the Bosnian conflict, the range of opinion among church leaders was very wide. For example, it included the views of HH Patriarch Pavle of Serbia and the Synod of Bishops of the Serbian Orthodox Church. Serb church leaders were under severe domestic political pressure, and at times condemned 'violence and crimes from whatever side they come'.[47] But, whereas a torrent of passionate protest accompanied the Croat retaking of Western Slavonia and the Krajina in May and June 1995,[48] little seems to have been said about Serb-perpetrated atrocities after the fall of Srebrenica in July. Serbs were seen as the victims of European history.[49] The Russian Orthodox Church's official pronouncements on the war seem to have been all about peace, but at a lower level clergy and bishops expressed solidarity with their Slav brethren, the Serbian Orthodox. There was no criticism of atrocities.[50]

We now turn to consider responses from British church leaders. This is not to suggest that the views of British Christians can be taken to represent the views of Christians elsewhere, but is to offer an accessible case study. British opinion in general was divided, and 'opinion in the churches has in part reflected these divisions of opinion which cross all party-political lines, except that no church leader or representative body has advocated withdrawal of the UN or the British presence'.[51] Strenuous attempts were made to co-ordinate activities and to act ecumenically, for example through the Balkans Working Group of the Council of Churches for Britain and Ireland (CCBI). But there was no agreed 'Church of England' position, largely because 'the General Synod and the full House of Bishops have not debated the issue and tried to establish such a position'. In Williamson's judgement the ecumenical approach was broadly speaking to support the *non-forcible UN peacekeeping option*, with its stress on political/diplomatic solutions and continuing humanitarian efforts, although it was recognized that this option had manifestly failed to end the conflict or the atrocities, and there were continued misgivings about it.[52] In the face of such uncertainty, it is understandable that critics such as Adrian Hastings, then Professor of Theology at Leeds University, should condemn what they regarded as mealy-mouthed temporizing. For example, a CCBI report of January–February 1993 was seen to have ignored 'the central fact' that 'a crusade of extermination, human and cultural, was being carried on by Serbs against Muslims', while the message adopted by the World Council of Churches at its January 1994 Johannesburg meeting was similarly castigated for refusing to condemn the perpetrators, hiding instead behind vapid statements that 'violence and brutality are being committed on every side, Serb, Croat and Muslim'. Hastings concluded:

The overall impression of these and other documents is of an amazing inability to face up to the reality of evil and to grapple responsibly and clear-mindedly with a moral crisis comparable to the Holocaust. On the one hand the ecumenical desire not to upset the Serb Orthodox Church and, on the other, willingness to swallow whole the political line of the Foreign Office and the European Community, have completely nullified any prophetic voice on the part of central church leadership.[53]

Three main points can be made in answer to such criticisms.

The first point is that the churches were not silent or inactive on the Bosnian conflict. From the beginning visits were made to Bosnia, expressions of outrage were unanimous and strong representations were made to the British Government to do everything possible to halt atrocities. A message from Cardinal Basil Hume to the British Prime Minister of 7 August 1992 can be taken as representative:

> We are faced with atrocities in Bosnia, some committed in the name of 'ethnic cleansing' which is horrifying and totally unacceptable, and they cannot be allowed to continue. It is not for me, as a Churchman, to define what would be politically and militarily acceptable, but people are looking for an early response which needs to be effective and sustainable in bringing humanitarian relief to those who are suffering, particularly the Muslim community, and also a cessation of hostilities.[54]

British Government policy was at times strongly criticized – for example, over failure to accept greater numbers of Bosnian refugees.[55] The churches were active from the beginning in humanitarian initiatives, care of refugees and efforts to promote peace and reconciliation.

The second point is to repeat that the Christian churches did not speak with one voice. Nevertheless, strenuous efforts were made to respond ecumenically, including solidarity with Jewish and Muslim representatives and communities. This was co-ordinated, for example, through the Conference of European Churches (CEC), the World Council of Churches (WCC), the Lutheran World Federation, and the Council of Catholic Bishops' Conferences in Europe (CCEE). Humanitarian aid in former Yugoslavia was co-ordinated through Action of Churches Together (ACT), working with the UN High Commissoner for Refugees (UNHCR). Within these frameworks, Christian Aid, CAFOD, the Methodist Church and Quaker Peace and Service (QPS), among others, were heavily engaged in humanitarian and reconciliation work.[56]

The third point is that many Christian leaders found it impossible to pronounce on political options, particularly those to do with a possible use of military force. In a joint letter to *The Times* on 14 July 1995, at the time of the Srebrenica atrocities, the Archbishop of Canterbury, the Archbishop of Westminster, the Moderator of the Free Church Federal Council and the Chief Rabbi condemned these outrages: 'events in recent days have highlighted once again the barbarity of those who murder, terrorise and oppress people in Bosnia'. They went on to say that 'as religious leaders we are not competent to judge between the agonisingly difficult military and political choices which are now facing the international community', but at the same time they asked 'how long will such actions be allowed to continue?'. In particular, as Clements and Williamson put it in November 1995: 'issues relating to the use of force in conflict situations indicate the clear need for deeper ethical reflection based on specific situations of violence. The question of the ethics of armed intervention poses real and unresolved dilemmas'.[57] It is difficult to find consensus on these issues within the Christian churches. Nevertheless, by the late summer of 1995, there seemed to be a large body of opinion which supported the taking up of the enforcement option, first perhaps by the reconstituted UNPROFOR, then by IFOR:

We in the Church of Scotland share the widespread anguish over events in the former Yugoslavia, and make the following statement.... So terrible is the plight of the victims of this conflict that no immediate means of ending the violence apart from the commitment of United Nations troops seems available. We share the moral dilemma of Her Majesty's Government and the United Nations, and we recognise that a decision to authorise the use of force to create safe havens and to protect aid deliveries may well bring other painful decisions in its wake.[58]

We end with a Christian response to the Muslim appeal of the Reis of Sarajevo quoted above. This comes from an 'Open Letter to All Victims of "Ethnic Cleansing" in the Former Yugoslavia', published as a full-page advertisement in the *Independent* on 5 August 1995. Called the 'Sarajevo Charter', it was widely endorsed by large numbers of signatories, including the Bishops of Oxford, Hereford and Barking. Here was an unequivocal call to undertake forcible humanitarian intervention:

We have watched you – the residents of Bihac, Gorazde, Sarajevo, Srebrenica, Tuzla, Zepa, and other 'safe areas' – as you have been hunted and pursued in your own country from one threatened enclave to another. We have seen you congregate in these 'safe areas' in which the United Nations and the authorities of the world have guaranteed your protection. And now we have seen you bombed in your houses and finally taken from your homes and places of refuge. As the world powers appear to have abandoned you, we invoke another power, the voice of ordinary people world-wide, whose outrage on your behalf places us beside you.... We call upon the leaders of all parties in the conflict to place the protection of human life before all other considerations. We call upon the governments of our countries and the United Nations to take urgent and decisive action to protect the lives, communities and territories of all those in former Yugoslavia who are threatened. We call for the enforcement of peace; the opening of corridors for food and relief; asylum for refugees whose lives are in danger; the raising of money and goods for humanitarian aid. And we call upon individuals and organisations to speak out and help in whatever way they can.

JUST HUMANITARIAN INTERVENTION

The terrible events in Bosnia which followed the outbreak of war in April 1992 shocked and outraged Muslims and Christians alike. Both were unanimous in condemning the atrocities, in expressing solidarity with the innocent victims, and in supporting relief efforts. Both agreed that governments as well as individuals have duties of concern across international borders in the face of such suffering, and a *prima facie* right to act accordingly through appropriate channels and by appropriate means. Neither recognized the statist non-intervention norm as an impervious barrier behind which governments or factions can practice ethnic cleansing or genocide with impunity. Both invoked an older solidarist tradition in which the subjects of others are not 'outside that kinship of nature and society formed by the whole world'.[59] Finally, when it came to the question of the use of force to protect threatened populations, there was widespread, albeit on the Christian side not unanimous, agreement that the mediaeval category 'defence of the innocent' remained in principle a just cause for forcible intervention. Restrictionist readings of contemporary international law which only recognize self-defence and collective action to maintain or restore international peace and security as legitimate exceptions to the ban on the threat or use of force are, therefore, rejected. This is already a considerable measure of agreement.

At this point, however, divergencies appear – not only between Muslims and Christians, but within the two faith communities as well. There seems to have been near unanimous Muslim demand for forcible international action to halt the assault on the new Bosnian state, to lift the arms embargo so that the Bosnian government could defend itself, and to protect the vulnerable. UNPROFOR through to July 1995 was dismissed as a palliative, and even the belated adoption of forcible measures thereafter was seen as inhibiting Bosnian government advances at the moment it appeared to have the upper hand. The governments of predominantly Muslim countries, however, seem to have been reluctant to do much themselves to convert these demands into political reality. No doubt this was partly because of Western political and military preponderance and the limited capacity of Muslim countries to act with any effectiveness independently. But even within these limits little effort was made. Perhaps behind this lay traditional suspicions of Western military interventions and unease about implications elsewhere (for example Sudan) where it was Muslims who were the oppressors.

The Christian response to the Bosnian tragedy was even less coherent than the Muslim response, not only because of the dissenting interpretation of events on the part of leaders of the Serb Orthodox Church (and, to some extent, of other Orthodox churches), but also because of differences of opinion about the efficacy and ethical implications of different political and military options. Christian churches in the West shared much of the uncertainty current within Western society in general. The greater capacity of Western governments to act forcibly made the choices real, but for that reason the dilemmas all the more difficult to resolve. Not to intervene forcibly might constitute being an 'accomplice to massacre', but forcible intervention was seen to involve risks of the kind noted above. This was reflected in many of the pronouncements of British church leaders, in particular the common refrain that the humanitarian abuse was unacceptable and must be stopped, but that how this was done involved difficult political and military judgements that ecclesiastics were ill-equipped to make.

It is here that the question of forcible humanitarian intervention links up with the wider commonalities and differences discussed in Chapter 4. Behind wide-ranging disagreement about specific humanitarian intervention policy options lies the quite extensive common ground between the just war and *jihad* traditions noted earlier. We have seen how both traditions broadly recognize extreme humanitarian need as a just cause for forcible remedial intervention when host governments are either incapable of alleviating the suffering or are themselves responsible for it. Where much of the disagreement arises is over the other criteria which need to be satisfied if forcible humanitarian cross-border action is to be finally justified. Just cause on its own is not enough.

A number of authors have tried to clarify the situation by applying traditional just war criteria to the question of forcible humanitarian intervention.[60] Fisher, for example, in addition to just cause, discusses criteria of competent authority, last resort, and, above all, the proportionality of anticipated good and harm, including probability of success. On the general issue of forcible humanitarian intervention, he concludes (with suitable caveats) that when 'people are threatened with large-scale torture, massacre or even genocide... the prevention of such suffering would constitute a just cause for humanitarian intervention'.[61] On the particular issue of Bosnia he thinks that the 'allies' actions in former Yugoslavia appear... on the whole justifiable against the just war criteria', although 'doubt must... inevitably persist as to whether by taking more decisive action earlier on, the West could perhaps have prevented more of the suffering that ensued'.[62] Somewhat similar stipulations are found in the so-called 'Mohonk criteria' for humanitarian assistance, including provision for forcible action, subscribed to by both Muslims and Christians: 'Where the government or other authority is unable or manifestly unwilling to provide life-sustaining aid, the international community has the right and obligation to protect and provide relief to affected and threatened civilian populations in conformity with the principles of international law'. But *prima facie* just cause is tempered by five other criteria. Military forces should (a) be used as a last resort, (b) be employed only in exceptional circumstances to protect and relieve, (c) be used sparingly because of their disproportionate human and financial cost, (d) comply with decisions of the appropriate civilian authority, and (e) respect the independence of humanitarian organizations.[63]

In fact, it seems that traditional just war criteria must be adapted in a number of ways in the case of forcible humanitarian intervention, amounting overall to a radical revision of contemporary statist norms in favour of older solidarist values. First, *just cause* is extended beyond restrictionist interpretations of what Michael Walzer calls the current 'legalistic paradigm' to revive early Muslim and Christian categories of defence of the innocent. Second, so far as concerns *legitimate authority*, there is quite wide agreement that UN authorization is preferred for genuine collective humanitarian action, and that transparency and accountability are important, although there remain as yet unresolved problems to do with legitimate agency. We will return to this below. Third, there are difficulties with the criterion of *last resort* if it is interpreted as meaning that other remedies, such as economic sanctions, are preferable and must be extensively tried first. Economic sanctions have questionable efficacy and are likely to deepen the sufferings of those they are intended to help. Early forcible action might in some cases be the best course of action, as, in the view of many, was the case in Bosnia. Fourth, on *reasonable prospect of success*, in addition to the normal requirement that military objectives must be readily attainable (which may have been the case with the delivery of humanitarian aid in Bosnia, but, given force dispositions, was not the case with the protection of safe areas), there is the further criterion of sustainability. This is widely seen to be essential in cases of humanitarian intervention in volatile conflict zones, with criticism of the idea that there is likely to be a 'quick military fix'. It is the long-term interests of the civilian population that should be paramount and intervening forces need to be sensitive to them. Fifth, the criterion of *proportionality* demands that anticipated harm must not be disproportionate to likely good, which is particularly difficult to calculate in cases of humanitarian intervention, where humanitarian factors have to be weighed against non-humanitarian factors. This links to a sixth traditional just war criterion: that the military action must be undertaken *with a view to a just peace*. Here there has been much criticism of cases in which political crises are treated as purely 'humanitarian', so that troops find themselves embroiled in intense conflict situations without a realistic political goal. Indeed, there may well be tension between humanitarian and political requirements. Seventh, there have been difficulties with the *in bello* requirement of *discrimination* in cases where UN troops have been accused of infringements of international humanitarian law, because the UN is not itself a party to any of the relevant treaties. It seems particularly important that there be clear safeguards against this in cases where the military action is itself claimed to be humanitarian.

In addition to adaptations of existing just war criteria, however, forcible humanitarian intervention also seems to require additional ones. For example, there is, eighth, the central humanitarian principle of *impartiality* in responding to humanitarian need (although not necessarily the principle of strict political neutrality in cases where one side may be seen to be mainly responsible for atrocities). Ninth, there is the principle of *complementarity* between military and non-military components. In humanitarian interventions military forces must co-operate with non-military humanitarian agencies, and should, where appropriate, be seen to serve them. Tenth, there is the vital principle of *consistency*. Partiality and double standards in choosing where to intervene and where not to intervene are common accusations of existing practice. Cases of egregious humanitarian abuse where not only has there been no forcible intervention, but not even determined non-forcible measures, have abounded, including Chinese oppression in Tibet and Indonesian excesses in East Timor. The impression widely given has been that great powers intervene and fail to intervene as suits national interest or the political requirements of incumbent governments. The whole enterprise of humanitarian intervention is discredited as a result. It is not clear how generally acceptable processes of selection can be instituted. As noted earlier, together with the unresolved issue of legitimate agency, these remain the main weaknesses in current attempts to find a coherent international response to large-scale humanitarian challenges. In face of these, many who acknowledge a right and duty of forcible humanitarian intervention in principle, in practice rule it out under present conditions.

In the words of one Muslim contributor, for example:

> For justified humanitarian intervention to be viable, there will have to be fundamental changes in international politics and in international authority structures. (1) International politics should cease to be the domain of the powerful. As long as global political decisions are shaped primarily by the interests of a handful of powerful élites in powerful states, intervention will almost certainly reflect their dominant foreign policy preoccupations...and have little to do with justice for the powerless. (2) For intervention to be viable, the institution that is given the task of intervening must also reflect the interests and aspirations of the human family as a whole...A genuinely democratic UN will bestow the right to determine whether a situation warrants intervention or not upon the UN General Assembly, rather than the Security Council. (3) In intervening, the General Assembly should go beyond merely 'keeping the peace'. To make intervention viable there must be a clear

commitment to 'enforcing the peace'. The UN force that we envis-
age would have the authority to take firm military action against
the oppressor. Without these changes in international politics and
within the international system as a whole, it will not be possible to
apply Islamic principles of humanitarian intervention.[64]

These are radical requirements. In its deepest implications the issue of
humanitarian intervention reaches down to questions about the very
nature of the international collectivity. It pulls in two directions. In
one direction lie the requirements of the 'humanitarian' component.
These are exemplified in the principles and practices of bona fide
humanitarian agencies and are embodied in the principles of humanity, impartiality (with qualification), neutrality and universality. This
represents the solidarist vision of a genuine international community
of humankind. In the other direction lie the realities implied by the
forcible 'intervention' component. These capabilities can be provided
only by powerful states. And here the strong tradition has developed
that soldiers risk their lives for their countries, not for the good of
humanity. When 18 US Rangers were killed in Somalia on 3 October
1993, for example, Senator John McCain received a letter from a
distraught father: 'in his grief he asked for answers as to why his
son had to die. American soldiers have always been prepared to give
their lives for the safety and security of this nation; without a higher
purpose for such sacrifice, their deaths would be pointless and hollow'.[65] The question of humanitarian intervention adds a further layer
to Niebuhr's 'ethical paradox of patriotism' in which 'individual
unselfishness' is transmuted into 'national egoism'.[66] In humanitarian
intervention, national egoism is in turn transmuted into solidarist
unselfishness, and individual soldiers are asked to risk their lives,
not for their countries, but for humanitarian goals. They are to
become 'knights of humanity'.

We have arrived at the most sensitive point in the tension between
statist and solidarist sentiments which lies at the heart of the debate
about humanitarian intervention. Both Muslim and Christian traditions teach that forcible humanitarian intervention should be undertaken in response to extreme threats of large-scale human suffering
which can be alleviated in no other way. The *jihad*/just war requirements for effective and legitimate humanitarian intervention are, however, stringent. If internationally acceptable processes and
mechanisms are to be found, therefore, then Muslims and Christians,
making up perhaps two-fifths of humanity, clearly have a critical role

to play within the international collectivity as a whole in finding them. This might be seen to constitute a final overarching *jihad*/just war criterion for legitimate forcible humanitarian intervention, the principle of *universality*: that the criteria which govern just humanitarian intervention should be endorsed by the international community.[67] As Hashmi puts it, it is important that 'during this period of development, principles of humanitarian intervention be based on as truly a universal and cross-cultural consensus on fundamental human rights, and the legitimate means to enforce them, as possible'.[68]

NOTES

1.   We leave open the difficult question whether religious groups are being persecuted as such or for other reasons.
2.   Article 2 (7) reads: 'Nothing contained in the present Charter shall authorize the United Nations to intervene in matters which are essentially within the domestic jurisdiction of any State or shall require the members to submit such matters to settlement under the present Charter; but this principle shall not prejudice the application of enforcement measures under Chapter VII.'
3.   Fernando Tesón, *Humanitarian Intervention: An Enquiry into Law and Morality* (Dobbs Ferry, NY: Transnational Publishers, 1988), p. 4.
4.   Richard Harries, 'Human rights in theological perspective', in R. Blackburn and J. Taylor (eds), *Human Rights for the 1990s: Legal, Political and Ethical Issues* (London: Mansell, 1991), pp. 1–13 at pp. 6–7.
5.   See, for example, the extensive bibliography on Islam and human rights at the end of Alison Renteln, *International Human Rights: Universalism versus Relativism* (Newbury Park: Sage, 1990).
6.   The same is true in the West. For example, Michael Walzer abandoned his communitarian objections to the possible justification of intervention when 'the violation of human rights ... is so terrible that it makes talk of community and self-determination ... seem cynical and irrelevant'; Michael Walzer, *Just and Unjust Wars* (London: Basic Books, 2nd ed., 1977/1992), p. 90.
7.   The United States called them 'acts of genocide', in order to avoid the obligation to act against 'genocide, as such under the *Convention on the Prevention and Punishment of the Crime of Genocide* (1948).
8.   For example, the Bangkok Declaration of the Regional Meeting for Asia stressed 'the universality, objectivity and non-selectivity of all human rights and the need to avoid the application of double standards in the implementation of human rights and its politicization, and that no violation of human rights can be justified' (Article 7). In the tradition of the 1981 African Charter on Human and Peoples' Rights

(Banjul Charter), the 1993 Tunis Declaration of the Regional Meeting for Africa similarly affirmed the universality of the concept of human rights (Article 8).

9. Ephraim Isaac, 'Humanitarianism across regions and cultures', in T. Weiss and L. Minear (eds), *Humanitarianism Across Borders: Sustaining Civilians in Times of War* (London: Lynne Rienner, 1993), pp. 13–22 at p. 13.

10. There are three other principles (independence, voluntary service, unity) which apply more narrowly to the Red Cross/Red Crescent movement itself: *International Review of the Red Cross*, November–December 1984, pp. 328–30.

11. 'The sovereign has no earthly judge, for one over whom another holds a superior position is not a sovereign.... Therefore it was inevitable that the decision between sovereigns should be made by arms'; Alberico Gentili, *De Jure Belli Libri Tres* (New York: Oceana, 1964/1598), p. 15.

12. Hugo Grotius, *De Jure Belli ac Pacis Libri Tres* (Oxford: Clarendon Press, 1935/1625), Chapter XX.

13. See Hedley Bull, Benedict Kingsbury and Adam Roberts (eds), *Hugo Grotius and International Relations* (Oxford: Clarendon Press, 1990).

14. John Vincent, *Nonintervention and International Order* (Princeton: Princeton University Press, 1974), p. 26.

15. Emmerich de Vattel, *The Law of Nations or the Principles of Natural Law Applied to the Conduct and to the Affairs of Nations and of Sovereigns* (Dobbs Ferry, NY: Oceana Publications, 1967/1758), introduction.

16. One example, mentioned in Chapter 1 of this book, was the ambivalence of Gladstone, who swung from stern non-interventionism to the impassioned advocacy of humanitarian intervention to stop the Bulgarian massacres at the time of the Midlothian election. For a fuller account of the humanitarian intervention debate see Oliver Ramsbotham and Tom Woodhouse, *Humanitarian Intervention in Contemporary Conflict* (Cambridge: Polity Press, 1996), Chapter 2.

17. Lori Fisler Damrosch, 'Changing conceptions of intervention in international law', in L. Reed and C. Kaysen (eds), *Emerging Norms of Justified Intervention* (Cambridge, Mass.: American Academy of Arts and Sciences, 1993), pp. 91–110 at p. 93.

18. Interviews with Robert Beresford (Committee for Justice and Peace of the Catholic Bishops' Conference), Keith Clements (formerly Co-ordinating Secretary for International Affairs, CCBI), Myriel Davies (UNA), Pat Gaffney (General Secretary, Pax Christi), Bruce Kent (International Peace Bureau), Catherine Perry (QPS), Martin Summers (East European Desk Officer, CAFOD).

19. Thus, for example, J. Boyle, 'Natural law and international ethics', in Terry Nardin and David Mapel (eds), *Traditions of International Ethics* (Cambridge: Cambridge University Press, 1992), pp. 112–35 at p. 123. See also John Finnis, *Natural Law and Natural Rights* (Oxford: Oxford University Press, 1980).

20. Papal pronouncement at the International Conference on Nutrition, 5 December 1992, quoted in R. Coste, 'The moral dimensions of

intervention', *Harvard International Review* (Fall 1992), pp. 28–9 and 67–8 at p. 28.

21. M. Haas, *The Asian Way to Peace: A Story of Regional Cooperation* (New York: Praeger, 1989).

22. Quoted in Garry Klintworth, 'The "right to intervene" in the domestic affairs of states', *Australasian Journal of International Affairs*, **46** (1991), pp. 249–66.

23. Vincent, *Nonintervention*, p. 271.

24. A. Al-Ahsan, *The Organization of the Islamic Conference* (Herndon, VA: International Institute of Islamic Thought, 1988), p. 36.

25. Sohail Hashmi, 'Is there an Islamic ethic of humanitarian intervention?', *Ethics and International Affairs*, **9** (1993), pp. 55–73 at p. 55.

26. *Ibid.*, p. 62.

27. Zaki Badawi, transcript of interview with the editors, 1996, p. 6.

28. Hashmi, 'Is there an Islamic ethic of humanitarian intervention?', p. 63.

29. *Ibid.*, p. 65.

30. *Ibid.*, p. 68.

31. Badawi, interview transcript, p. 7.

32. Quoted by Hashmi, ibid., p. 70. Citing the case of some Europeans who fought on the side of the Muslim Algerians against French colonial oppression, Mutahhari comments 'the *jihad* of such people was even more sacred than that of the Algerians, because the Algerians were defending the cause of their own rights, whereas the cause of others was more ethical and sacred'. This echoes the ethical conclusions of Gentili and Grotius cited above.

33. *United Nations Peacekeeping: Information Notes* (New York: UN Department of Public Information, June 1994), p. 83.

34. Chandra Muzaffar, 'Responses', private communication with the editors, 1996, p. 2.

35. 'A couple of sorties on Belgrade very early – not on Sarajevo but on Belgrade – would have caused Milosevic to collapse very quickly, attacking legitimate targets not areas of civilian population. The threat should have been against the real culprit, not a proxy; and it was obvious to everyone that Milosevic was the real culprit', Zaki Badawi, interview transcript, pp. 4–5.

36. When the 'safe areas' were designated as such under SCR 836 (14 June 1993) the UN Secretary-General, advised by the UNPROFOR commander, estimated that an extra 34 000 troops would be needed to implement the policy properly, with 7600 required to begin implementation under a 'light option'. In the end only the 7600 reinforcements were authorized, and they took more than a year to be deployed.

37. I. Khan, *Muslim News*, 26 March 1993, p. 3.

38. E. Ahmad, *Boston Review*, June/August 1993, p. 5.

39. Not always welcomed by the Bosnian Muslims (*The Times*, 6 November 1992). On the question of individuals acting in default of government response, Zaki Badawi comments that this is allowed under Muslim law and ethics: 'Those individuals had the support of quite a number of scholars. It is only when there is ambiguity that scholars would shy away from giving support. But when there is an obvious case

of people being ill-used by others, it is legitimate to go in and try to help them'; interview transcript, p. 1.
40. Although in April 1993 OIC states promised $83 million emergency assistance, and in July seven OIC states offered troops for UNPRO-FOR. Troops from Jordan, Malaysia, Pakistan and Turkey were sent.
41. Hashmi, 'Is there an Islamic ethic of humanitarian intervention?', p. 72.
42. 'These are essentially sick people. General Mladic needs a psychiatrist or somebody to put him in jail'; Zaki Badawi, interview transcript, p. 8.
43. For President Ozal of Turkey: 'if the aggressor had been the Bosnian Muslims, probably the situation would have been completely different now', *Independent*, 12 January 1993.
44. As reiterated on numerous occasions by Prime Minister Mahathir Mohamed.
45. *Jordan Times*, 1 July 1993.
46. *Jordan Times*, 16 July 1995.
47. Holy Synod of Bishops of the Serbian Orthodox Church, *Appeal to All International Factors*, 12 December 1995.
48. 'Fifty years have passed since the victory over Nazi fascism. . . . Where is the place for our people this fiftieth anniversary jubilee? Always and consistently on the side of justice and freedom, we see our people today without justice and freedom; always faithful to its allies as fighters for peace and humanity, today we see our people cast out, expelled into the desert of the twentieth century, accused of the sins of others'; Holy Synod of Bishops of the Serbian Orthodox Church, *Message for Public Assembly 70*, May 1995.
49. 'As we write this, tragic news has reached us: on May 25 and 26 NATO again bombed the Serbian People in the Serbian Republic in order to force them to recognise these artificial borders and to force them to their knees; bombs are falling on those same regions where the Ustashi and Hitler's soldiers once killed the fathers of those who are suffering now.' The Serbs are described as 'the only European people without its own internationally recognised state'. Holy Synod of Bishops' *Message for Public Assembly 70*, May 1995.
50. Information communicated by Xenia Dennem, Keston Institute.
51. 'The Former Yugoslavia', information sheet, The Council of Churches for Britain and Ireland, September 1995.
52. 'Letter to the House of Bishops', General Synod of the Church of England, Board of Social Responsibility, 17 August 1995, pp. 1–2.
53. Adrian Hastings, 'SOS Bosnia', *Theology*, **47** (778) (1994), pp. 242–4.
54. Press Release, 7 August 1992, reprinted Lambeth Palace.
55. Letter from CCBI Presidents to the Prime Minister, 6 November 1992.
56. CCBI Information Sheet, September 1995, vol. 1.
57. Keith Clements and Roger Williamson, 'Peace and reconstruction in former Yugoslavia: Aims and priorities for the Churches of Britain and Ireland', p. 2.
58. Church of Scotland Press Office, 14 August 1995.
59. Gentili, *De Jure Belli Libri Tres*, p. 15.
60. For example, Hugh Beach, 'Do we need a doctrine of just intervention', in *Council for Arms Control* (London: Council for Arms Control,

1993); David Fisher, 'The ethics of intervention', *Survival*, **36** (1) (1994), pp. 51–9, and 'The ethics of intervention and former Yugoslavia', in Roger Williamson (ed.), *Some Corner of a Foreign Field* (Basingstoke: Macmillan, forthcoming); K. Himes, 'Just war, pacifism and humanitarian intervention', *America*, **169**, 14 August 1993, pp. 10–15, 28–31. Beach and Fisher apply just war criteria to intervention in general, not just to humanitarian intervention.

61. Fisher, 'The ethics of intervention', p. 56.
62. *Ibid.*, last paragraph.
63. The 'Mohonk criteria for humanitarian assistance in complex emergencies' emerged from a *World Conference on Religion and Peace* held at Mohonk, Canada in 1994.
64. Chandra Mustaffar, 'Responses', p. 2.
65. John McCain, 'To intervene or not to intervene?', *Armed Forces Journal*, September 1994, pp. 67–9 at p. 67.
66. Reinhold Niebuhr, *Moral Man and Immoral Society: A Study in Ethics and Politics* (New York: Scribner, 1932), p. 19.
67. For further discussion of the way in which just war criteria need to be adapted to accommodate forcible humanitarian intervention, see O. Ramsbotham, 'Towards an ethical framework for humanitarian intervention', forthcoming.
68. Hashmi, 'Is there an Islamic ethic', op. cit., p. 56.

8 Conclusion

Before drawing together some of the main threads in this book, it will be as well to recall that the study group was formed out of concern with suggestions of a looming post-Cold War confrontation between Islam and the 'Christian' West:

> We are facing a mood and a movement far transcending the level of issues and policies and the governments that pursue them. This is no less than a clash of civilizations – the perhaps irrational but surely historical reaction of an ancient rival against our Judeo-Christian heritage, our secular present, and the world-wide expansion of both.[1]

Bernard Lewis's sombre warning was taken up by others, notably Samuel Huntington in a well-known article: 'the next world war, if there is one, will be a war between civilizations'.[2] Huntington gave six arguments in support of this claim: (a) differences between civilizations are real and basic; (b) in a shrinking world interaction between civilizations is increasing; (c) economic modernization and social change are separating people from local identities and weakening the nation-state as a source of identity; (d) the West is at a peak of its power, but non-Western civilizations are increasingly returning to their roots in challenging Western hegemony; (e) cultural differences are less negotiable than political or economic ones; and (f) economic regionalism is increasing. Huntington saw faultlines between civilizations as the flash-points for future conflict, in particular noting the 1300-year-old rivalry between Islam and the West: 'This centuries-old military interaction between the West and Islam is unlikely to decline. It could become more virulent.'

Some individual Muslims have echoed the idea. Even Akbar Ahmed, in a sophisticated account of postmodernism and Islam, ends up with a similar dichotomous confrontation:

> There will be, increasingly, little elbow room, limited space, on our planet; this is because of the nature of the postmodernist era. The West, though the dominant global civilization, will continue to expand its boundaries to encompass the world; traditional civilizations will resist in some areas, accommodate to change in others. In the main, only one, Islam, will stand firm in its path.

Islam, therefore, appears to be set on a collision course with the West.[3]

Behind these mutually antagonistic constructions lie, on the one hand, the fact of radical Islam, seen as a threat in some quarters in the West,[4] and, on the other hand, the widespread resentment among many Muslims at what is regarded as continuing Western hegemony, arrogance and geopolitical exclusionism:

> [T]he Muslim masses are feeling insecure in relation to the function-ing of the international system because of the double standards in international affairs. The expansionist policy of Israel has been tolerated by the international system. The *Intifada* has been called a terrorist activity while the mass rebellions of East Europe have been declared as the victory of freedom. There was no serious response against the Soviet military intervention in Azerbaijan in January 1990 when hundreds of Azeris were killed while all Western powers reacted against Soviet intervention in the Baltic Republics. The international organizations, which are very sensitive to the rights of small minorities in Muslim countries, did not respond against the sufferings of the Muslim minorities in India, the former Yugoslavia, Bulgaria, Kashmir, Burma, etc. The atomic powers in some Muslim countries like Pakistan and Kazakhstan have been declared a danger, when such weapons have been accepted as the internal affairs of other states such as Israel and India. Muslims, who make up about 25% of the world's population, have no per-manent member in the Security Council and all appeals from the Muslim World are being vetoed by one of the permanent members. The Muslim masses have lost their confidence in the international system as Neutral Problem-solver after the experiences of the last decade.[5]

In this book we do not engage with these wider political issues, but are concerned to disentangle Muslim–Christian ethical thinking from them. Islam cannot be identified wholesale with the programmes and actions of particular radical Islamist groups, nor can isolated acts of terrorism be regarded as a 'clash of civilizations' in any serious sense. Equally, Christianity cannot be identified solely with the secu-larized political interests of Western governments. Indeed, those who posit the idea of a 'clash of civilizations' can be seen to be already at odds over this. Huntington, for example, argues in terms of eight civilizations, three of which are Christian (the Western, the

Slavic-Orthodox and the Latin American), a fourth (the African) is both Christian and Muslim, a fifth is Islamic, and the other three are Japanese, Hindu and Confucian. In contrast, Lewis identifies 'our' 'Judeo-Christian heritage' and 'secular present' as two aspects of the same expanding civilization, whereas Ahmed describes the dominant global civilization as 'the West' and identifies it, not with Christianity, but with a 'secular materialism' which 'has rejected belief altogether'.[6]

These are complex issues which we do not go further into here. Others have done so elsewhere.[7] Our aim has been more modest, namely to stand back and explore our own understanding of our Christian and Muslim inheritance. We have been concerned to trace traditional Muslim and Christian teachings on questions of war and peace, and to assess commonalities, differences, and applications today, including the fundamental question posed by James Turner Johnson: does the defence of values by force remain a moral possibility?[8] Our conclusions are no doubt limited by the fact that we are a British group, as also by other specificities and exclusions which make up our identity. Those who have contributed to the book are listed at the beginning. These conclusions represent a consensus within the group. No further claims are made.

Chapter 1 sketches the long and complex history of military and cultural interaction between the two religions. Acknowledging bloody episodes of conquest, massacre and crusade, the emphasis is nevertheless on shared cultural roots, long periods of peaceful coexistence and interchange, and the huge variety of manifestations of Muslim and Christian civilization across time and space. The astonishing richness and variety of both Muslim and Christian cultures, enduring down the centuries and spread across every continent, give the lie to any simple idea of a unitary confrontation between them.[9]

Chapters 2 and 3 trace the evolution of Christian and Muslim thinking about peace and war, showing how, from very different starting points and despite quite different traditions of exegesis from founding texts, both religions came to engage with similar problems and to grapple with similar difficulties. Jesus did not have political power, but later Christians from the time of Constantine did. Muhammad, after ten years of prophetic mission in Makkah without political power, subsequently founded the first Islamic state in Madinah. Since then, both traditions have had to apply the teachings of their faiths to the political requirements of the day, including questions about the control of political violence, the legitimacy of waging war, and the limits within which it can justifiably be fought. Despite the differences in provenance and historical experience, these have been common themes in Islamic as in Christian ethics, politics and law.[10]

More recently, historical experience has diverged again. With the eclipse and eventual collapse of the Ottoman empire, Islam entered a long period of political decline from which it has only recently begun to recover. The Christian West, on the other hand, entered a period of unprecedented global expansion, which is only now, perhaps, beginning to be challenged. At the same time, unlike Islam, Christianity lost its dominant position within an increasingly secularized Western culture, introducing what perhaps remains the biggest single discontinuity between Islam and Christianity today. This also fundamentally affects the central theme of this book, raising the question how far the revived interest in just war doctrine in the West in the nineteenth and twentieth centuries reflects specifically Christian thinking and motivation.[11] In Chapter 2, in the section on 'modern applications', Christian contributors did not debate this issue in general terms, but justified the designation 'Christian approaches' by confining attention to explicitly Christian contributions. Within these terms, Christian pacifist as well as Christian just war positions were discussed.

In Chapter 3 Muslim contributors face a comparable problem, namely doing justice to the variety of recent Muslim responses to the nature of contemporary politics, including the development of the modern secular state. Here the main distinction is between what might be called radical and mainstream interpretations of *jihad*, with contributors to this book favouring the latter. In particular, whereas, as is often pointed out, the writings of Muslim jurists from the classical period may suggest that *jihad* only applies against non-Muslims, this is not seen to be a proper reading of the original teaching in the Qur'an and Hadith. A careful reading of these texts shows that *jihad* applies universally against any who threaten evil, whether Muslim or non-Muslim. These are important conclusions, permitting considerable overlap with the Christian just war doctrine outlined in Chapter 2.

Finally, one of the most notable features of Chapters 2 and 3 is the extent of the internal controversy and differences of interpretation revealed within the two faith communities. Indeed, it is possible to argue that there has been more divergence within them than between them, once again leading to significant qualification of the idea of two monolithic civilizations opposing each other.

Chapter 4 is the central chapter of the book. In it, the two traditions are brought together for comparison. Common and divergent themes are traced and a surprising degree of convergence is found, particularly regarding the ethical constraints governing both resort to war and its conduct.[12] This is not surprising in view of the fact that the Qur'an explicitly confirms the ethical content of previous scriptures, and the two traditions share a common cultural history as set out in Chapter 1, which reached its peak in the rich interchange in al-Andalus up to the thirteenth century. The conclusion to Chapter 4 should be read as part of this conclusion, so we will not repeat it here. Instead, we will add a few comments on the nature of the overlap and complementarity between the concepts of *jihad* and just war which the study group discovered. To the extent that the just war tradition is often equated with dominant Western cultural categories subsequently universalized through secularized international law, Islam is wrongly seen to be faced with the alternatives of resistance or capitulation. This is not how we view the situation. Instead, we see a complementarity between the Muslim concept of *jihad* and the Christian concept of just war in which each brings out features already implicit in the other.

On the one hand, criteria for the justified use of force already found in the tradition of *jihad* are articulated more clearly than is usually the case, when prompted by comparison with the Christian tradition of just war. These are not alien imports. A strong claim can be made that Qur'anic injunctions preceded the articulation of Christian just war precepts.[13]

On the other hand, what is sometimes criticized as the rather legalistic and one-dimensional form in which traditional Christian just war theory has come down to us, is enriched and transformed when reinterpreted in the light of *jihad*. For example, at a March 1992 symposium on religious attitudes to the use of force in international affairs in the wake of the Gulf War, a number of well-known participants criticized the just war tradition on the grounds that (a) it embodied an unsophisticated and unhistorical view of what causes war, (b) it lacked an adequate focus on whether war serves justice by not looking closely enough at alternatives, (c) it was damagingly detached from any doctrine of *jus post bellum*, the nature of the just peace for which just war should be fought, and (d) it was not sufficiently concerned about the evils inherent in warfare as an institution or the associated moral failings of governments and social systems.[14] Earlier chapters of this book attempt to refute these charges. Either way, it can be argued that a fuller account is given in the tradition of *jihad*, which, as explained in Chapter 3, includes the use of force within a wider concept of struggle 'in the way of God'. Military *jihad* is set within the context of spiritual and political *jihad* and is inseparably a part of it. This enrichment of what is often a secular-ized just war doctrine in fact makes explicit what is already implicit in the Christian tradition. As emphasized in Chapter 4, both the *jihad* and just war traditions are built on the foundations of the concept of a just peace. The Islamic tradition 'stresses, not the simple avoidance of strife, but the struggle for a just social order. In its broadest sense, the Islamic view of peace, like its Western counterpart, is in fact part of a theory of statecraft founded on notions of God, of humanity, and of the relations between the two'.[15] Similarly, Thomas Aquinas, in his version of just war theory, as outlined in Chapter 2, emphasized under 'right intention' that the purpose of war was to promote good, combat evil, and 'intend' a just peace – eminently Islamic sentiments.

Chapter 5 sketches some of the main *ad bellum* and *in bello* pro-visions of modern international law, and shows how they are conson-ant in general terms with much of the common central teaching in both traditions described earlier.[16] This is again not surprising, since both traditions have, in their different ways, contributed over the centuries to the development of what is now called interna-tional law. But that is not to say that Muslims and Christians are entirely at ease in an international system which, in many eyes, still overwhelmingly privileges the secular sovereign state, as shown with reference to the question of humanitarian intervention in Chapter 7.

Chapters 6 and 7 apply conclusions from earlier chapters to two recent cases in which Muslims and Christians were faced with su-premely difficult choices about the use and non-use of force. Saddam Hussein's brutal occupation of Kuwait in August 1990, and the murderous war in Bosnia which began in April 1992, challenged Muslims and Christians alike, with Muslims perhaps confronting more difficult problems of political decision-making in the former case, and Christians in the latter.

In Chapter 6, applying common *jihad*/just war criteria, Muslim and Christian contributors offer assessments of the 1991 Gulf War. There is universal condemnation of the Iraqi take-over of Kuwait, but difference of opinion about the forcible international response. One Christian contributor argues cogently that the subsequent war to expel Saddam Hussein was legitimate by just war criteria, but two others in a joint contribution question this, mainly on grounds of 'right intention'. Here is an interesting disagreement about whether 'right intention' should be subsumed under 'just cause', as the first writer argues, or whether it should stand as an independent criterion capable of ruling out the use of force even if there is a just cause, as the others claim. On the Muslim side, one contributor sees the Iraqi invasion of Kuwait as contrary to Islamic international law, and 'the alliance of Kuwaiti–Western powers' in opposing him as 'legal'. Others, in a joint response, take a different line, offering a wide-ranging critique of Western, and in particular United States, policy and conduct during the Gulf crisis. This reflects widespread Muslim response at the time.[17] It is immediately apparent that, in rejecting the legitimacy of the war as fought, the specific events between the Iraqi invasion of Kuwait on 2 August 1990 and the ceasefire of 27 February 1991, which formed the exclusive focus of enquiry for the first Christian contributor, are here seen within a broader historico-political context, and it is the latter which provides the main grounds for rejection. This opens up a rich area of debate for those undertaking the daunting task of deriving a joint Muslim–Christian *jihad*/just war doctrine. The fact that the two Christian contributions were in disagreement about the legitimacy of the 1991 war, and that (less directly) the two Muslim contributions also seemed to be at odds, suggested to the study group that once again this could not be interpreted as a simple 'confrontation' between Christians and Muslims.

All of this prompts a familiar but difficult question. What are we to make of the fact that application of agreed general *jihad*/just war criteria may lead to opposite conclusions about the legitimacy of particular wars? Christian just war theory has been critized by both pacifists and realists on these grounds, seen as an empty formal categorization devoid of content and open to abuse when used as spurious ethical justification by governments. It is true that *jihad*/just war criteria are to some extent formal and therefore vulnerable to differing substantial interpretation, but this is the case with all general sets of criteria. The conclusion in this book is that they nevertheless lay down essential restrictive principles derived from Muslim and Christian tradition going back many centuries, which, however much abused in practice, may still serve to limit the unbridled exercise of force and help to ensure that its use is subordinated to the overarching goal of contributing to a larger peace. As suggested in

Chapter 5, these common principles are now largely incorporated into modern international law and codified as an agreed body of detailed legislation, although this still lacks means of enforcement and needs further tightening.

Finally, in Chapter 7, a different approach is adopted in considering the question of humanitarian intervention in Bosnia. From a survey of the literature, supplemented by interviews and internal discussion, a broad consensus emerged about the issue in general, albeit with some differences of opinion about its application in the case of Bosnia. Here, in contrast to the Gulf War, more Muslims than Christians appeared to think that force should have been used earlier. Application of *jihad*/just war principles is shown to support the idea of justified humanitarian intervention, but only on strict conditions which adumbrate the possibility of a future, more solidarist international community.

To sum up. In this study group both Christians and Muslims were prepared to dissociate themselves from their projected identities as envisaged in the 'clash of civilizations' hypothesis. Christian participants rejected identification with the secular interests of Western governments. They sought to derive just war teaching from explicitly Christian, not secular, sources. Many of them were critical of the policies of particular Western governments and of the so-called Western sovereign state system in general. Muslim participants were equally forthright in refusing identification with Islamic political extremism. While recognizing the importance of returning to spiritual fundamentals, and acknowledging the sense in which *jihad* embraces the struggle for political justice, they condemned all use of terrorist methods by governments and by insurgent groups, and rejected the association of *jihad* with forcible military conversion to Islam. The Qur'anic injunction 'there is no compulsion in religion' was seen to anticipate the anti-crusading Christian tradition going back to the time of Vitoria that difference in religion is no just cause for war. More broadly, it was concluded that there is neither a uniform Christendom, nor a uniform Islamic civilization confronting each other. As the earlier chapters of this book show, there is much overlap between Christian and Muslim mainstream cultures, not least on the crucial issue of war and peace. Indeed, they have more in common with each other than with the secular societies with which they coexist. The much vaunted clash of Islamic and Christian cultures is thus a myth.

NOTES

1. Bernard Lewis, 'The roots of Muslim rage', *Atlantic Monthly*, 266, September 1990, p. 60.
2. Samuel Huntington, 'The clash of civilizations?', *Foreign Affairs*, 72 (3) (Summer 1993), pp. 22–49. Huntington defines a civilization as the 'highest cultural grouping of people and the broadest level of cultural identity people have short of that which distinguishes humans from other species'.
3. Akbar Ahmed, *Postmodernism and Islam: Predicament and Promise* (London: Routledge, 1992), p. 264.
4. Such as the Taleban in Afghanistan, the military Islamic government in Sudan, the revolutionary Islamic government in Iran, the Armed Islamic Group in Algeria, Hamas in Palestine, Islamic Jihad in Egypt, Hizbollah in Lebanon. Judith Miller sees Islam as incompatible with Western values of pluralism, democracy and human rights and advises the US Government to combat radical Islam directly ('The challenge of radical Islam', *Foreign Affairs*, 72 (2) (1993), pp. 43–56); Leon Hadar, on the other hand, denies that Islam is a unified political phenomenon and sees radical Islam as the language of political opposition to corrupt governments in the Middle East, concluding that the US government should stop supporting these regimes ('What green peril?', *Foreign Affairs*, 72 (2) (1993), pp. 27–42).
5. Ahmet Davutoglu, *Civilizational Transformation and the Muslim World* (Kuala Lumpur: Mahir Publications, 1994), pp. 103–4. Quoted in Richard Falk, 'False universalism and the geopolitics of exclusion: The case of Islam', unpublished conference paper. Falk eloquently endorses and expands Davutoglu's theme.
6. The full quotation is: 'On the surface it is more than a clash of cultures, more than a confrontation of races: it is a straight fight between two approaches to the world, two opposed philosophies. And under the great complexity of the structures involved – the layers of history, the mosaic of cultures – we can simplify in order to discover major positions. One [the West] is based in secular materialism, the other [Islam] in faith; one has rejected belief altogether, the other has placed it at the centre of its world-view'; Akbar Ahmed, *Postmodernism and Islam*, p. 264. This passage carries on directly from the passage quoted earlier.
7. For example, John Esposito, *The Islamic Threat: Myth or Reality?* (New York: Oxford University Press, 1992) and Fred Halliday, *Islam and the Myth of Confrontation* (London: I. B. Tauris, 1996).
8. James Turner Johnson, 'Threats, values, and defense: Does the defense of values by force remain a moral possibility?', in William V. O'Brien and John Langan (eds), *The Nuclear Dilemma and the Just War Tradition* (Lexington, Mass.: D. C. Heath, 1986), pp. 31–48.
9. For an idea of the range of Islamic civilization see Marshall Hodgson's three-volume *The Venture of Islam: Conscience and History in a World Civilization* (Chicago: University of Chicago Press, 1974).

10. John Kelsay, in the introduction to *Just War and Jihad: Historical and Theoretical Perspectives on War and Peace in Western and Islamic Traditions* (co-edited with James Turner Johnson, New York: Greenwood Press, 1991), notes how, despite differences, Islam shares with the West the central notion of 'war as a rule-governed activity', p. xv.

11. It is worth recalling that a similar question can be asked about the inception of the Christian just war tradition from the time of Constantine, in so far as it borrowed heavily from earlier non-Christian Roman writings, notably those of Cicero.

12. We may note in this respect the similar conclusion reached by John Kelsay on 'certain persistent commonalities' between the Western and Islamic traditions: 'Both speak to the effect that war must serve legitimate aims; both are concerned to limit the resort to and damage of war. Both worry about problems posed by the human capacity for self-interest and self-deception; in this regard, both try to motivate the moral conscience of humanity as a means of discriminating between just and unjust action', *Islam and War: A Study in Comparative Ethics* (Louisville, Kentucky: Westminster/John Knox Press, 1993), p. 5.

13. 'In connection with the Qur'anic presuppositions about the existence of universally objective moral values "ingrained in the human soul" (91: 18), one might say that Islamic revelation foreshadows the just war concepts conceived or grounded in natural law of modern Western theorists'; Abdulaziz Sachedina, 'The development of *jihad* in Islamic revelation and history', in James Turner Johnson and John Kelsay (eds), *Cross, Crescent, and Sword: The Justification and Limitation of War in Western and Islamic Tradition* (New York: Greenwood Press, 1990), pp. 35–50 at p. 47.

14. These and other points are summarized by David Smock in 'The utility of just war criteria: A Christian perspective', in his book *Religious Perspectives on War: Christian, Muslim and Jewish Attitudes Toward Force After the Gulf War* (Washington DC: United States Institute of Peace Press, 1992), pp. 5–14.

15. Kelsay, *Islam and War*, p. 30.

16. Although, as argued by some, the just war tradition is more permissive of the use of force in international affairs than is the UN Charter. It is partly on these grounds, for example, that Robert Johansen regards just war theory as now 'out of date', in Smock, *Religious Perspectives*, p. 10.

17. For further detail on mounting popular Muslim resentment against the anti-Iraq coalition in 1990–1, see James Piscatori (ed.), *Islamic Fundamentalism and the Gulf Crisis* (Chicago: The Fundamentalism Project/ American Academy of Arts and Sciences, 1991).

Index of Qur'anic Verses Cited

Index of Biblical Citations

General Index